Dr. Angela Longo's
QUANTUM WAVE GUIDED LIVING

Exchange My Patterns, Changes Everything

The EEEZY Way:
Emergent,
Entanglement,
Eternal,
Zestful
You

BALBOA
PRESS
A DIVISION OF HAY HOUSE

Balboa Press books may be ordered through booksellers or by contacting:

Balboa Press
A Division of Hay House
1663 Liberty Drive
Bloomington, IN 47403
www.balboapress.com
1 (877) 407-4847w

Because of the dynamic nature of the Internet, any web addresses or links contained in this book may have changed since publication and may no longer be valid. The views expressed in this work are solely those of the author and do not necessarily reflect the views of the publisher, and the publisher hereby disclaims any responsibility for them.

The author of this book does not dispense medical advice or prescribe the use of any technique as a form of treatment for physical, emotional, or medical problems without the advice of a physician, either directly or indirectly. The intent of the author is only to offer information of a general nature to help you in your quest for emotional and spiritual well-being. In the event you use any of the information in this book for yourself, which is your constitutional right, the author and the publisher assume no responsibility for your actions.

Any people depicted in stock imagery provided by Getty Images are models, and such images are being used for illustrative purposes only.
Certain stock imagery © Getty Images.

Print information available on the last page.

ISBN: 978-1-9822-2937-5 (sc)
ISBN: 978-1-9822-2938-2 (e)

Library of Congress Control Number: 2019907355

Balboa Press rev. date: 10/22/2019

CONTENTS

PART TWO:
KNOWING MY ETERNALBEING

PART THREE:
UNDERSTANDING THE ENERGY OF YOUR TRIUNITY

WHAT PEOPLE ARE SAYING ABOUT

I am in appreciation and awe of your gifts and offerings. Your system of Relationshifting is powerful, effective and eminently practical. You helped me a great deal in our session yesterday to start transforming the root of some of the limiting patterns in my life around money, spirituality and relationships. I see the Light shining through the parts of me that have continued to live in the proverbial box. I have started practicing what you led me to write down and I feel the benefits already. I intend to integrate this approach into my acupuncture practice as I work with it for myself.

The value of your life work is evident - and I would recommend all practitioners of the medical and healing arts to read your book once it is released!

Darren Starwynn, O.M.D.

Phoenix, Arizona

With my first relationshifting session, the pain I had for years in my shoulder left and hasn't returned in 2 weeks, even after long hours at the computer which normally brings on a recurrence.

Maren Schmidt

Author of Montessori books and online workshops for parents Big Island, Hawaii

I am embracing how I 'slump' inside and paralyze myself in relationships with men. I shifted this to, 'I power-ize myself'. One shift and, surprisingly, I watched my mate shift also. It's easy now, that when I perceive an internal collapse on the horizon, I move to Heartwave, 'I power-eyes myself.'"

Janet Redmond, *Clinical Psychologist T.A. Trainer New Zealand*

I have done 30 to 40 years of alternative health modalities. However, when I do heartwaving, I feel an immediate sense of strength and completeness. I feel different in physiology and a greater sense of well being."

John Hamilton

Kiwi, New Zealand

This method worked what seemed like a miracle on me. I had dealt with gradually increasing upper abdominal pain for 9 days till I could hardly sleep when I went to Dr. Longo. After that initial Relationshifting session the pain was reducing down to 40% in a way I had never experienced. She said my pain WAS my BATHWAVEs (beliefs, actions, thoughts...). Relief was instantaneous with the shifts. This is a new concept for me beyond cause and effect. Later after the acupuncture, the pain was already reduced by half. Over the next two days, continuing on my own with my quantum shifting, all abdominal pain left me.

I don't yet understand how it works, but I intend to learn more. My results were too fantastic to ignore."

Mark Schmidt

Big Island, Hawaii

I cannot believe how much my thinking has changed since I have moved to Hawaii. Angela has enlightened my life resplendently and therefore, physically.

For instance, on a recent cruise, I had an upset stomach for over a week. When I came home, I used herbs and moxa in my life along with mirroring and heartwaving. Within two days, I was feeling 100% again.

I can't thank you enough, Angela, for opening my eyes to my eternalbeing "Elation" and the life "we" now have an adventure with!

Dr. Kristal Blacksmith, *Professor of Biology*

Kamuela, Hawaii

Relationshifting

Quantum Resplendency

- Living My Triunity Is Resplendency (Quantum Equivalence)
- Understanding BATHWAVEs on My Four Body Levels
- Rewriting Love Letters I Give Myself with Bathwaving Tool
- Getting Ass-ets in Gear by Shifting the Eight Bottom Lines
- Read and Name My Eternalbeing
- Living Anew as Emergent Mirror-Calls (Miracles)
- Awareness of Radiant Entanglement
- Communion of Personalbeing and Eternalbeing as Illuminatedbeing for Resplendence

__Haiku for Hi Q (Heart Intelligence Quotient)__
When I dare to bare
my heart naked,
I turn my scared into sacred.

My Prayerful Heartwave

May I stop discontenting myself.

May I be aware of the recurring pattern of actions of my true desires that reveal my unique eternalbeing, for that will free my resplendence to glow abundant gifts of which miraculous manifestation is one.

May I be aware of accessing the unlimiting 'informotion' of entanglements that is born of faith in myself and others.

May I value and use everything that I source and have, therefore, give myself.

May the triunity that I am—personalbeing, eternalbeing, and resplendent illuminatedbeing—be eternally radiant and aware.

May I share the emergent understanding of resplendency; that I am new and different in every moment while enjoying the fruits of my harvest.

May I face and embrace my 'mirror-calls' as a gift of my resplendency, and when challenging, replace them with the grace of my desires.

And only as needed, may I muster the power to decide whether to shift or not to shift.

May I have confidence wherever I am, understanding that it is truly where I have chosen to be.

Encourage resplendency as the conviction of my bones, and free myself to sing, dance, appreciate, shine on and openly care for each person I meet.

It is the resplendency of each and every one of us.

Ah men, ah women, ah children, ah way of quantum based resplendency!

PREFACE

Dear Reader,

Even though I am not a writer—I am a very practical hands-on Traditional Chinese Medicine (TCM) doctor and trained biochemist—I have felt compelled to tell my story.

This story encompasses my learning as a Ph.D. in biochemistry; my work as a TCM doctor focusing on understanding my bodies' energy systems and healing with acupuncture and herbs; and my own journey of healing liver cancer with a variety of new tools.

What I discovered is a way of living I call Quantum Resplendency since it is based on qualities of the quantum world. It is a life full of awareness of the miracles that we have and guide us to an existence that is contenting, fulfilling, expansive, understanding, and cherishing.

Relationshifting is a set of tools that will help you shift your patterns of struggling, conflict, isolation and illness into "resplendency". Resplendence means to be radiant and glorious. Relationshifting to Quantum Resplendency is about helping you cross a bridge into a new way of living. This book is a handbook of resplendency and what to do once you are aware of it.

To help you over this bridge I will show you tools and techniques that I have used with myself and with clients over the past twenty years. These tools include the following:

- *Bathwaving*, which is an easy to use technique to shift old non-productive patterns into an open and resplendent way of being.
- Understanding *BATHWAVEs*, which are my self-created energy patterns manifested from my beliefs, actions, thoughts, habits, words, attitudes, values and emotions.
- Reading my *Love Letters*, which are messages I unknowingly send to myself to help guide me to living resplendency.
- Understanding my *Triunity*, helps me to see that I am actually three beings in one nest, and how and why we have neglected seeing this larger picture of ourselves.
- Reading and naming my *Eternalbeing*, the larger unique purpose of my life.
- Muscle testing to help me access my perceptions and patterns and the universe's recordings of everything that has been.
- Replacing the *Eight Bottom Lines*, the eight survival mechanisms, that keep me from transforming my BATHWAVEs to living resplendency.

As I discovered, used and refined these tools, I was surprised at how quickly they could work. I found, along with my clients, that I could shift old behavior patterns in a matter of minutes instead of years, simply by using the Bathwaving technique I will show you in Chapter 4. However, it does take three months of reminding myself to make them habits. This might take eight minutes twice a day.

As part of this handbook, I think it is important to include some scientific background into why these tools work so quickly. Their efficacy is due to the quantum nature of our living.

I consist of both 'particles' and quantum waves, and I have two "beings" that are the equivalence of this 'particle' and quantum wave existence. It is the communioning, or sharing of thoughts and feelings between these two beings—personalbeing and eternalbeing–that manifests the third aware being in my triunity, the resplendent illuminatedbeing. As I began to work with my triunity–instead of unwittingly working against it for most of my life–various struggles, conflicts and illnesses seemed to melt away.

I will give detailed explanations of the different relationships within our triunity. These discussions about various aspects of triunity are to guide you in this new way of living resplendently. I don't want you to get across the bridge without a map. When you are living in the resplendent way you will see that life is EEEZY, a term I use to say that living is an Eternal, Emergent, Entanglement as Zestful You.

Many of my discussions are to help you help yourselves and others, since once you discover and live your triunity, my experience has been you may want to help others relationshift to resplendency.

The third part of this book includes information about the Five-Element System used in Chinese medicine. I have found this system to be illuminating about various relationships in all aspects of living, and I wanted to share it with you. You can relationshift without knowing about the Five-Element System, but it is a handy tool to help you understand some of the dynamics of any situation.

I've divided this book into three parts–Seeing My Triunity, Knowing My Elernalbeing and Understanding the Energy of My Triunity. Worksheets are included within the chapters and also in the appendices for handy reference.

My desire is to share the discoveries that work due to the equivalences from the quantum nature of the universe and our own quantum nature of 'particle' and quantum wave, adorned and virtual, personal and eternal, leading to living the wholeness of the triunity of resplendency.

Dr. Angela Longo
July 2012

PART ONE:

SEEING MY TRIUNITY

I am my own Fortune Cookie

I am a
Resplendent, Illuminated TriUnity

CHAPTER 1

"YOU ARE YOUR OWN FORTUNE COOKIE"
OR
LIVING IS EEEZY

From Waitaha to Quantum World

Driving down a rural road in Aotearoa, New Zealand a bird brushes my camper van window and flies up a mountain. Even though it is close to dusk, every fiber in my being says, "Follow that bird."

It is sunset as I drive five kilometers, following the bird up a steep stark gravel road. Warning signs about approaching logging trucks are my only directional aid. Trusting my instincts, I come upon a Boy Scout lodge with strange tattooed people standing around a fire. I ask, and they permitted me to set up camp there.

My hosts invite me to join them around the fire, and a hundred or so people say 'karakia', a prayer. We take turns speaking from our hearts. As we linger around the fire, they inform me that the philosophy and prayer I had shared with them agreed with the ideas of the two-thousand-year-old Waitaha who brought wisdom to Aotearoa. This group of people gathered to study this ancient wisdom.

The next day, we head to the original site of their Temple of the Wisdom of the Four Winds to meditate and karakia. I share Relationshifting and the Bathwaving technique with many of them and my impromptu evening drive up a mountain road begins the deepening of new friendships, all thanks to that sweet New Zealand bird in flight.

The Waitaha way of interacting recognizes the importance of birds: birds interact with each other and honor the dawn with songs of beginnings. I began connecting to these people through my interaction with a bird. The birds, with Waitaha's understanding, honor the sunset, with songs of renewal and rebirth through our night's dreams, which are communications between our unique beings.

To the bird that brought me to this gathering, I say 'Kia ora', meaning thank you and I love you, bird, for connecting my eternal dream of networking, reweaving and translating this ancient Waitaha wisdom. 'Kia ora' for giving me a song for a new beginning.

It is my unique resplendent illuminatedbeing reminded by that bird that brings this book to you. It is that bird that showed me the emergent way to begin telling my journey of the past twelve years.

Dr. Angela Longo

Out of the jungle and into the light

Twelve years ago, I was given a life sentence of liver cancer by a diagnosis with an energy machine out of Europe called the QXCI machine (Quantum Xrroid Consciousness Interface). With my illness, I felt lost in a jungle with only a machete—which was "cause and effect." I kept working. I invented a cause and effect technique using my skills as a traditional Chinese doctor. The cause and effect technique did help me to clear enough of the jungle, so that I could blaze a path and begin seeing the forest and not just the trees. As I stepped back and saw the big picture of my life, I realized that *I was the jungle*, and I could begin transforming my scary fearful jungle into my Garden of Eden.

For years while I was coming out of the jungle, I had to sit on an O-ring pillow because I had such a bad rash. I had to detox with herbs. Cause and effect provided time, as I stood back and realized that I could be the reason for my frightful jungle as I was my Garden of Eden. I had to be the reason. Somehow I was the glorious world and the horror story at the same time.

With my knowledge of the body's energy systems used in Traditional Chinese Medicine (TCM), along with my background in biochemistry, I began to see how quantum physics might provide an understanding. I was two natures at the same time–an unseen character and a visible "adorned" physical body. I began to experiment with different techniques to help me leave the old, replacing with the new, not only to survive, but thrive.

Now that I have personally used these techniques, which I call *Relationshifting*, and now Quantum Wave Living, and share them with clients for twenty years, this way of living has been called resplendency. Resplendency means to shine, to be radiant or glorious.

Struggle, conflict and illness are the inevitable ways of life when I hold on to the old patterns, believing that everything happens because of cause and effect. The quantum world shows us that there is living beyond cause and effect.

I wish to share with you these techniques which conform to the quantum world. For this knowledge I am very grateful. It is understandable why the physicists turned their back on this new quantum world of particle/quantum wave because it defied cause and effect. It challenged everything we knew. It defies the way we think and act. It defies our old science. As a chemist I knew it defies entropy and the laws of thermodynamics.

With a biochemistry Ph.D. degree from the University of California Berkeley, I was able to expand my awareness to a whole new kind of science. The quantum world, as Heisenberg says, has a difficult time proving the truth. We can only live it. And in the living, as the saying goes, the proof is in the pudding.

It encourages me to vision living life as I truly desire and relish it, and finally, beginning again, we can 'delight' in it—'de-light'. It is not an accident that the word "delight" has the root of "light" in it. Light has this quantum nature of a physical twoness of 'unseen' wave; and palpable 'particle' (photon). We need to realize that we are a physical threeness like everything else in the universe that

2

is both 'particle' and 'quantum wave'. When we live both of these ways our life in communion, a third resplendent awareness is emergent and that completes the triunity of us.

Seventy-five percent of the clients that come into my acupuncture clinic have already given up on living. Or they have 'unconsciously' given up, like I did twelve years ago before my diagnosis of liver cancer.

The cancer recipe is: being unconscious about giving up, together with believing we are victimized by cause and effect; we have a sickening situation. It takes years of doing that to create this condition in our body, so don't worry. A lot of us, are living in denial, and as the joke goes, that's not the river in Egypt.

Denial is responsible for the unconscious, which doesn't even truly exist. We have created it and buried things we did not want to know in it, and that is what rises up and bites us in the ass, just as it bit me on my ass. Please excuse my off-color humor. I'm sorry; if I don't laugh at myself I'll take all this so seriously, then I'll judge it and that gets me quite ill. And I will find myself back in causing and effecting again. Fortunately, I can make a quantum shift again and again into my radiant way of living.

Please follow me, as I followed that bird one evening in New Zealand, to find out how you can Relationshift my life out of a jungle where you struggle for survival to the life beyond your wildest dreams, a resplendent illuminated life.

At times with my tale you may wonder where we are going, but I hope you will follow the path, as I followed that bird, to learn these techniques that have shown me to a new way of living.

Let's learn how to Relationshift to a Resplendent Way of Living!

What is Relationshifting?

Relationshifting is a set of tools that will help you shift everything mired in struggle, conflict and illness. We will replace it with a way of living that is freeing, contenting, fulfilling, expansive and loving and resplendent.

This book presents personal, clinical and social tools. These tools are stepping stones to help you bridge to resplendent living. Most people can't make a "quantum leap" to this new way. There are obstacles along the way that will come to light as you learn these Relationshifting techniques. These tools bring the basic principles of the quantum world into our daily living. Implementing these principles on a day-to-day basis frees me from the old scientific belief that 'cause and effect' dominates us.

This book presents more than theory. I became a biochemist in the first 27 years of my life and have become a very practical Traditional Chinese Medical (TCM) doctor and professor for the past 43 years. After the diagnosis of liver cancer twelve years ago along with an autoimmune skin condition,

I needed something new and fast to transform my life and restore my health. With the aid of ideas from the quantum world these daily living Relationshifting tools are what emerged as I regained my health and in the process transfigured my life, as I said previously, out of the jungle, into the light of day along with the dark of night.

I also introduce many new terms and when a word is first used, it will be in italics.

Some of what you will learn to apply from the quantum world is this:

- You have three natures: adorned, virtual and 'whole'. These natures echo or resemble the state of the quantum world which are "particle" and quantum wave from whose interactive conversation is 'wavicle', brand new wave/particle. Our resplendent state is new to us and when combined with our adorned condition offers us more than we can even imagine. Discoveries applicable to the nature of matter and light are beginning to be put to conscious use in our living. Quantum theories of entanglement, emergent, and eternal can now be put into practice to make our lives resplendent, allowing us to live the life beyond our dreams.
- You will be shown a method to identify and name this other you, the unique physical invisible eternalbeing of you, that is akin to the 'quantum wave pattern' of the physical atoms which compose our bodies.

Relationshifting techniques work without deep understanding of the quantum world.

My clients, friends and myself have used Relationshifting techniques successfully by simply doing them consistently developing a deeper understanding over time. I did not relate them to the quantum world until later with hindsight.

An overview of Relationshifting techniques

My life is my journey. My relationships, my daily experiences, my symptoms of illness, my emotions, and my dreams give me a treasure map to the whole me and to the tools that can be used supporting all my desires.

Mirror-calls are miracles

All my responses to experiences are reflections or *mirror-calls* (think miracles!) of my resplendent living. I might also think of these events as wake-up calls to the life of my dreams. The only requirement to be able to understand my mirror-calls and in turn read my treasure map is *authenticity*. Authenticity can be a challenge for some to achieve. It was for me, but I will also show you a technique called *Bathwaving* that helped me immensely in valuing and living this essential authenticity.

Recognizing my own issues perhaps as emotional triggers in these reflected patterns is called a mirror-call. When I realize that everything in my living is there to serve my personal expansion, allowing me an unlimited mode of being, life does, indeed, appear miraculous.

BATHWAVE

BATHWAVE is a simple technique, scientifically based to transform any situation I perceive as an obstacle to living beyond my greatest dreams. My obstacles may be circumstances I put in my own way, or these state of affairs may seem as if others are responsible. One of the maxims that Heartwaving (previous name for Bathwaving) will help me wake up to is this: *No one else can put anything in my way.*

Bathwaving involves a process of recognizing patterns in my life and then changing those patterns using words and movement. Each Bathwaving exercise takes less than a minute to do.

Learning to use these Relationshifting tools, to read my treasure map and thereby discover the richness of my life is not a spiritual journey. In the words of the Dalai Lama, "There is no need for temples, no need for complicated philosophies, or religion. Our own brain, our own heart is our temple".

I might add that the universe is the 'temple' or playground of my three beings...and you will learn to play with fun in this wonderland when you become aware of quantum tools I call *Emergent, Eternal, Entanglement, for a Zestful You*, or for short, *EEEZY.*

I do not just look inside myself to know myself; I look all around me. Look at my life. Look at how I respond and/or resist living. These are the clues on my treasure map to my resplendent living. I'll give you easy ways to use Relationshifting tools and techniques that open the way for resplendency.

Love letters

Relationshifting sees my response everything and everyone who comes into my life as offerings to myself as a *love letter* in a benevolent universe. A love letter is 'translatable' in whatever form they appear. Love letters also reflect my own perceived patterns, and I reveal how to shift any of these patterns I wish with the Bathwaving technique. Mirror-calls are love letters, in the form of my relationships, emotions, physical symptoms, dreams, daily events, and more.

In this book I'll show you how to understand the *love letters* that are all around you. The love letters that I give myself all the time are calling me to resplendence, yet I didn't know how to understand them. The language of resplendent living is new to me, though the 'words' have surrounded me my whole life. Relationshifting helps me become aware of what I am *really* saying to myself. Relationshifting may help you express the authentic you every moment and have your life surprise you with fresh insights and synchronicities every moment.

Quantum Shift

This mode of living and being in tune with my quantum wave and 'particle' natures, and quantum being, is called Resplendency. When I am ready to make a quantum shift through Bathwaving I may find that the person at work, who bugs me, is no longer a pain in the *okolae, bottom in Hawaiian.*

Instead the grouch is showing me a pattern of obstruction within myself that is ready for me to move. After relationshifting myself in private, they may even stop yelling at me.

The dogs howling unremittingly from my neighbor's garden, bothering the heaven out of me, are reflecting the part of myself that hounds me.

The women who repeatedly show up in my life to sabotage me, may be a mirror-call of my own jealous feminine or personal self-saboteur.

Part of my journey through this book will be assistance in translating the meaning of those mirrors, those reflections of myself and my behavior patterns. Depending on my response to a mirror-call, the next step is quantum shifting my old pattern into a new pattern of my own resplendent desire.

BATHWAVE
Beliefs Actions Thoughts Habits Words Attitudes Values Emotions

BATHWAVEs

Once I am clear about the pattern I see in my mirror-call, I will describe the simple, but exquisitely effective technique that I call Bathwaving to transform the pattern.

My mental, and often, emotional patterns can be remembered by BATHWAVEs—an acronym of Beliefs, Actions, Thoughts, Habits, Words, Attitudes, Values and Emotions. Mahatma Gandhi once told us that it is from these BATHWAVEs that we weave our destiny. My destiny IS me, my molecules, health, wealth, events, relationships, and more. My BATHWAVEs are self-created patterns as data and in-*form*-ation which is prior to energy. Information carries with it a type of quantum field in and around me that Chinese medicine describes.

We can see different energy fields now using special photography techniques that I will describe in one of the early chapters of this book.

For most of humanity and history, I believe that we each select some of these BATHWAVE patterns in the first three to seven years of our life. We call this our *original story*. Once a person has reached adulthood only such things as trauma, severe sickness, near-death experiences and the like, catalyze real change in an individual.

It has been said that experiments over the past century with everything from lengthy psychoanalysis to the world of psychedelic therapy have yielded only partial results in bringing about the positive change that so many people desperately long for in their lives. Resplendency as quantum wave living may provide a quantum leap of difference that I was asking for.

As a beginning tool, Bathwaving a pattern may sound like saying a positive affirmation, but the technique with repetition over time begins to open me to integrate my 'particle' and quantum wave natures for a quick yet lasting transformation.

Eight bottom lines

As you can well imagine, every person's BATHWAVEs are different. Amazingly enough, there are eight general activities, which I refer to as the eight bottom lines, that are old habits of coping mechanisms that prevent Relationshifting and drain our energy.

These eight bottom lines are survival pattern mirror-calls, asking us to replace them using Bathwaving or any other method that works for you. These eight bottom lines are fundamentally judgments and include accusing, blaming, complaining/criticizing, lying, hiding, denying, defending and justifying. These eight BATHWAVEs require longer repetitive attention. For instance, accusing and denying took me years to shift and hold. It is worth the effort I have put into it. Luckily for you, I now see clients shift their bottom line BATHWAVES in weeks versus the years that it took me thanks to new processes and quantum discoveries.

Muscle testing

Applied kinesiology has also had its place in helping me to both test and empower first myself and then other research assistants. As I found positive results with muscle testing, gradually, I applied this work in my practice. If you are not yet familiar with muscle testing, I encourage you to go to the appendix section of this book and start developing this self-help technique, as a functional way for testing my stuck energy patterns, my BATHWAVEs.

Muscle testing is useful in verifying that I have successfully transformed my BATHWAVEs pattern also.

It is not always easy for the conscious mind to accept that I am carrying around some heavy baggage in the 'BATHWAVE' department, which is why we need to muscle test the universe's recording.

For example, one might consider oneself a 'recovered alcoholic' and still find oneself stuck in a pattern of self-numbing or denial, which will, as I can imagine, cause all kinds of problems in one's daily life. The things that I refuse to deal with—either by lying to myself, simply hiding them, or without awareness denying them, which is how I end up with an 'unconscious'—are what will surface as sickness, problems and struggles. These BATHWAVEs based on lying, hiding and denying require a whole different way of muscle testing with oneself or others, which I will explain later in the chapter about these "eight bottom lines".

Understanding our triunity from its quantum world equivalence

The quantum world is revealing to me that first there is a pulsating quantum wave that manifests new "particles" as fast as the speed of light in our bodies. The equivalence of this emergent miracle state consists of the unseen eternal 'quantum wave' and the material 'particle' both giving rise to a new "wavicle" transforming my body. Once I understand that I am this triunity like everything else in the universe, I begin to use my quantum wave nature to understand my eternalbeing and my particle nature as my *personalbeing*. When I live both of these ways, and learn how my eternalbeing and personalbeing work together, my triunity is emergent miracles, and my life is greater than I have ever imagined.

Looking through Heart Shaped Glasses
is my Personalbeing Particularizing.

Looking through Star Shaped Glasses
is my Eternalbeing Visioning the Recurring Me.

Looking through Heart/Star Shaped Glasses
is my Resplendent Illuminatedbeing Living
the EEEZY Quantum Resplendency.

Living our triunity

The equivalence of the nature of my being can be understood in the physical nature of light and atomic "wavicles", which have a quantum wave nature and a 'particle' spinning nature. What I neglect to see is that I am much more than just my mindful physical body, or my 'particle nature'. I will describe a technique to recognize my quantum wave nature and a technique to trust that. Once I become aware of my wave nature and interact with it, I discover that each of us is a 'resplendent illuminatedbeing', a triunity relationship of particle, quantum wave and emergent illuminatedbeing awareness.

Each of my lives is an expression of the interactions among the three beings of my triunity. Awareness of the conversations between my triunity becomes my resplendent way of living.

Eternalbeing

We each have an eternalbeing. Once I become aware of my eternalbeing's actioning, my direction and purpose in life becomes clear though it is not a goal. I'll describe a simple, yet effective way to discover my eternalbeing's theme. I have been living my eternalbeing's theme all my life, but mostly unaware. Imaginatively living my eternalbeing's theme is the resplendent way.

Tongue maps

Looking at the tongue is a Traditional Chinese Medicine diagnostic technique. What I have found is that observing our tongue is an interesting way to view a map of our lifetime of *love letters* to ourselves, a map that changes slowly with our transformations.

Translating these love letter tongues is quite easy using the tongue map drawings included in this book. Each picture of a tongue has an organ associated with it. And each organ has a BATHWAVE shifting table of their related BATHWAVE understandings to use with Bathwaving. Sticking out my tongue and saying "ah!" will have a whole new meaning for you.

Tongue map reading is presented in Part Three: Understanding the Energy of My Triunity.

A few aces for the game of living

As you learn about Relationshifting, I'll give you more than four aces to put up your sleeve. I do want you to have every advantage!

The 'Ace' of Bathwaving process can be described metaphorically, as a dance or a song of shifting consciousness, using four of our five senses: first we *face* (notice the ace in face?) the obstruction, as we *embrace* (another ace) it. At a quantum level our loving intention to appreciate and shift our obstruction will literally melt the information pattern into raw 'data'. At that point we *replace* (yet another ace!) our obstructive BATHWAVE with our reorganizational *grace* (fourth ace!!) of our true desire.

We'll also learn about the Ace of Diamond Shining in this book. I hope you will see all these aces as a good deal in the game of life.

The next 2 aces will be given in the next workbook as I ran out of space in this book…note the 'ace' in space is important in the ace of the diamond chain gang…

The proof is in the pudding

As I unfold these techniques for my use, I will refer to current scientific theory to support my point of view, but not to prove it. Thanks to Werner Heizenberg's Uncertainty Principle, which he formulated as a young 23-year-old quantum physicist, I abandoned the older western scientific approach. I understand clearly, that we cannot prove anything in this universe. Even as Copernicus was rejected for daring to suggest that the earth revolved around the sun, so any arguments, fought over today in scientific circles, will first be proved then be toppled, as our universe seems to expand to fit our ever increasing awareness.

I invite anyone who wishes to join this expansion and add to it with their awareness. As each one of us is a mirror-call for our life, we can individually shift patterns and then relax as we watch our living transfigure. Relationshifting is a technique for being the change you want to see. It is experiential. It is not enough to simply read this book. You really have to explore and experiment with each aspect in order to find out for yourself how easy it is to exchange mirror-calls (miracles)!

You'll learn that living the resplendent way is EEEZY: eternal, emergent, entanglement for a zestful you!

CHAPTER 2

"STRESSED SPELLED BACKWARDS IS DESSERTS"
OR
RELATIONSHIFTING OUR RELATIONSHIPS:
AND EVERYTHING IS RELATED!

Living backwards

With a diagnosis of liver cancer twenty years ago, my life was in the balance.

At that time, as a Traditional Chinese Medical practitioner for 30 years, I had been living in an unconsciously perceived 'stressed' world seeing problems and struggles around me, while having an extraordinary success with them in my clients. Neither had all my knowledge of the world, my work, the alternative books I had read, the documentaries I had watched, nor the religions I was practicing prevented this diagnosis of liver cancer. All my efforts to live a healthy life hadn't worked.

Was I ready to turn around the way I was living and relating in order to live the true benevolent nature of the universe? I obviously needed to do something new and different.

I was ready to take a quantum leap to change my life.

May I first say that I have always been living the resplendent way—that we all are living the resplendent way–though I obliviously was working against myself by not knowing about my two being existence, which I will explain in more detail in this chapter.

In hindsight—which is always with 20/20 vision–I was living it all backward. A pillow that I found in a thrift store told me*:*

Stressed spelled backward is desserts.

I had to laugh out loud as I hugged this pillow with an important message for me. As I'll explain in more detail later, this type of synchronicity is part of resplendent living's way of *"entanglement"*.

In other words, I now see that all situations are like this: they are relationships of the reflection or mirror-call (miracle) of myself guiding me to resplendency which is the essence of my authentic sweetness and contentment, no matter the situation. Twelve years later I am turning around my cancer, the concept of stress, and my way of relating. I am sharing this with my clients internationally and I want to share this with you. In order to understand the philosophy behind Relationshifting, we need to grasp the enormity of the new reality revealed by the basic quantum world.

Everything in the Universe
is made up of Particle/Wave

Particles are Body Surfers!

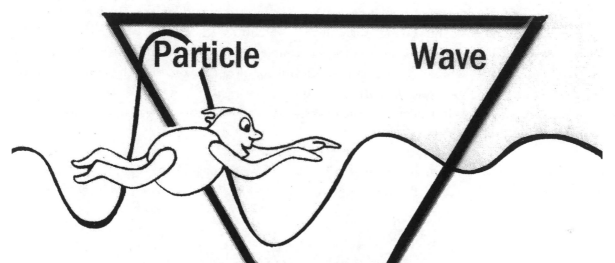

Particle　　　　　　　**Wave**

Resplendent Wholeness*

a Triunity...

*electrons, protrons, neutrons, quarks,
bosons and light, which are the building blocks
of atoms, which we are!

Emergent from my two being existence is my triunity

Communion is the word we use to signify bringing together our two-being existence. Our physical particle being is referred to as our personalbeing. Personalbeing would be our spirited mindful body that experience time and space, cause and effect, life and death.

Second, our physical quantum wave nature, the unique unseen being we each have, is labeled eternalbeing. Eternalbeing is our recurring eternal pattern in a wave-like manner. Quantum waves extend throughout the universe instantly. Hence, it is beyond time and space as well as cause and effect. Even Einstein called the entanglement theory of this wave nature "SPOOKY" because it was beyond cause and effect as well as time and space.

To continue, the illustration of this equivalency in the quantum world is the two natures of sub-atomic material and of light. The interplay of the two natures has appeared a paradox, thus the *Quantum World via Heisenberg,* which notes that simply observing something instantly shifts the observed. Yet this sub-atomic interaction is a clear mirror of our true nature: the particle and the quantum wave, the personal and the eternal. The quantum wave is always there, yet if you don't look for it you won't see it, as it happened in the old physics. Knowing it with awareness is the radiance of resplendence, to be explained.

Our eternalbeing, just as real and distinct as a quantum wave, must be looked for to be known. I will poetically introduce eternalbeing's commonality as the *diamond shining* or *eternal doing* running through our life:

Our Diamond Shining:

What is ever presenting about you?
Eternally recurring in all accomplishments you do?
What ignites your heart and sees you through?
Forever, it gives you a clue.

In the chapter called, *Eternalbeing Naming and Reading,* I'll show you how to identify your unique actions of eternalbeing and name it with practical techniques I call reading your quantum wave pattern, Eternalbeing, or the Ace of Diamond Shining.

Relationshifting transforms me to mindfully live the full knowledge and communion of my personalbeing and my eternalbeing.

Everything IS related!

All reality is related, in every way and everywhere I look, starting from a quantum world point of view to the macroscopic wholographic universe.

In other words, as written eloquently by physicist Dr. Fritjof Capra in his book, *The Web of Life (1996)*: subatomic particles are not 'things' but interconnections between 'things'. And these 'things', in turn are interconnections between other things and so on. In quantum theory, we never end up with any 'things', we always deal with relationships.

Nature, Capra continues, does not show us any isolated building blocks, but rather appears as a complex web of relationships...

This idea of a complex web of relatings begs some questions:

- Could our personalbeing be a web of relatings of which we are the authority expressing the patterns we desire?
- Is everything in our spirited mindful body related?
- Would being aware of these relatings be beneficial?
- Would these patterns of relating reveal a hidden nature to ourselves?

As Werner Heisenberg, one of the founders of quantum theory, put it: The world thus appears as a complicated tissue of events in which connections of different kinds alternate or overlap or combine and therefore determine the texture of the whole. Capra, F. (1996)

A particle is a set of relatings

The American physicist, Henry Stapp said:

An elementary particle is not an independently existing unanalyzable entity. **It is, in essence, a set of relationships that reach outward to other things.** Capra, F. (1996)

This 'reaching outward to other things' is the equivalence of our radiance of resplendent illuminatedbeing that we will describe in detail and diagram in a later chapter.

In the past, we have believed that the properties and behaviors of parts determine those of the whole; the situation is reversed in quantum world. It is the whole that determines the behavior of the parts. That would be the whole pattern or web...Frijof goes on to write, that the pattern of life, we might say, is a network pattern capable of self-organization. This is... at the very forefront of science. Capra, F. (1996), Jantsch, E. (1980)

The systemic properties of a particular level are called 'emergent' properties since they emerge at that particular level. Systems thinking is contextual thinking, Capra, F. (1996), and since explaining things in terms of their context means explaining them in terms of their pattern of associations, we can also say that systems thinking is pattern thinking or web-aware.

Relationshifting uses the pattern

Relationshifting is pattern thinking, therefore, systems thinking and web-aware. Ultimately, as the quantum world shows so dramatically, there are no parts at all. This is one reason that Relationshifting can work quickly and dramatically.

What we call part is merely a pattern in an inseparable web of relating. Therefore, the shift from the parts to the whole can also be seen as the shift from objects to relating. In the systems thinking view we can realize that the objects themselves are networks of relating imbedded in larger networks. *For the systems thinker the relating is primary.* Capra, F. (1996)

The perception of the living world as a network of relatings has made me think in terms of networking which is another key characteristic of systems thinking. This network thinking has influenced not only my view of nature but also the way I work with health, well-being and relationships. It is the cornerstone of Relationshifting, and is central to Traditional Chinese Medicine (TCM).

About physicist Geoffrey Chew's bootstrap philosophy Capra continues:

The material universe is seen as a dynamic web of interrelated events. None of the properties of any part of this web is fundamental. They all follow from the properties of the other parts, and the overall consistency of their interrelation determines the structure of the entire web. Capra, F. (1996)

This is not static like a spider's web but a constantly moving flow of energy. It is beginning to describe what our individual resplendency is like. This is also the reason, that I have consciously changed the word relationships to relating.

It is the dynamic interrelating verbs that we are focusing on in relationshifting. The story is only relevant to reveal the verb patterns of us: whether it is contracting or expanding us, whether it is repulsing or attracting us, diminishing or enhancing us.

Later in Part Three of this book I'll explain this constantly moving flow of relating energy by describing in detail the Five Element Theory used in Traditional Chinese Medicine and what that all means to you and Relationshifting.

The Five Element Theory never ceases to amaze me. For me, the understanding of these relatings has become a reality in 40 years of practicing this elegant science. Understanding body energy flows was one of the important bridges to Relationshifting, and to the resplendent way of living. More later.

Confused? Einstein was too

If this feels unsettling to any of you, don't feel alone. You are actually in good company with Einstein, who described his feelings from these ideas from the quantum world: "It was as if the ground had been pulled out from under one, with no firm foundation to be seen anywhere, upon which one could have built." Capra, F. (1996)

Capra conjectures that in the new paradigm,.. all scientific concepts and theories are limited and approximate. Science can never provide any complete and definitive understanding.

Relationshifting realizes that the triunity of the individual, revealing our emergent nature has always been the tour de force of pattern creating in the world. It has been poorly understood and applied. This book among others is a submission of simple practical methods to reveal and live the new pattern paradigm each in his own creative way.

Shift a part, shift the whole

To view a physical reality is actually to view of web of relatings and, therefore, when we pay attention to our relationships, or symptoms, or dreams, or events... and we shift one within ourselves, using techniques of Relationshifting, we are clearly shifting the whole web of our reality, which includes our well-being.

Experiencing the ways of the quantum world is easier by using Relationshifting techniques and by following the step-by-step methods demonstrated in the following chapters. The chapter called "Some En-chatted Evening" describes an on-line chat where I helped a family friend to relationshift some issues.

Shifting a little impacts our whole life

The criteria of systems thinking are all interdependent. Nature, to mention Capra again, is seen as an interconnected web of relationships in which the identification of specific patterns depends on the human observer and the process of knowing. This pattern of relatings is described in terms of a corresponding network of selections or ingredients that we make, none of which is any more fundamental than any other. Capra, F. (1996)

These ideas from above describes to a tee the philosophy supporting Relationshifting.

In the pattern of our living, we can jump into any portion and focus on what to shift or be creative with, and we impact our whole life. Capra, F. (1996)

Patterns are 'informotion' becoming energetic

'Informotion' is a pattern of information whose design represents incipient energy, yet was prior to this energy before patterning. These would represent the living I Ching patterns that we provide ourselves. Some of these pattern designs may resemble a well-known set of patterns to the Traditional Chinese Medicine practitioner, of the energetics connecting each of our organs. A meridian is like an electric circuit connected to each organ in our body, like the electrical cords connected to each of the appliances in a home. Measuring the integrity of the meridians can reveal the deeper health issue along with the treatment in acupressure/acupuncture, and provides yet another map for Relationshifting. I'll discuss this in more detail in Part Three.

These patterns can be observed in the physiological energy levels in the Meridian System, which are seen in the *tongue maps* presented in this book. All of these are the cause and effect methods of the energetic world.

Resplendence works on the data/informotion world and is prior to all this and expresses 'Fiat' or a command function. A self-evident BATHWAVE pattern is evident in all areas of our living.

A wholographic film reality

Since all phenomena of us are related, in order to understand any event, we can make use of the concept of a *wholographic film*. We can focus on one piece of the photographic film of our lives, which is 'alive for us', or any moment, in order to gain understanding of another part and the whole of our life.

In other words whatever I do in one area of my life, I do in every area of my life. For instance, when we are able to understand our mirror-calls, we can begin to own and shift the immediate moment's issue in our relationships and, thereby, transform our whole life because of this wholographic film reality. As an old Chinese philosopher once said "In all things, lie all things."

My life is a dynamic pattern

I now understand why some Native American friends called the Wise Woman in myths, *Spider Woman*, because she is a weaver and the web of the spider would be a pattern or reflection (mirror-call) of the nature of her reality. You see a web, you know that a spider is involved. Our life is like a living web of informotion and data with us as its essence as the weaver and re-weaver.

Resplendency is our instantaneous "google function"

Resplendence is the process outside of the old concepts of time and space. Resplendency is our instantaneous "google function" of everything, everyone and every time with no charge. Our DNA is our quantum computer. Entanglement is the quantum equivalence. Bathwaving is a bridge of cause and effect for reweaving my life's pattern if I am blocking living resplendency. Resplendency itself does not require the bridge.

According to Relationshifting, the pattern I weave and reweave is like a melody, which is an eternal melody I begin to choose as I enter this life. Though the qualities of the pattern itself can change, just as the key that a melody is played in may change, the basic melody can be heard and is recurring. My one choice is my eternalbeing action of my resplendent way. We each choose a unique and individual pattern or essence to our pattern much the way each species of spiders has their own specific pattern within their instinctual knowledge.

Unlike the spider, though, our pattern is dynamically emergent. Our patterning eternalself has unlimited creative expressions.

This pattern of data may be in the shape of a *fractal* image much like all of nature. Nature repeats a fractal pattern infinitely going inwards molecularly, and infinitely expanding outwards into the galaxies. An amazing understanding of this universality is that our being reaches the whole universe as we express ourselves.

What is my pulsating radiance?

Radiance is automatic for our quantum wave reaching outward to other things and returning to center spinning to turn around and radiate outward again.

Pulsating radiation is what we are actually. Our body is the place of turning around to radiate, connect and communicate our eternal unique actions as illuminatedbeing.

My pattern is unique and emergent

How I weave my pattern is unique to me and is reflected back to me in my doings/accomplishments of which I am proud. This eternal pattern is less obvious or obscured in my symptoms, dreams and how I feel about my relationships and daily events. These patterns can be understood with Relationshifting.

Applying the Relationshifting techniques to recognize and communion with my unique eternalbeing gives me great freedom and grants me the golden opportunity to change my old patterns. I am able to instantly transfigure and expand my web, and thus my reality, into what I truly desire every moment. I do not have to be stuck in an old unfulfilling picture pattern. With Relationshifting, I experience my ability to be creatively 'in charge' of my true selves. Living truly becomes "eeezy", secure and sustainable. With awareness of resplendency, relationshifting is instantaneous.

My BATHWAVEs as patterns

The success of treating conditions of the body as relationships has been exemplary for thousands of years in its effectiveness in a cause and effect way.

For each of us, our beliefs, attitudes, thoughts, habits, words, actions, values and emotions form a pattern.

I call this pattern my BATHWAVEs, an acronym for Beliefs, Attitudes, Thoughts, Habits, Words, Actions, Values, Emotions.

Our Triunity

This pattern is a contextual expression of our interactions between *our triune beings:*

1. Our **personalbeing** interacting with its BATHWAVEs (environment),
2. Our **personalbeing** interacting with another physical part of us that we know less about, *our* **eternalbeing** (our true recurring quantum wave-like pattern of me), emergent from #1,
3. Our **resplendent illuminatedbeing** (RIB), emergent awareness of the interactions of personalbeing and eternalbeing in all moments of our living.

Don't worry, you can live this without understanding it. These interactions will be discussed throughout this book.

My BATHWAVE pattern repeats itself fractally throughout my body and social systems, adorning my elemental organ systems as well as my personal and social relationships, and more.

I do my own Relationshifting to expand my life and my BATHWAVEs. Later, as you fill out the *five element questionnaire* you will begin to see which elements and therefore organs are deserving your attention and support in Bathwaving transforming work. The five element questionnaire in Part Three and the appendices helps you read another form of the love letters that you send to yourself.

Also, our social relationships provide hours of bathwaving fun, as we shift our BATHWAVEs to serve/ prepare readiness for our resplendent nature.

With this book I seek to inspire with a practical and radical new method to create glow in my relationships, my health, my dreams and life events and to live whatever you desire in full resplendency.

I hope to give you step-by-step instructions to put Relationshifting into action with Bathwaving, understanding my BATHWAVEs, and reading my love letters among other techniques.

Even though it's based on the quantum world, I don't have to be a rocket scientist to use Relationshifting to redirect my life to my eternalbeing dreaming.

Summary

I hope that in this chapter it's clear that everything is relating: that there is a wholographic film reality in the universe. My BATHWAVEs (beliefs, actions, thoughts, habits, words, attitudes, values, and emotions) create patterns that describe a unique being malleable to transform as my dreams. And my body is comprised of a system beyond energy which is data and informotion in a quantum resplendent way. I'll be talking more about that in the next chapter.

Later I'll show you how my BATHWAVEs are functions of my 'wave nature', or my 'resplendent' eternalbeing. We'll do an exercise, which I call "Finding my diamond shining" to discover the unique actions of my eternalbeing, which is revealed in the 'spaces' between accomplishments of which one feels proud.

My Eternal Theme

When I design my day as a communion with my ETERNALBEING, the air flows easily over and through my cells releasing the repast that I chew over and over and over again.

And I am free to dance wild, fearlessly sustaining the music of Padma's starry voice, and Becky's heartfelt hip swayings, saying that I may RE-WEAVE the web of my friendships now and forever revealing their eternalbeings, as I express my recurring ETERNAL THEME....

though played in unlimited multitudinous keys.

By 'Angelinking' Longo 6/22/11

I am a Love Letter to Myself

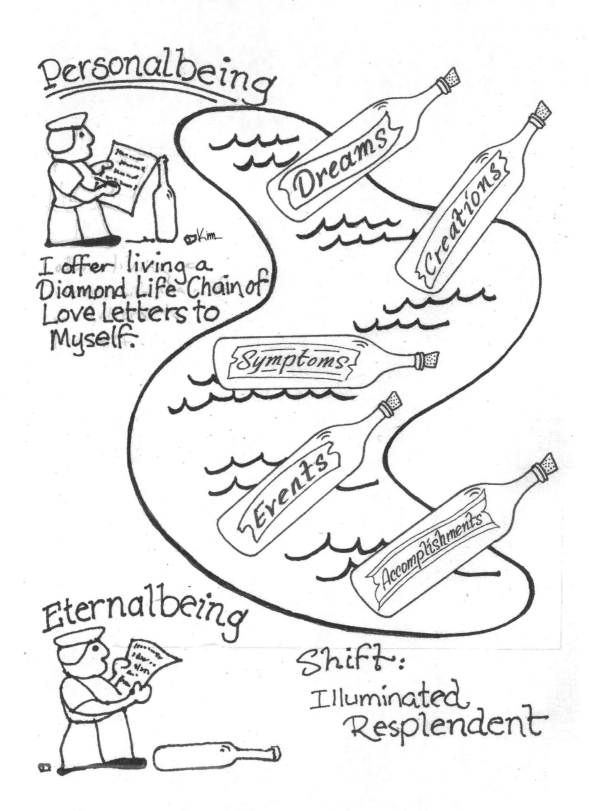

CHAPTER 3

IT'S ALL LOVE LETTERS TO RELATIONSHIFTING:
PREPARING THE STAGE ON WHICH TO BATHWAVE MY RELATIONSHIPS' LOVE LETTERS

Haiku for Hi Q (Heart Intelligence Quotient)

When I dare to bare
My heart naked,
I turn our scared into sacred.

Learning to understand 'love letters' as a bridge to resplendency

What if I knew that I was always giving myself 'love letters' every moment of my life? I may be, yet I may not know how to understand and read them?

What if I knew that my pain, conflict, struggle, anger, doubt, grief or fear of the moment, could shift in minutes, or perhaps moments, once I had the skills to read my love letters?

Would I be interested in learning to understand my love letters?

This book will be a guide to learning how to use the tools of my Relationshifting which helped me perceive the miracles (mirror-calls) opening my resplendent living.

In this chapter I cover some of the basic ideas needed in order to be able to *read my love letters, which are messages to myself about what I truly desire in order to begin again as my resplendent self.*

Five important ideas to know to begin Relationshifting

The five concepts I needed to know to begin Relationshifting follow:

- **First idea, 'likes attract'.**
There are no opposites attracting as they taught me in the old science classes. *Magnets attract magnets, so 'likes' attract.* The positive and negative poles just tell me what direction the electrons are flowing creating polarities (which are different than opposites) in the attraction, hence magnets attract magnets. Direction of attraction does not imply opposites.

What I attract to my life is like me. How I react to what I attract is mirroring me in some way, which will be explained simply, later in the book.

- **Second idea, living is like a Whologram.**

This is my preferred spelling of hologram because it reminds me that the 'whole' picture is perceived in every piece. Let's say I take a wholograph of me which is a 3D picture of all of me and what I am doing. If I break the whologram into 100 pieces, the whole picture of me is present in each of the 100 pieces of the picture.

This means that whatever I do in one area of my life I do in every aspect of my life. I can know myself by what I perceive in any part of my life.

- **The third idea is to check whether a sentence is true or not, it has to be true forwards and backwards.**

If we take the wholographic film idea in reverse it would say, 'whatever I do in a piece of my life is in the whole picture of my life'. Since this is true for me, the original wholographic film idea is true for me.

It follows that with Bathwaving I can face and embrace and shift what bugs me in a small piece of my life and the whole picture of my life is impacted. This is huge idea to understand and live.

I can start filling my cup with the small graces of what I truly desire. As the cup overflows it will eventually dilute out the unwanted stuff and only the grace we have been pouring in will remain. The Ace of Heartwaving is one such cup filling technique free for the doing. Simple, fast and easy, it is learned in minutes, to be used for a lifetime. You'll be introduced to this technique in the next chapter.

- **Fourth idea is everything is shiftable...am I ready to shift?**

I can know my most recent BATHWAVEs (beliefs, actions, thoughts, habits, words, attitudes, values, emotions).

The importance of knowing my BATHWAVEs is written by many human beings. Here is my own favorite version originally written by Gandhi-ji:

> *"Keep my Beliefs my choice because*
> *my Beliefs become my Thoughts,*
> *my Thoughts become my Words,*
> *my Words become my Actions,*
> *my Actions become my Habits,*
> *my Habits become my Values, and*
> *my Values become my DESTINY"... or YOUNIVERSE.*

Rearranging the first letter of each of this recipes' ingredients with an added dash of Attitudes and Emotions, I figured out an acronym to remind me of *what manifests my destiny, which is me...* BATHWAVEs (Beliefs, Actions, Thoughts, Habits, Words, Attitudes, Values and Emotions).

- **Fifth idea is my favorite...Entanglement Theory:**

I have access to anything or anyone I wish to know thru my DNA, according to latest research. Entanglement 'googles the universe' for me as soon as I set the context (ask my question).

Whatever option I choose to do and be, my whole universe mirrors it for me simultaneously. What a novel idea...and versa vice. Whatever mirror-call I am reacting to, I can know that I dialed it up for my resplendency. Resplendency translates loosely as 'to shine and be glorious as our radiance'. I'll give more practical explanations of resplendency later.

Whatever I wish to know is what I am 'entangoing' with, enabling me to know things I have never known before. There are a few illustrations of this in subsequent chapters.

Let's put these five ideas into action!

My True Desires

I keep overflowing my cup with my true desires...

self limiting patterns

quiet anger

fears

Soon ᵥᵥᵥ Cup only containing True Desires

Kim

I Keep Filling My Cup Full of My True Desires

This is a story that is very important to me. It repeats a quantum principle that is new to me.

> After traveling far, I walked up to the door of a school in which I desired entrance, and upon knocking, a window in the door opened and a person said, "You are not prepared, come back later" and the window closed.
>
> Upset, I walked away wondering, "What does that mean, I'm not prepared? I've studied and worked my whole life to be ready to enter this particular school of mysteries."
>
> So I started walking back the way I had journeyed from my home and asked people, "What do you think it means that I am not prepared?" No one knew until a little child in the group stepped forward and said, "I know, I know, I know" but then the child ran away.
>
> Everyone looked at each other and shrugged their shoulders but somehow I knew that that was my answer. That somehow the words 'I know' had prevented me from being prepared. So, I spent time thinking that I had to un-know things to be accepted into the school, but the problem is there isn't any way to un-know because once we know, we know what we know.

It took me a while to understand that this story encourages me to bring my full cup to a teacher, no matter what is in it. As the teacher is pouring fresh water into my full cup, I can allow the cup to overflow.

When I asked the story teller, Roger B. Cotting, what the fresh water represented in my life, he said it was living my true desires. With the diagnosis of liver cancer, I told him I must not know my true desires, when he smiled and agreed.

At this moment I was ready to begin again with the quantum wave living because, he explained, it would reveal the pattern of my true desires. Eventually, everything I am pouring into the cup of my desires replaces the old beliefs that were in the cup and creates the clarity of what I really desire in the cup.

That is the principle upon which this book is written. There's nothing to empty or clear from my cup in order to read this book. There is nothing to get rid of. Clearing would require a judgment. All we have to do is keep filling our cup with our true desires. And our cup runneth over until all that is left inside is what we have been pouring in.

Bathwaving: A Relationshifting tool

The technique of Bathwaving is not a clearing technique.

Bathwaving is basically acknowledging what is in our full cup, in an embrace, with the unconditional love of who we are and where we are.

In doing this loving embrace, we open the cup to receiving what we really desire. Otherwise we would have to judge and call what is in the cup 'poison' which would work against us since the cup is our body.

To learn how to do Bathwaving, you'll need to be aware of my current BATHWAVE, meaning my belief, action, thought, habit, word, attitude, value or emotion…that is alive for you in this moment. This process I call the BATHWAVE Loving Transformation or BLT.

Once you have expressed my current BATHWAVE in a simple clear sentence, like "I am worrying", the next step is called "Face It and Embrace It".

With "Face It and Embrace It" I simply, yet lovingly, stroke my body while saying out loud that you love where you are at in the moment:

> "I face and embrace that I am worrying my head off and I am ready to begin again with something new and different."

This is the acknowledgement that my cup is full and ready to receive.

We see how to open my cup to receive in the second part of Bathwaving. This part is called "Replace It with My Grace", where you pour in easily understood words what you truly desire, like "I relax and the world is beautiful".

Saying these words out loud in three tenses of our 'languaging brain', is "Replacing It with My Grace". Along with a key movement circling our midline, these two activities comprise the second part of Bathwaving which I call 'Quantum Shifting'.

If you learn best through visualization, picture your BATHWAVE pattern—that option that you have chosen in this moment—as a snowflake pattern melting back into water with my embrace, as you face and embrace my BATHWAVE in Part I. Then I can reshape my pattern as I desire with quantum shifting in Part II, replacing with grace.

In summary: Bathwaving, a Relationshifting tool, is comprised of four basic steps:

- BATHWAVE Loving Transformation (BLT): Being aware of my current belief, action, thought, habit, word, attitude, value and emotion or BATHWAVE mirror-call that I desire to transfigure
- Face It and Embrace It
- Replace It with my Grace: reshaping words for a new beginning
- The Quantum Shift

Learning to open the cup—to face and embrace who I am—will also be useful in reading this book, particularly to understand the communion of my personalbeing and eternalbeing.

The idea of Relationshifting is a modernization of some ancient ideas all brought together. These concepts presented in this book are supported by the ancient science of TCM (Traditional Chinese Medicine) and ideas of the Waitaha, while grounded in the modern sciences of the quantum world and biochemistry.

In the next chapter I show how to Bathwave. One of the reasons Bathwaving works is that information repatterns through movement of desire.

Information as Movement in Relationshifting

> *The detail of the pattern is movement,*
> *As in the figure of the ten stairs.*
> *Desire itself is movement …*
>
> T.S. Elliot, *The Four Quartets*

The nature of information pattern is motion

The more I worked with Relationshifting, I began to understand the nature of information patterning that I am creating in our lives. It is really about the 'verbs', or action words, that move me.

The most important part of information patterning is the movement it creates in my life, which is the movement of desire, as described in the T.S. Elliot poem above.

I am always expressing these motions or verbs through my living. *When I begin to see the pattern of my BATHWAVEs—beliefs, actions, thoughts, habits, words, attitudes, values, and emotions— I can restructure my motions to be as I truly desire.*

As I began to focus on the 'verb' behind the BATHWAVE I had profound shifts and living transformations.

This involved doing the simple Bathwave of facing and embracing whatever BATHWAVE I felt necessary. Each time I saw that I was always really facing and embracing a movement. Then with the grace of a new movement, I replaced it with the action I really desired. I felt as though I was living the title of the book, *I Seem to Be a Verb*, co-authored by Bucky Fuller.

Living is motion

My experience is that the very essence of living is motion. What keeps us motivated and functioning is the motion of our desires. Scientifically, when matter stops moving, atomically stops vibrating, it becomes black holes. Motion is quite basic or we would all fall into boring black holes.

Informotion

Motion, then, is what I am really facing and embracing in Part One of my Bathwaving.

It's important to again note that I am embracing it and loving it, and not clearing it or getting rid of it, as I used to say in the old days. The quantum world says, "Energy can neither be created nor destroyed in the universe."

I finally understood that I can't clear anything from the universe and I don't really need to clear anything. I may convert my information, back to "raw data", and transfigure it into new Informotion. On a physiological level I am probably making new glial-neuronal synapses.

> **I have coined a necessary new word 'informotion' to describe this phenomenon just by replacing the "a" with an "o".**

Instead of thinking I am embracing what I want to change, I am really loving it. At times, I'll laugh as I embrace it, because I can't really believe that I love this motion that I've decided to shift. But after I stroke my body lightly, that sense of disbelief disappears, as does a feeling of silliness or embarrassment.

This light sense of touch is noted in physiology to be an important factor that supports developing the limbic system by connecting it from the cortex to our feeling brain. In a baby, it's the light touch that keeps the baby moving, thriving, and developing. Without that light touch or stroke, the baby would die as noted in Ashley Montagu's book, *Touching*. This light loving touch reorients the limbic system to a new framework, allowing new information to enter.

For visual and energy buffs, since I am mostly made up of water (75-85%), I can imagine that this light loving touch may be melting a pattern, much like a 3D fractal snowflake pattern. For those who have studied or experienced the patterns of meridian sensations along the body with acupuncture of Chinese medicine, this visualization might be useful. I also include visualizing my quantum wave pattern transforming delightfully throughout the universe instantly.

This touching sensation would physiologically be translating to the limbic brain's reorganization. My old pattern of glia/neuron networking might melt into prior data. Our skin resistance changes as has been tested. The informotion network dismantled into its original data can be reassembled in Part II of Bathwaving using the quantum shifting technique.

These old BATHWAVEs, in Part I, are the context in which my existence was structured.

These BATHWAVEs are motivating me or hindering me. When I amawa re of them, whether from tongue maps, relationships, symptoms, dreams, events, accomplishments…I can look for the verb in our BATHWAVEs which is what I really want to replace.

It should be clear that this is not psychology nor intended to be. It is closer to 'dancing the pattern fantastic' and akin to chi gung. Shifting our BATHWAVEs would have to be called info gung (informotion gung), or rewriting the "I Ching of myself."

> **When I face this motion—this action in our BATHWAVEs–and embrace it, I can activate these old flows with ease and replace them with a grace of my new glow/desire. These desires are sustaining and supporting my glow into my desirable next moment.**

Entangling my shifts with others

The discovery of Entanglement Theory is what gives me this new miraculous understanding of the nature of reality. With every pattern shift done with ease, verified by my muscle test, or skin resistance test (as in lie detector) or just by my energetic noticing, I am *entangoing* as I desire with my universe.

As I quantum shift in Part II, **I become aware that everything with which I am in entanglement, "which is my world", will experience the shift instantly, simultaneously, in the moment and in the same way. Free will rules their choice whether they hold it or not. The encouragement is given.**

The knowledge of entanglement is so new and different, that Einstein labeled it Spooky Theory.

With free will, people in my world can choose not to hold the shift, if they so wish. However, my shifts are for my well-being, as well as theirs, therefore, it will be rare, that they will not shift.

One such instance might be when we are self-sabotaging. When we shift self-sabotaging to being self-supportive, and a person is in entanglement with us they also feel self-supportive, and it is a good feeling. Whether this person keeps that self-supportive good feeling is not my business. It has taken me many Bathwave shifts to change my understanding of this free will idea to *'everyone knows what is best for themselves, even when they ask for my opinion or support'*.

Relationshifting enables me to know and transfigure myself, by reading and understanding all the 'love letters' I have been giving myself.

By facing and embracing, and replacing with grace, everything that I desire to shift, I have a life that is desirable by me.

I also can know and manifest my true unique eternalbeing (EB), as I desire.

When personalself and eternalself interact and relate, living becomes easy, self-sustaining, secure, expanded, miraculous, and fun, namely resplendent. The method for perceiving my eternalbeing will be described in a later chapter and bears no resemblance to anything spiritual.

Eternalbeing is more like the one frame of a movie that describes the whole movie, though does not reveal the characters, nor the location, nor the era, nor the plot. All of these, is the realm of the personalbeing (PB).

Dr. Lam Kong tells the story:
"For one with no experience;
Ice, Water and Steam are 3 different things..."

"Wisdom reveals that the ice,
like body, water, like mind, steam,
like shen (spirit) are all the same."

Personalbeing describes the who, where, when, and what of our living.

Eternalbeing describes the 'how to do' that inspires me in my living, and really stands alone as the overview of my diamond patterning...which is why it is in Chapter 11 called the Ace of Diamond Shining or Eternal Being Reading and Naming

Reading my love letters

To be able to read any of my love letters, it helps to understand what the old mystical schools were talking about when they said we had 'four bodies'. The best explanation of this phenomenon was given to me in story form by my great acupuncture teacher, Dr. Lam Kong, from China, now working in Oakland, California along with his three trained children.

When we were trying to describe to him what 'holistic health' was back in the early '70s, as the 'integration of the body, mind, and spirit in medicine', he finally understood what we meant and began to tell us this story in Pidgin Chinese.

The three bodies story

"If you take a person who knows nothing and show them a block of ice and say, "Ice!" they will touch it, and feel how hard and cold it is. Then, you take it away. They smile and say, "Ice," as they think of this block, that's hard and cold.

Then you bring them a bowl of water and put it in front of them. They put their finger in it and say, "Water!" As the submerge their fingers in the water, it sticks to their fingers. They mess with the water and it starts to splatter. Then, they tip the bowl and watch it flow. They smile and say, "Water", and so they think they have learned something new.

You bring them a Thermos with some steam in it. You take off the top of the Thermos, carefully, under their face. They are taken back by this heat. They try and grab at it, but they can't, and you say, "Steam", and they think, they know three new things now. 'Ice' is hard and cold. 'Water' is sticky and flowing. 'Steam' is hot and disappears. So they think they know three different things".

Dr. Kong smiled and looked into our eyes, with a twinkle in his own eyes, he said:

"With a little *"lolegee"* they learn that all these three things are really the same thing, not different. The ice represents the body since it is solid. The water is like the mind and emotions. The steam is like the 'spirit', (called 'Shen' in TCM which, resides in the 'heart'). With a little "lolegee" we know that the body, mind, and spirit are the same *thing*."

Dr. Kong smiled big and we looked at each other and said, "Well, we want some of this lolegee. What is it?"

We started looking up "lologee" in his Chinese/English dictionary. He pointed to a word, yet it didn't say anything that looked like lologee. What the Chinese characters said was wisdom and contemplation. Finally, Dr. Lam Kong looked up a different word and there it was, 'knowledge', pronounced "lolegee", in Chinese pidgin. Yet, what he also meant, was wisdom and contemplation.

With a little knowledge, wisdom, and contemplation, we learn that these three different forms as body, mind, and spirit, are really the same patterns. It is only their appearance that is different.

This also applies to the fourth body which would be the quantum world form of water in our story above. Quantum world is on the level of the atomic components of water: hydrogen and oxygen. This level is about the 'particle'/quantum wave nature of the electrons, protons, and neutrons etc. of which hydrogen and oxygen are made. We will learn that in my world, it would be the wondrous condition of the eternalself's 'informotion' patterns of our unique illuminatedself.

Let's get practical in the rest of the chapter and compare the love letters on each 'body' level to give you the ability to understand the speed and efficacy of working with each level.

Three of the four bodies that we need to understand resemble the ice, water, steam story about being the same in different forms. Now we can add the fourth–Quantum Informotion that contains the informotion blueprint reflection of the other three bodies. And it is a dynamic quantum blueprint.

We have four bodies to read love letters

We can read our present love letters in each of these four 'manifestations'—our physical body and mind, our electromagnetic meridian system, our spirited chakras, and our eternalbeing. Yet when it comes to Bathwaving to make a quantum shift, it is most effective to read the first three—body, mind and spirited self–and shift the fourth, our informotionbeing. I have gained faith in and trust in "quantum waves structure matter" theory according to the laws of the quantum world of the fourth body. (the Bathwaving Informotrix).

I'll tell you why now.

The classic four 'body' system

The equal though different level 'bodies' are, first, the physical body. As Einstein along with others says matter is made up of energy that is just moving slow enough so that we can touch it.

Working with this physical love letter is like sending the love letter snail mail to the you-niverse. Slow, but maybe sure? Of course. But we are usually working on many levels, which I hope to explain.

The second level body is made up of the Meridian System in the ancient Tradition of Chinese Medicine. They are the electrical meridians or chords from each of the organs which plug the organ into the energetic system of the body, or chi system in Chinese. They are all connected like individual electrical circuits to the main big circuit and switch box, much like a house has. That energy body or EMF (Electromagnetic Field), extends out probably like a magnetic field, about a half-inch to one inch from the body, depending on how strong my chi force is. Research using Kirlian photography has captured countless photos of this body. Working with this second body is like sending love letters by phone or Western Union.

The third body is the one that is the summation of organ tissues and endocrine glands' fields. It is still an energetic field in nature though a more diffuse field that has been seen with radio telemetry. This field is named the 'aura' and extends about eight to nine feet out from the center of the body. It can be measured and mapped by a SQUID (Superconducting Quantum Interference Device). It looks like a big donut-shaped field, a torus, and has been described by various artists and mystics sometimes as a pear-shaped structure that surrounds the body. Google a radio telemetry photo.

Most of the organs and hormone systems of the body have fields including *nuclear spin forces** associated with them. The interplay of all of these fields creates this structure and is used in a lot of faith healing and energy (chi gung) healing treatments. This is the internet method of sending love letters. Fast and sure.

The fourth body has been poorly understood, even by mystics, and it was mislabeled as the 'causal' body. I say mislabeled because what I live at this level is simultaneously manifested in all the other three bodies, without the cause and effect time lag. This fourth 'body' is made up of 'data and informotion" patterning which is prior to energy and becomes the informotion which forms the energy/matter of the other level bodies.

This informotion might be in the form of the eternalself's BATHWAVE's, which like a bridge, or stepping stones, link or download into the other three level 'bodies' or energy structures. As we said earlier, this fourth body is a pattern or blueprint or matrix for the energy/matter of the first three bodies.

Wouldn't you want to read love letters of this miracle blueprint: love letters that can transform the other three bodies instantly, faster than cause and effect? Wouldn't you want to be able to respond to those love letters with that same instantaneous awareness?

This is the miraculous (mirror-call-us) way of sending resplendent love letters. We will learn how to use quantum methods with the Relationshifting techniques.

Qualities of the 'LL' 'Field' of the fourth body

There is another field I would like to tell you about, the 'LL' Field. Pearsal P. (1998)

Research has been done on this non 'force', which is called, in some books, the fifth "field", though, it is NOT an energy field.

It is often referred to as a matrix in literature. I might call it the Informotrix (I), which you might think of as a "I point" of our living.

The research done at Princeton University described seven qualities of the 'LL Field'.

- The first quality of this matrix 'LL' (I am adding an L to signify Love Letter) is that it is '**instantaneous**'.
- The second quality of this LL matrix is that it is **free of limits. It appears everywhere all the time, with us at its center.**
- The third quality is that **nothing outside of us stops it or can change it**. Therefore, it's a powerful Love Letter.
- The fourth quality is that it is **accompanied by the four other fields, the electromagnetic force, the field of gravity and the two nuclear forces which are the weak force and the strong force of the nucleus.** It is a Love Letter with fusion!

- The fifth quality is that **it fills all space as vibrating data becoming information transmitted within and to all people and things**. So everyone and everything receives our Love Letter of the LL Field. Can't get much better than that!
- The sixth quality says that the heart's field is 50,000 times stronger than the brain's field. This fact is about energy fields and implies that the LL field is probably way beyond the power of either of these fields.
- The seventh quality is that it has **no entropy, contradicting the second law of thermodynamics. This means that it does 'not fall apart or diminish ever'**. It's the Love Letter that 'keeps on giving'.

Dr. William Tiller has noted that this "field" is simultaneous with biophysical changes. Pearsal P. (1998) and Tiller, W. (1997)

Whatever is in this LL field manifests in all our four level 'bodies' simultaneously.

This fits Einstein's recommendation that in responding to what problems we are facing today, we may want to use another method of thinking than the one we were at, when we created the problems.

Even the qualities of the 'LL" field are all reflective of the quantum world!

Are you getting excited about learning to understand and read the love letters you are writing to myself on another level than you may be presently thinking?

That is what Relationshifting is about: Using the awareness and understanding of my unique 'LL' Field to transform my life into resplendent living.

With Relationshifting I'll be able to write the Eternal Love Letters of my dreams. The LL Field is the area to which Relationshifting through the tool of the Bathwaving technique wishes to prepare my bridge to resplendent living.

The LL Field could also be called, in terms of Relationshifting, the place where my personalbeing and eternalbeing commune to create awareness as illuminatedbeing.

Let's take a look now at some studies of some of our four bodies' phenomena. Perhaps these studies will help you see the relatedness of our four bodies.

Heart coherence: A third body phenomenon

So much is misunderstood in the field of science. For instance, we believed in the past that the brain was the most powerful and important organ in the body because it was the seat of thought. Here are a couple of studies that point us in a different direction.

The most recent research done by Dr. Roland McCrady at Heartmath Research Center has demonstrated some new information in this area. For instance, the heart's electromagnetic force

(EMF) is 5,000 times stronger than the brain's EMF and the heart has nearly as many nerve cells and glial cells. Pearsal P. (1998) 62-74. He also showed that when you have an intuition, it registers in the heart's torus field before it registers in the brain's electromagnetic field, (EMF). It was also shown on a biological level that heart cells in tissue culture, which means grown on a dish in a fluid, if separated beyond a certain distance on the plate from other heart cells, would die. But that if they were close enough to each other, they would continue beating like heart cells. Childre, D. (2004) (Heartmath. com) That's right. Alone each cell dies, yet when in proximity they beat together in unison and live. This is called being in coherence. Coherence appears to be a quality that occurs in the third 'body'.

Heart coherence is when the heart rate variability is in sync with itself. In other words, when all my heart cells are beating in unison with each other, you have a smooth curve showing my heart rate variability. When two people are in close proximity, say holding hands, their hearts will go into coherence as long as there's no irritation or conflict between them.

Kirlian photographs: A second body phenomenon

Research from scientific laboratories have verified a lot of the energetic sensations that people have in the presence of people they like versus people they are in conflict with. Kirlian photography done at UCLA by Dr. Thelma Moss also verified some of these findings, looking at the second energetic EMF body. This form of photography originated in Russia by Dr. Semyon Kirlian used a photographic plate that had a voltage drop across it and could show the presence of acupuncture points at the fingertips. (Moss, T. (1980) and Gennaro, L. (1980).

Dr. Moss's study found that when people's fingers were placed on the plates and they felt loving toward each other, the electromagnetic fields close to the fingers would connect. When the people felt conflict and judgment towards the other, the electromagnetic fields would deviate away from the other person. These were all reported in scientific studies, but not common knowledge, say, in news broadcasts or newspapers. The results of Kirlian photographs is a second 'body' or level manifestation.

Perhaps the best experiment was done with a leaf and shown in this chapter. The leaf was cut and a Kirlian photograph was taken immediately. Where the piece of the leaf was cut off, there was still an electromagnetic field picture of that missing portion of the leaf appearing on the plate.

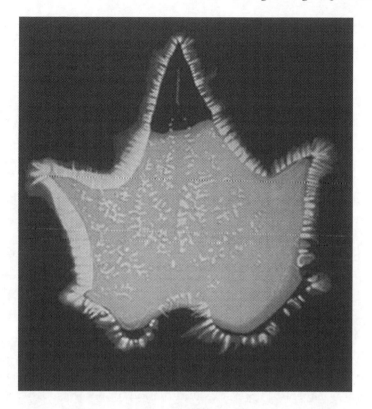

Acupuncture points, seen in Kirlian photos, and used in Traditional Chinese Medicine, can be used to harmonize the organs and the health ridding the body of various pains and diseases.

These studies help us know that our second and third level energy bodies are verifiable.

Back to the fourth level body

The point I am making here is that these four level bodies are akin to the ice, water, steam, and quantum waves, in that they are actually all the same identical self, though they are in different forms. Like one melody played in different keys.

This fourth level of the data and information, the fourth body, took my interest 12 years ago. After practicing Chinese medicine for 28 years, I was diagnosed with a QXCI machine (Quantum Xrroid Consciousness Interface) as having liver cancer. After three more evaluations with the machine, I was also diagnosed with lung cancer and liver cancer as two of my top ten ailments. I wasn't about to dismiss these diagnoses.

I thought I was doing everything to support my health and well-being, according to orthomolecular dietary therapies, herbal regimes, acupuncture treatments, and religions. After I began treating myself alternatively an autoimmune skin condition erupted, which was very telling, literally. They were all love letters, though I didn't know that at the time.

With these diagnoses I knew that I needed to integrate information/data of the four level bodies with all that I had learned. I began a process of documenting my BATHWAVEs and their 'impact' in my system.

Einstein is quoted as saying that energy can neither be created, nor destroyed. Therefore, a belief–which becomes an in-formed energy pattern–can neither be created nor destroyed. A belief's form can be 'trans-formed'. With this idea, I formulated a technique and called it the BATHWAVE Loving Technique (BLT).

There is a YouTube demonstration that might help you learn it if you can watch it called Bathwaves I and II. It is the same technique with the old name. I'll describe how to do it in the next chapter.

BATHWAVEs are the eight phenomena that mentors seem to agree are manifestations of who we are. This wisdom is also reflective of the eight bagua (trigrams) of the I Ching (pronounced e-ching).

I had studied Educational Kinesiology with Dr. Carla Hannaford, noted research physiologist and author, so I knew the importance of integrating the brain, body, and energy-Hannaford, C (2002)–the first, second and third level bodies–to be in charge of our lives. Her books inspire countless educators, scientists, and parents, including myself, to practical tools for enhancing learning and transformation. Hannaford, C (2010). I was inspired to use this information to synthesize a system, to encourage my free expression.

I was convinced from neuroscience that a soft, gentle touch of the whole body coupled with awareness and speech was enough to remodel the limbic system and possibly the pre-frontal cortex. This information formed the movements and language used in the Bathwaving techniques of Face It and Embrace It, and Replace It with your Grace.

The neuroscience behind the techniques will be discussed in detail in a later chapter called, How Low Can You Limbic?, named after a stick dance that we loved to do when I was in my 20's, called the Limbo Dance. Dancing has encouraged my self-expression and therefore supported my sanity and health throughout my present 70 years of life.

Summary

To change my living I need to be able to read my love letters.

I receive love letters via all of my four bodies.

Relationshifting techniques help me learn to recognize certain phenomena as love letters that may be manifesting on different levels:

- the physical via illness or health;
- the mental, via thoughts and ideas that are contained in BATHWAVEs;

- the social, via the people situations and relationships I attract to myself; and
- the Bathwaving informotion, via dreams and daily events.

All these love letters understand our true desires and give ourselves encouragement to change by making a quantum shift.

Resplendency of the fourth body underlies the three bodies and creates a type of link to the data/informotion or resplendent 'building' informotion for our physical, mental, and energetic bodies. Years ago I wrote, "Don't be the force. Be the field... of love." Now I write, "Don't be the field. Be the creative entanglement of data and informotion for my resplendency."

Now that I have set the stage, let's move on to learning about my eight bottom lines that prepares me to see our BATHWAVEs clearly.

Thanks for staying with me as I explained the foundational understandings of why Relationshifting techniques, Bathwaving among them, work in an easy way. As I've mentioned, in the next chapter I'll describe how to do the Bathwave technique.

Bathwaving
Part 1: Face and Embrace

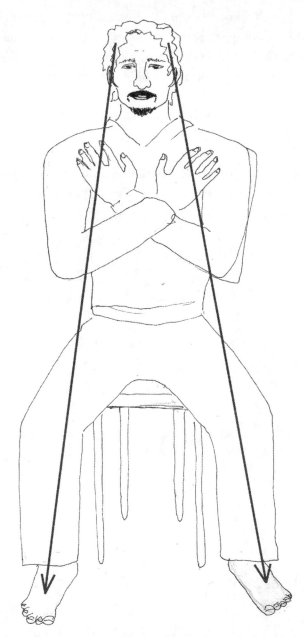

**Lightly and quickly hugging the body,
saying out loud what you are
facing and embracing.**

CHAPTER 4

ACE OF BATHWAVING THE EIGHT BOTTOM LINES
OR
GETTING OUR ASS-ETS IN GEAR

Philosophy for Success:

Keep my belief positive,
because my beliefs become my thoughts,
my thoughts become my words,
my words become my actions,
my actions become my habits,
my habits become my values,
my values become my destiny.
~Gandhi

As I mentioned previously, this quote by Gandhi led to the acronym BATHWAVE from Beliefs, Actions, Thoughts, Habits, Words, Attitudes, Values, and Emotions.

Discovering that these eight manifestations configure our personalbeing, our spirited mindful body, gives us a structure with which to begin understanding the love letters I give myself.

Eight is the number of the building units (Bagua) of the 64 chapters of I Ching. The I Ching is a blueprint that has been correlated with the 64 codes of the translating molecule (tRNA, 'translator RNA'), of our DNA, the molecule containing our genes and entanglement capability. Eight seems to be an important number in helping us make changes. You can see the correlation in the diagram I have created. Schonberger, M. (1992).

Staying in the BATHWAVE

Seeing the acronym BATHWAVE, it is very easy for me, and I hope for you, to keep these basic forms of self-expression in my awareness. It makes a good chant: BATHWAVE: Beliefs, Actions, Thoughts, Habits, Words, Attitudes, Values, and Emotions. Composer Jaiia Earthschild has written a song using BATHWAVEs as a theme!

Just as 'light' and the building blocks of all of our atoms (electrons, protons, etc.) seem to have two states, one technique for Relationshifting is named Bathwaving, to remind me of the emergent three natures of my being, reflected in my atomic whologram. 'Heart' for my particle nature as the central organ of my personal 'particulate' system—my first three level bodies—and, of course, waving for my 'wave' nature eternal pattern found in my fourth level body.

Bathwaving
Part 2: Replace with Your Grace

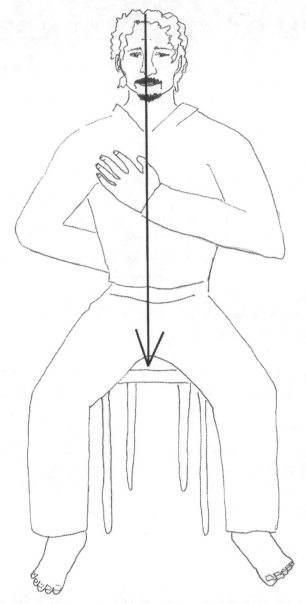

Hands stroke your midline Starting behind your heart.
One hand goes over head to front, down to chair.
At same time, say what you desire in each tense:
I can relax. I will relax. I relax -or-
I can, I will and I relax.

BATHWAVE Loving Transformation is the name of Part 1 of the Heartwaving technique and Part 2 is called the Quantum Shift. I've also nicknamed this technique the Ace of Heartwaving since all four words describing the process end in 'ace'. I face and embrace in Part 1, then replace with the grace of my true desire called the quantum shift in Part 2 which traverses the heart. See illustrations to help visualize this process.

Part 1 is a melting down of our former BATHWAVEs/information back into raw data. You might think of it as a computer program that is dismantled back down into its basic language components. Quantum Shift, Part 2, is the reconstruction of a new program. Perhaps I could continue with the visual idea of a snowflake pattern in the water of my body. Part 1 would be melting the snowflake pattern back to amorphous water, before creating a brand new pattern which would reflect my own design in the Quantum Shift.

Visualizing the material to be transformed

Heartwaving, the alternate name for the technique especially part two as it goes around the central body through the heart, transforms beliefs, actions, thoughts, habits, words, attitudes, values and emotions that I recognize through my love letters as not being healthy for my resplendent self.

Being a visual learner, I usually picture the BATHWAVE informotion as a fractal diagram much like the three-dimensional snowflakes, but a little bit more of a spiral, based on Fibonacci's number series called the Golden Mean. Since all biological forms evolve according to this structure, I have imagined this Heartwave Informotion Matrix (HIM) as a 3-D fractal. This would be the masculine aspect of our BATHWAVE pattern. The feminine aspect might be called the Heartwave Energetic Resonance (HER). I'll talk more about the feminine and masculine aspects in a later chapter.

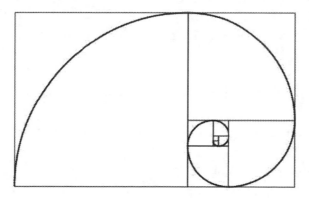

[Figure 4-1]

As yet, HIM/HER defies the ability to be photographed directly. However, it is generally accepted in science that the universe is a hologram, which means that if you break it into many pieces, each piece would contain the whole picture as the original one which is why I spell it whologram. Amazing isn't it? Our universe would be wholographic in nature across space (form) and time (movement). HIM/HER would be a wholograpic piece of my life and would outpicture my whole life.

All life on earth, from plants to humans, has been shown to follow the evolutionary form of a fractal (a repetitive spiral design) infinitely spiraling inward in our molecular/atomic structure to DNA and eternally spiraling out into galactic structures.

It is a plausible hypothesis that these material forms have an energetic blueprint reflecting an eternal repetitive pattern. The exciting hypothesis is that our fourth 'body' (beyond energy) with BATHWAVE informotion/data in-forms the first three 'bodies' with a design pattern translating into the spiraling fractal. It is a reasonable conjecture and useful in doing any transformative technique for visual or mathematical types. See figure.

More about the Bathwave technique

Back to the Bathwave technique: once we understand the BATHWAVE information we wish to change, we use four of our five physical senses in doing the transformation:

1. speaking the BATHWAVE out loud, for instance: "I face and embrace that I worry and I am ready now to shift that and do something different...",
2. listening to my words,
3. visualizing an image of embracing and loving my worrying since it did get me to where I am now,
4. feeling as I lovingly touch my skin and feel the emotion, if any, associated with it.

The first part of the BATHWAVE uses a quick light loving touch over the whole body–front, back and center–while speaking my current BATHWAVEs and embracing it. This is further explained physiologically in the chapter, "How Low Can You Limbic?", as a limbic and possibly neocortical reorganizer.

The front of the body mirrors what I am facing 'ahead of me' which signifies our BATHWAVEs about the 'future'.

The back of the body mirrors my 'past' BATHWAVEs since it is what is 'behind' me.

Where the front and back meet along my sides represents my BATHWAVEs about the 'present'.

I *muscle test* before and after every BATHWAVE.

(See appendix A: O ring muscle test.)

Aches, pains, itches...and other such symptoms can be understood using this informotion about front, back and sides of the body, and then dated by calibrating their location on the body into an approximate era of our life. The feet would signify distant 'past' on the back or distant 'future' time on the front, and the head, more present time or *'nonce'* time, referring to the present moment.

The quantum shift

The second part of the Bathwave, the Quantum Shift, uses a light stroke around my midline or central nervous system. This is based on the Cup Story of pouring the water of true desires into my cup, replacing the old.

The midline is part of the second level energy body, in Chinese Medicine. It is called the microcosmic orbit of the Ren (Conception Vessel) and Du (Brain Governor) meridians. It is the main electrical energy circuit of your body. On the third energy body, it is the core of the three meter torus of my heart's EKG field. On the fourth level 'body' I might say it's the quantum wave pattern on my heart-drive of the body's universe modem, akin to the hard drive of a computer which is where reprogramming would occur.

When I reshape a Quantum Shift sentence to my new desire, I need to use three tenses to reprogram our nervous system, since the brain has been built upon my old belief of 'past' and 'future' existence. I use the potential tense word 'can', future tense word 'will' and present tense, when speaking the new statement of my shift.

For example for the BATHWAVE: "I WORRY." the quantum shift might be:

Potential tense: I can relax, do my best, and the world is beautiful.

Future tense: I will relax, do my best, and the world is beautiful.

Present tense: I relax, do my best, and the world is beautiful.

Or they can be said in one sentence out loud: I can, I will, and I relax, do my best, and the world is beautiful touching around my core once.

The present tense statement needs to be repeated daily for three weeks to three months to make them habits. We recommend saying at night with eyes closed and then again in the morning with eyes open.

Quantum shift movement

Place one hand on my back above and behind my heart and other hand on my back from below my heart. Move top hand over the head midline, over the face to throat, past heart and lower abdomen past the groin to the chair if seated, while the other hand moves to the back bottom of the spine to eventually meet the other hand below the pelvis. If seated just move both hands to the chair and move the pelvis on chair to complete the cycle.

Modern philosophers and physicists are beginning to agree that this 'nonce' moment is the only time that exists. According to Quantum Entanglement Theory, when we shift and change things in the present, the past and the future are also surprisingly changed. This is called the 'entanglement of time'. Entanglement throughout space has been demonstrated and described in the chapter, "Entango While We Are In Entanglement", Chapter 7.

Reading our mirror-calls

To begin our study of translating our mirror-calls as we recognize our BATHWAVEs that we wish to replace and shift, we need to ask ourselves what 'verb or motion' has created an obstacle to my authenticity and prevented me from facing myself in my "mirror"?

With years of clinical experience and study, Relationshifting reveals there are eight basic blockages that are commonly sabotaging our ability to face and shift our beliefs, actions, thoughts, habits, words, attitudes, values and emotions. These I refer to as the eight bottom lines.

Before you begin going into a detailed study of myself according to tongue maps, symptoms, dreams, relationships and daily events, it is helpful to shift these eight basic blockages or obstructions to movement and thus transformation. Then we can begin the translation of our universe's love letters that we have given ourselves.

Bridge of the Eight Bottom Line Mirror Calls of Resplendence.

Eight awakening mirror-calls of our resplendency

We call these eight transformations, the basic eight awakening mirror-calls of our resplendency. The first three are related and called the ABCs, which are Accusing, Blaming, and Complaining and seem to occupy approximately 45% of my 'resistance' energy. The next three 'lie, hide and deny', usually comprise another 45% of my resistance to transformation. The last two obstacles are defending and justifying that make up the last 10% of my resistance pie.

Let's go through all eight basic awakening mirror-calls (miracles).

1. Accusing
This is the subtle 'judging' of our minds that will keep us accusing for most of our lives.

It took me years to understand and shift out of this function. Finally, I learned about Parmenides, a philosopher from before the time of Plato who, paraphrasing, was far ahead of himself when he said:

Humankind creates words that don't even exist, and then we spend our whole lives struggling against what doesn't exist.

The idea of evil was one example Parmenides mentioned. When a philosopher asked me to find something in the universe that I could hold in my hands that was a bad, I couldn't. There were only thoughts of some behavior patterns that come from our misunderstandings or desperation, that I know now are all shift-able. When I faced and embraced that I believed bad existed. Replacing it with, bad cannot will not and does not exist. I embraced judging bad and good, then I began to free myself.

It helps if I see and understand the mirror-call (miracle) nature of reality. For as I begin to understand the quantum shift that **'the universe is benevolent and good in not interfering with our transformation of these mirror-calls'**, I begin to appreciate myself in a deeper way.

"Appreciating" might be another quantum shift for whomever or whatever I am accusing. This book is a translation primer of all of the gifts I give myself that are the mirror-calls for my resplendency.

Before we leave this arena, **we need to ask whether we are accusing others or whether we feel accused/judged by others?**

The second option means we are accusing/judging ourselves which is mirrored by others. Use the O-ring muscle test to get answers.

When this is true for me then I might embrace that I don't value myself or that I am hard on myself. These BATHWAVEs might move to the quantum shift: "I value myself" and/or "I am being gentle with myself'" or I love myself unconditionally. The one that I need to put in will muscle test weak until I put it in. After the quantum shift it tests strong unless I have something else blocking it to shift.

Shifting our BATHWAVEs is the treasure hunt that leads one from accusation to self-actualization.

2. Blaming
Blaming is an obvious one, and it comes with the territory of modern media, which only reports the struggles and conflicts in the world. When I embrace that there's no need to blame, just to understand the nature of reality and entanglement, blaming can be eased and I can replace it with 'blessing'.

When "**I Face and Embrace I am blaming others for the way things are,**" **I might replace it in Part 2, with the quantum shift, "I can, I will, and I bless others for being a mirror-call of my resplendent nature."**

Then I have to check with muscle testing if I feel blamed which would be the mirror of self-blame. After embracing self-blame, the quantum shift might be: "I can, I will and I do understand and bless myself."

3. Complaining and Criticizing

This one is occupying the largest percent of most of my life, and can be embraced again and loved as a less than empowering habit of my daily routine.

Instead, I can 'connect' and 'communicate' with whomever until it becomes empathy with the person or thing I was complaining about, and who is sometimes 'us'. This will be explained later.

My quantum shift might be that I desire to understand what a person is going through.

Relationshifting these awakening mirror-calls profoundly transforms relationships without the need of confrontation.

4. Lying

These next three bottom lines are easy to remember because they have a little rhyme within them. Lying, Hiding, Denying.

Lying is really about deceiving myself or others about the way I believe things really are.

The quantum shift is that "I am open and honest with myself at all times" which serves me to a much greater degree.

5. Hiding

Hiding from myself and others, being invisible, and not being seen or heard, can be a tactic of survival for children.

As I enter adulthood I can embrace this, realizing that I no longer need to hide my voice or my being. I can speak my desires and step up to the plate however I choose, and those would be worthy quantum shifts. *"I am visible and speak my desires."*

The Relationshifting method would help me own and understand the hiding as what I do with myself.

6. Denying

This motion of denial has created the 'unconscious' of Western psychology. Since I don't really want to know everything, I 'unconsciously' deny things from my awareness without knowing it.

With courage, honesty, and commitment, the unconscious does not really need to exist. I can embrace this denial function, replacing it with the quantum shift that **"I am aware of everything about me"**.

The unconscious of others is not my business unless they are mirroring me. Then I need to be clear what they are denying and then use Relationshifting to see what needs to be shifted, and Heartwave **that it is still about me denying whatever their relationship is to me.**

This may or may not feel good at first, yet it does as soon as I face and embrace things, which takes only seconds. Bathwaving my eight bottom lines is in the long run desirable for my well-being, my wisdom, and my relationships.

I have heard it said that what is in my unconscious is what usually kills us. I had at least 15 faces of anger in my unconscious with my liver cancering. Whew! And I still Bathwave the triggers behind those emotions sometimes.

I cannot muscle test these last three—lying, hiding and denying—in the normal way for myself because I would lie, hide or deny about it and give myself the wrong answer!

There is a method I devised using the circular fingers muscle testing, to determine whether I am in denial. *I choose a name of someone whom I trust, and ask if I can 'ask about me from their position'* (and adopt their 'internet Heartwave whol'ogram space' for a moment,) muscle testing for the answer about me. This can get the correct answer for me.

For instance, when I muscle test I say may I test as Jessica, I get a yes. Then I muscle test the question, "Is Angela in denial?" I get an accurate answer. If "yes", I need to 'embrace' this denial out loud with the final quantum shift, "I am open and aware of everything about me".

7. Defending

When I feel or believe that I am being attacked, I will go into defense mode. Lawyers and judges are very, very good at this. They are paid to be.

I do not ever need to defend myself, unless I am in that field or career.

I can embrace that I tend to defend that which I believe in, but I realize it's a waste of my energy. I might replace it with, "I am fine just the way I am" or "I enjoy being the way I am" or "Everything is good, just as it is."

8. Justifying

We do this when we want to prove ourselves. Nobody needs justifying. Some people get paid for justifying: managers, CEO's, people who run things are paid to justify and do cost benefit analysis. However, in our lives we do not need to do that, outside of the field of business.

In my daily life, energy can be depleted justifying what I am doing. I do not need to explain to others or myself. Let's embrace justification and put in that "I can, I will, I do as I desire," or "I can, I will, I do act on my desires."

These eight obstructions or depletions of our energy or chi, once shifted, open the way for energized rejuvenation and a deep practice of Relationshifting and a study of Bathwaving. This has lead me to health, wealth, and wisdom of my relationships along with my basic relationship with myself as my personal and eternalbeings commune with my illuminatedbeing.

If I have difficulty shifting any or all of them I am not alone. Repetition is common for these deep patterns. Give myself twenty-one days to ninety days to feel stable with them. With my active awareness they will diminish and I will be able, for example, to shift from justifying to "doing what you desire" in a moment.

Summary

The eight manifestations of my personalbeing, BATHWAVEs, can be transformed to more loving and beneficial BATHWAVEs by using the Heartwaving technique.

First, I identify those BATHWAVEs presenting in the moment that are obstacles for my well-being.

Second, I use BATHWAVE Loving Transformation, (BLT), to face and embrace my current BATHWAVEs.

Third, I replace with grace my current BATHWAVEs with my desired BATHWAVEs by stating my desires while using the quantum shift stroking motion.

Fourth, I read my new quantum replacements every day for twenty-one days to ninety for solid results in living my desired BATHWAVEs.

Fifth, I use muscle testing every few days to verify that I am maintaining the shift.

Remember, that some of these patterns have been with me for many years, and it may be easy to slip back into these old patterns if I don't keep awareness.

As I become more aware of my BATHWAVEs, I should be on the lookout for eight basic awakening mirror-calls, my eight bottom lines, that create resistance to my ability to live resplendence. These eight mirror-calls are important, as they help me see what I desire to transform.

In the next chapter, I'll talk about how to recognize my basic relationship mirror-calls, the miracles that happen every day.

Ace of Heartwaving

Bathwave Loving Transformation (BLT)

A QUANTUM MOLECULAR MOVIE SHIFTING TECHNIQUE

It's all shiftable material. Are you open and willing to shift?

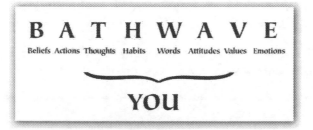

Part One:
Face It and Embrace It

- *Stroke body from head to toe*
- *Say, feel, and think of what you want to shift at the same time.*
- *Keep eyes open*

BACK = PAST
FRONT = FUTURE
SIDES = PRESENT

Don't miss a spot!

Part Two:
Replace It With Grace

- *Say what you desire three times:*
  - *with verb "can" (potential tense)*
  - *with verb "will" (future tense)*
  - *with present tense*

Quantum Shift

At the same time do a simple stroke across seven nerve hormone chakras:
With one hand on forehead and other hand on back of neck, move to top of the head, down to ears, to throat, past heart to lower abdomen while one hand moves to the bottom of the spine.

• Drink as much water as possible •

OPTIONAL MUSCLE TEST: *Put thumb and baby finger on your weakest hand together to form a ring. Put index finger from other hand in center of ring. Say your name and test the strength of your ring. It will be strong if you have drunk enough water. Say "I am a cabbage" and test. It will be weak (unless you are a cabbage). Use this test to test the efficacy before and after bathwaving and quantum shifting.*

Eight Basic Bottom Line

Mirror-Calls
(Miracles)

AWAKENING RESPLENDENCY

"Ace" / Heartwaving

PART ONE: *Bathwaves:* Face It and Embrace It;
Speaking and feeling while lovingly stroking body

PART TWO: Replace it with Grace/*Quantum Shift*
Circle mid-line with hands while saying quanta. Must test for shift.

Bathwaves ⟶	*Quantum Shift*
1. ACCUSING I accuse people of things. I judge myself and/or others. I feel something is against me or blocking me. I feel accused or judged by others.	1. I appreciate people or things. I love myself and others unconditionally. The Universe is good and benevolent and works to help me. I feel valuable. I feel gentle with myself.
2. BLAMING I am blaming others. I am blaming myself. I feel blamed.	2. I bless others for the way they are a mirror-call of my resplendency. I bless myself. I stop blaming myself.
3. COMPLAINING/CRITICIZING I am complaining about/criticizing myself and/or others or situations.	3. I am complimentary with myself and others. I complement and commune with myself and others.
4. LYING I deceive myself and/or others.	4. I am honest and open with myself at all times. I am open and honest with others with discernment.
5. HIDING I am hiding from myself and/or others.	5. I am visible and speak my desires.
6. DENYING I have been burying things under and "unconscious" rug unknowingly.	6. I am ready, willing and able to know everything about me.
7. DEFENDING I am defending or explaining myself or others.	7. I am fine being just the way I am.
8. JUSTIFYING I am justifying and proving myself to others.	8. I do as I desire. I am good just as I am.

Mirror-Calls of my Resplendence
Mother - Son/Daughter

His/Her BATHWAVE to face & embrace:
   I must still need a mother...nurturance
His/Her Quantum Shift:
   I can live self-nurturing
         I will live self-nurturing
               I am self nurturing

CHAPTER 5

BASIC MIRROR-CALLS (MIRACLES)
OF RELATIONSHIPS FOR RELATIONSHIFTING
OR
A TRANSLATION LIST OF RELATIONSHIPS

Bathwaving goes with me wherever I go.
Relationshifting goes where I can't go.
~Dr. Angela Longo

The gift of irritation

When I own and embrace the issues I have with our relationships, I begin to perceive that living is always a mirror-call of my resplendent living. How? Those situations that agitate me are essentially enlightening my nature.

Relationship triggers, those actions I dislike in others, are the mirrored reality of me that I can shift in my selves to heighten my awareness of my resplendence.

Learning to translate and replace the reflected BATHWAVE is the purpose of this chapter. There is a useful work page at the end of this chapter.

When I face and embrace what I observe others doing that bothers and irritates me, I see those behaviors in others as specific mirror-calls I can replace. This benefits both of us. When I own those 'bothersome' behaviors of other people as only reflections of my own BATHWAVEs (beliefs, actions, thoughts, habits, words, attitudes, values and emotions) I take one step over the bridge to resplendency.

As a Bathwave, I can begin to shift the mirror-call-us (miraculous) dance of my relationships to prepare for enlightening and revealing my personalbeing. When I can connect my personalbeing and my eternalbeing through the Heartwaving technique, my true communioning selves emerge.

The person with whom I have 'relationship triggers' is significant in its underlying meaning and mirror-call to me. Below I will look at some common relationship mirrors. Talking to a mirror may be useful.

The basics mirrors for my translation are (with appreciation to Jung and others):

- Mothers are about my (feminine side's) self-nurturance and self- care.

- Fathers are about my (masculine side's) self-guidance.
- Partners and friends are about my own beloved's self-love of the gender that they are.
- Children are about my creativity…masculine or feminine, depending on their gender.
- Authoritarian characters might be about my self-guidance/discipline in the gender that they are.
- Animals pertain to what that animal means to us specifically. When you have no idea, look at some dream book imagery, such as:
  - Cats might be about my feminine side.
  - Dogs, about unconditional love in my life.
  - Horses might be high ideals.
  - Birds, transcending or bird's eye view.

Translating and shifting model illustrations:

Mother relationship mirror

Angela saying:
"My <u>mother</u> irritates me (her child)."

Relationshifting (BATHWAVE) translation;
"My <u>self-nurturance</u> irritates my feminine creativity."

After facing and embracing this in Part 1 of the Bathwave technique, the Quantum Shift might be with "My self-nurturance can, will, and …:
"My <u>self-nurturance</u> supports my feminine creativity."

I re-mind myself by repeating the present tense quantum shift daily for three weeks.

Father relationship mirror

Angela saying,
"I feel my <u>father</u> doesn't love me (his child)."

Relationshifting (BATHWAVE) mirror-call:
"I feel my <u>self-guidance</u> doesn't love my feminine creativity."

Facing and embracing this feels good. The quantum shift might be with I can, I will, I…:
"I feel my <u>self-guidance loving</u> my feminine creativity."

I re-mind myself by repeating the quantum shift daily for three weeks to three months.

Partner or friend relationship mirror

Angela saying,
"My partner isn't romantic towards me."

Relationshifting translation of our BATHWAVE:
"My beloved masculinity isn't romantic towards my femininity."

After embracing this BATHWAVE, the quantum shift might begin with
"My beloved masculinity can, will, and … :
"My beloved masculinity is romancing my femininity."

I re-mind myself by repeating only the quantum shift above daily for three weeks.

Child relationship mirror

Daniel says, *"My son isn't listening to me (father)."*

Relationshifting BATHWAVE translation:
"My masculine creativity isn't listening to my self-guidance."

Embracing this in his body, he quantum shifts:
"My masculine creativity listens to my self-guidance."

Repeat quantum shift statement daily for three weeks.

Two true stories

Once I got the gist of this practice, I began to recognize some of my mirror-calls at the time they were occurring. I also began to perceive the miraculous nature of it all, in that I create the "mirror-call-us" to understand my true nature and the obstacles I may be unknowingly creating.

I'd like to share a couple of stories from people using their mirror-calls to change their lives, and more.

Mirror-calls of my Resplendence
Father - Son/Daughter

His/Her BATHWAVE to face and embrace:
I face and embrace that I still need a dad.

His/Her Quantum Shift to face and embrace:

I can live my own self-guidance
I will live my own self-guidance
I live my own self-guidance

Relationshifting a husband's mirror-call

Jessica called me, cold with fear. "I am in such a loving, compatible marriage, but lately, I have been having thoughts of leaving the relationship. These thoughts terrify me, because always in relationships before, they have signaled the end. Once those thoughts have come to me, somehow, sooner or later, the relationship deteriorates and eventually, I break up with the partner."

I asked her if she knew a reason she was thinking that way. "We haven't made love in months. The recession has put such a strain on our finances. I haven't had any income this year and I feel powerless and dependent on Don. He seems to be withdrawing to himself; there's no real romance between us at the moment."

As Jessica has been working with me for years, I was able to fairly easily point her toward the kind of Relationshifting that would yield results. First of all, I asked her if she knew what to do.

"I have been embracing that my beloved masculine side is selfish and withdrawn."

"Honey!" I cried. "That won't work, what are you doing?"

She took a deep breath. "I'm judging him as selfish," she said.

"Yes! And you are judging my own masculinity, in the same breath, the part of you that expects to make money?" I said.

First of all, we had to sort out our Relationshifting priorities. In looking at the big picture I could see that she was back into believing that 'bad' things were 'happening' to her. I asked her if she really believes that nothing bad happens in the universe. "Oh, yes, I've been working on that. I know it's all good," she said. But I sensed some denial.

Now, one cannot muscle test one's own denial; someone else has to do it for you (or you can become your own surrogate). I muscle tested for her denial and sure enough, first she had to embrace her denial lovingly and replace it with the quanta, "I am open to seeing the complete truth." Only then was Jessica ready to deeply and lovingly embrace her judgments completely, rather than individually dealing with one issue after another. She put in the quanta, "I unconditionally love myself, Don, and everyone."

Mirror Call - Partners

Her BATHWAVE to face and embrace:
I face and embrace that I am irritated by my masculine beloved.

Her Quantum Shift to replace with her grace:
I can understand that my masculinity supports me.
I will understand that my masculinity supports me.
I understand that my masculinity supports me.

As she did this quantum shift, she shared with me how she finds breathing deeply helps her to embrace herself internally, feeling her inner body, while she touches her outer body. At some point, she told me she felt terror in her solar plexus.

I asked her, what does it looked like? "It looks like a wide-eyed, terrified elf out of a comic strip and it's got its arms wrapped around my center of power. It is myself, Saboteur!" She named it Golly and I instructed her to embrace it with her new found unconditional love until it dissolved, like the Wicked Witch in the "Wizard of Oz", completely vaporized. Then she put in the quanta, "I am my power manifesting my desires." I asked her to name her eternalbeing and to commune with it. I will write more about this in the chapter on our eternal friend.

Jessica called later to say that 15 minutes after our phone session, she met Don and he gave her the deepest, loving embrace.

"Finally!" I said, delighted. "Oh," she said, "we really are almost always loving and affectionate." I told her that I often hear her justifying and defending her relationship and would she test herself to see if that is true?

She said, "Yes, and as I start to embrace all that justifying and defending, a deep feeling of insecurity arises." So she embraced that, too, and replaced it with, "I am secure in myself and in all my relationships."

At this point we were well on the path of healthy relating for Jessica. We were already seeing how it shifted things for Don as well. In intimate relationships, no matter how we try to hide our critical thoughts and feelings, our partners are always manifesting them as a mirror, so we can see them. When we face them and embrace them, and replace them with the grace of our true desires, we begin to believe in the mirror-call-us nature of relationship.

Mirror Call: Woman with Cat

Her BATHWAVE to face and embrace:
I face and embrace that I am feeling victimized being a woman.

Her Quantum Shift to replace with her grace:
I can be safe as a woman.
I will be safe as a woman.
I am safe as a woman.

Relationshifting the neighbor's dogs

This is from a client's e-mail:

My husband and I love peace and quiet. We are musicians and cherish our late afternoons and evenings playing and composing songs. So when neighbors moved in with seven dogs amongst two houses, our lifestyle was thoroughly impacted. The dogs barked in four-part harmony for two to eight hours daily for months. Phone calls and requests yielded no results. My husband became primal a few times late at night, roaring in ways that are by no means standard for him. His health and our happiness were at stake. I had been confronted once by one of the dogs, a large, trained hunting dog, as I returned from an early morning walk. The dog raised its hackles, growled, snarled, and bared teeth, and succeeded in accessing my roar so I was able to turn around a dangerous situation.

As the dog turned away, one of his owners came up, "He's a guard dog," he said. "He senses evil, and if my husband yells at my family again, I'm going to kick his ass!" "Oh, and Aloha to you, too," I thought, but I bit my tongue.

A couple of months later, the four-dog harmony went on continually from afternoon through the night. A phone call yielded nothing; the owners were away. By the next afternoon, 24 hours into this bark marathon, I went to the driveway to see if I could calm the dogs. I am an animal lover and was writing about animal magic at the very time that this happened. The four dogs in the pen were not exactly rolling on their backs, but at least they were paying attention to me when, as if from nowhere, all three of the big hunting dogs came rushing at me, slathering jaws, hackles raised, preparing to leap at me and bring me down like a local wild pig! My husband and I both roared this time. The dogs backed down and I went home and started packing up our house, wondering where we would move to and how we would afford it.

At midnight, I called again, as the dogs were still barking and this time, I told the owners that they would in fact have to pay for our move. I had had to call the police and the humane society and was 100% over the neighbors.

I called Dr. Longo. "What are the dogs telling you?" she said. "That I should move," I responded. "No, no!" she said. "Once you get the gist of this practice, you'll start to recognize some of your mirror-calls at the time they are occurring. You'll also begin to perceive the miraculous nature of it all in the "mirror that calls us" to understand our true nature and the obstacles we may be unknowingly creating. You need to be teaching my best friends about A, B, C's—accusing, blaming, and complaining. *(They were actually teaching her! A.L.)* That's the bared teeth, and it has to do with unconditional love. I have to go, you work it out."

Dr. Longo always lets me do my own homework, but isn't that what all teachers and therapists need to do? So I started facing, first of all, my own inner "hounds of hell," that had in fact been harassing me, telling me that things were not okay in my life and those hounds were being really cruel and loud and mean in my inner being. I embraced my inner hounds and not very long after, a friend arrived in a police car in serious need of help. She had been kidnapped and terrorized overnight by a crazed ex. So after letting her sleep and feeding her for a few days, I spent an afternoon Relationshifting for her, or with her. Her quantum shift was, "I love and cherish and trust myself unconditionally." As we *matured the quanta*, I found that I could not give myself the unconditional love that I was guiding her toward and so we worked together. Three hours into the process, we both stopped, too exhausted to go on. We had matured her quantum shift to 21 years. We had half a lifetime to go, but we had grounded her deeply in some profound shifts, and I had shifted along with her.

As you shift together, many people find themselves tingling all over, body hair rising, chicken skin or yawning. We were both experiencing all of these and more. So I had, without planning it, been an unconditional best friend to someone, just like Angela had advised.

Almost immediately after she left, there was a knock on the door. The neighbor who owned the three hunting dogs was at the door. We invited him in and he began a complete, unconditional "apology for the past year and especially the past months." He promised to make things right. He went out and bought runners for his dogs and a nice bottle of wine for us, which he delivered that evening. We have now had almost a week, the first week of consecutive days of peace and quiet without barking in over a year. Our lives have changed almost overnight for the better.

With a quantum shift, I changed myself within and the outer world changed with me. My howling inner demons had to be tamed first and then my friend's, and only then, could the neighbors control their dogs!

Summary

To sum up this chapter, once you begin using Relationshifting and Heartwaving you'll see my mirror-calls more readily.

An issue with my mother might be a mirror-call to take better care of myself. A problem with my partner might be a call to deal with an issue at work. A problem with a dog might be about best friends or unconditional love.

Once you learn how to look at my BATHWAVEs and see that the griefs, fears, irritants or overwhelming events in my life are actually reflections of myself, or mirror-calls, you'll see that these mirror-calls can begin to help you shift my life to one of resplendency.

Use the "Work/Play Page for Relationship Love Letters" at the end of the chapter.

In the next chapter, Some En-Chatted Evening, I'll give you an example of how you can relationshift anytime and anyplace.

Using the Work/Play Page for Relationship Love Letters

Steps for translating my situation or gripes (my BATHWAVEs) in any social relationship:

Translating example #1:

I get irritated every time I finish a phone conversation with her.

"<u>Angela</u> has <u>resentment</u> toward her <u>mother</u>." Basic translation is:

"My <u>feminine creativity</u> has <u>resentment</u> toward my <u>self-nurturance</u>."

Bingo! We have now found the BATHWAVE Mirror-call of my Love Letter to myself!

It's not about my relationship with my mother. It is about relationship with myself.

Take this statement and Bathwave it after muscle testing whether it is true or not.

In my case, it is true. Unconsciously my feminine side has resented having to nurture myself since I was a child. Muscle testing strong for this, I proceeded to face and embrace not only this statement but all BATHWAVEs that come up for me. While lightly stroking the length of my body front, back and sides I may say a simple statement to the point or it may sound something like this:

"I face and embrace that my feminine side has resentment towards my self-nurturance since I've always felt sorry for myself wishing my mother was there for me more than I really thought she was. I am really stuck in my own self-pity party. I am ready now to let go of this old feeling of resentment and self-pity, this old need I have for a mother to nurture me and I am desiring to shift it."

The new quantum shift might be simply "my femininity appreciates my self-nurturance".

> "My <u>feminine creativity</u> can <u>appreciate</u> my <u>self-nurturance</u>."
> "My <u>feminine creativity</u> will <u>appreciate</u> my <u>self-nurturance</u>."
> "My <u>feminine creativity</u> <u>appreciates</u> my <u>self-nurturance</u>."

This quantum molecular shift completes the first Relationshifting of relationships example.

Use this form to help you clarify your love letters:

Work/Play Page for Relationship Love Letters

Here is a simple form for you to use in translating the love letters you are giving yourself. When Relationshifting your mirror-calls attempt to be specific with the issue:

_____ has an issue (_____) with _____.

Example:
Angela has resentment toward her mother.

- *Mothers* are about our (feminine side's) self-nurturance.
- *Fathers* are about our (masculine side's) self-guidance.
- *Partners and friends* are about our own beloved self of the gender that they are.
- *Children* are about our creativity...masculine or feminine, depending on their gender.
- *Authoritarian characters* might be about our self-guidance/discipline in the gender that they are.
- *Animals* pertain to what that animal means to us specifically. If you have no idea, look at some dream book imagery, such as:
    - Cats might be about your feminine side.
    - Dogs, about unconditional love in your life.
    - Horses might be high ideals.
    - Birds, transcending or bird's eye view.

Translation inserts:
My masculinity or femininity (whatever you physically are) has an issue with *translation of person* from basic mirror call list.

_____has an issue(_____) with _____.

_____has _____with _____.

Example:
My femininity has resentment toward my self-nurturance.

Muscle test should be strong. This is the complete BATHWAVE to take with you to the Heartwaving technique. After doing Part 1 of Heartwaving it will be easier for you to come up with a useful quantum shift for Part 2.

Summary

To sum up this chapter, once I began using Relationshifting and Bathwaving I understood my mirror-calls more readily.

An issue with my mother might be a mirror-call to take better care of myself. A problem with my partner might be a call to deal with an issue at work. A problem with a dog might be about best friends or unconditional love.

Once I learn how to look at my BATHWAVEs and see that the griefs, fears, irritants or overwhelming events in my life are actually reflections of myself, or mirror-calls, I saw that these mirror-calls began to help me shift my life to one of resplendency.

Use the "Work/Play Page for Relationship Love Letters" at the end of the chapter.

In the next chapter, Some En-Chatted Evening, I'll give an example of how one can relationshift anytime and anyplace.

Mirror Call: Authority/Citizen

His/Her BATHWAVE to Face and Embrace:
    My self guidance scares me...
His/Her Quantum Shift to replace with their grace:
    My self guidance can be confident.
      My self guidance will be confident.
        My self guidance is confident.

CHAPTER 6

SOME EN-CHATTED EVENING
OR
RELATIONSHIFTING WENT TO VETERINARY
SCHOOL WITH LISA, IN A CHAT

This following texting conversation demonstrates how a young woman who knows the Bathwaving technique is guided to relationshifting fun, Hawaiian style!

I've known Lisa, her 6 sisters and brothers, and her parents for almost 19 years. Lisa is 23 years old, graduated from Stanford and is currently in veterinary school.

Hawaiian Style Pidgin unedited:

Lisa: hi auntie Angela
how r u

me: great..writing book on relationshifting!
how u?

Lisa: pretty good

me: coming home?

Lisa: finally a little break from school
for a few days
have a quiz this friday
then one test and 2 quizzes next week
then 2 take home finals and 5 in class
then done
quick 3 weeks
not comng home yet

me: oh good luck...... whew

Lisa: july or august
i need some heartwaves
my roommate is on my last nerve

me: how come

what she do?

Lisa: she is just so demanding
and if i tell her no she has a temper tantrum

me: does your feminine side demand a lot of yourself, and then does tantrum yoga

Lisa: oh that's a good one
then what do i put in

me: Quantum Shift(QS) might be 'My feminine side can, will, and is understanding and gentle with myself, generous too.'
one repetition only for each verb tense
Sent at 8:46 PM on Wednesday

me: how does it feel?

Lisa: i feel a lot better

me: cool.......read QS daily for 3 weeks

Lisa: she is always nagging me about every little thing
i don't get how she is the one person who can get to me
all the time

me: she is mirroring you, to help u shift
lol
true?

Lisa: i guess so

me: i am just writing about it

Lisa: another one?
if ur not busy

me: sure......shoot

Lisa: not sure how to phrase this one
so i am really good friends with a guy in my class
we are surgery partners
so we study a lot and hang out
it just seems to me that his girlfriend hates me
and everyone tells me she hates me
i interact with her and hang out with her

is it jealousy
how can i fix the problem

me: muscle test
Sent at 8:52 PM on Wednesday

Lisa: its just weird because she isnt the only one, some of his friends that are girls hate me too just because im friends with him but when they get to know me better they really like me i just dont know what it is about me that makes them hate me

me: the mirror is about the jealousy my feminine side feels about the masculine side's brilliance muscle test that?

Lisa: but is my feminine side jealous?
i dont get it
cuz it doesnt bother me that they do it
it's just really awkward
Sent at 8:55 PM on Wednesday

me: OK.... is my feminine side awkward with my masculinity??

Lisa: no

me: feels awkward

Lisa: i think its the brillance thing

me: yes
with my brilliance(masculinity)
embrace how you hate how awkward you feel with your brilliance

Lisa: ok
Sent at 8:58 PM on Wednesday

me: put in that "I feel comfortable, appreciate and respect my brilliance and everyone's brilliance"
Sent at 9:02 PM on Wednesday

me: one repetition of each tense
Sent at 9:03 PM on Wednesday

Lisa: much better

me: gr8!
can I use that in my book

Lisa: excellent

Relationshift anytime, anywhere

From this chat session, I began to understand the struggles Lisa was living inside herself. Our session also helped me see in a different light Lisa's chronic swollen lymph glands and tonsils that she had most of her life.

These Bathwavings are beginning to transfigure Lisa's chronic discomfort with her own personal gifts, and lighten up her demanding nature with herself.

Whew...I resembled Lisa and lost my tonsils at 21 years old. Thank you for the mirror-call (miracle) for me, Lisa.

If you are curious about how this young woman turned around her two most difficult relationship issues in a thirty minute chat, and if you are interested in learning how to Relationshift and do the same for yourself, you have the correct book.

And I hope you have fun learning it!

In the next chapter, we'll explore how you can learn to dance with your personalbeing and your eternalbeing, or entango with entanglement.

Boyfriend/Husband · Girlfriend/Wife

His BATHWAVE to face and Embrace:
My feminine side is not hearing my masculine
needs and desires.

His Quantum Shift to replace with his grace:
My own feminine side can hear and support my needs and desires.
My own feminine side will hear and support my needs and desires.
My own feminie side hears and supports my needs and desires.

CHAPTER 7

EN-TANGO WHILE WE ARE IN ENTANGLEMENT WITH RELATIONSHIFTING

Entangled waves mirror each other instantly.

~Schrodinger

Recognizing the entanglement of mirror-calls, in every moment, is what makes Relationshifting, instantly so profound.

~Dr. Angela Longo

Relationshifting instantly

As a research scientist and TCM doctor, I wanted to understand the phenomenal speed of change in my life and in my clients' lives that I was observing with Relationshifting.

I realized that I needed to consider the space/time paradigm shift predicted by the Entanglement Theory of quantum world. Entanglement was originally discovered when two electrons (particle/ waves) from an atom were separated by a great distance. One was perturbed and the other responded in a mirrored manner at the same exact time. This simultaneity defied the existing laws of cause and effect and space/time. Mind boggled, Einstein labeled the phenomenon as 'Spooky Theory'.

When BATHWAVEs are shifted for a painful condition, my clients and I have noticed that *the pain seems to disappear instantly with the transformation.* I began to understand that the 'pain', in that instant, *is the BATHWAVEs.* This challenged all the science I had been taught *all my life*. It blew my proverbial mind, and created a series of questions:

- Could I be living like the quantum world with a nature like a quantum 'wave' that exists in entanglement with myselves and my world?
- If so, would I be able to mirror myselves and my world instantly, thus defying cause and effect and the old concepts of time and space?
- Would there be an equivalent aspect of the self like the quantum wave nature of matter as compared to my "particle" personalself?
- Yet the quantum wave 'intimately localizes the new 'particle' which I call a "wavicle"... so maybe that's how miracles occur?
- Do I just have to know my eternalself (my quantum wave-like pattern, and as such, my personalself is manifested as I desire?

Employee   **Employer**

His/her BATHWAVE to face and embrace:
   I face and embrace that I am being really hard on myself...

His/her quantum shift to replace with their grace:
   I can be gentle with myself.
     I will be gentle with myself.
      I am gentle with myself.

With these thoughts I proceeded to develop methods and systems to assist myself and others in transfiguring obstacle patterns into supportive personal awareness with ease of living quantum resplendence. Translating relationships, daily events, symptoms, dreams, tongue maps and so on... into the love letters of BATHWAVEs, might serve one to choose to shift when desired.

Since all biological evolution occurs according to the golden rule of Fibonacci's Number Series, it seems reasonable to assume that the patterns of information or BATHWAVES, that we are shifting, may also be redirected in fractal designs that reflect the golden rule. As one transforms a BATHWAVE of oneself, according to Systems Theories, our whole pattern emerges transfigured.

According to Capra it seems ultimately—as quantum physics showed so dramatically—there are no parts at all. So what I call a part, is merely a pattern in an inseparable web of relatings. Therefore, the shift from the parts to the whole (in science), can also be seen, as a shift, from objects to relatings. From things to actions. From static to pulsating motion.

This idea, along with Entanglement Theory, explains how Western Medicine is shifting from treating diseases as part of a body, to transforming beliefs or other BATHWAVE patterns of a whole person. This also explains, how Traditional Chinese Medicine (TCM) works, in its five elemental relatings that connect every organ of the body to each other organ in a web of inseparable relatedness. No wonder TCM worked so miraculously and captivated my mind and body as soon as Dr. Kong shared it with me, for which I am eternally grateful. This Five Element related organ system will be shared in Part III of the book as a map of BATHWAVE patterns to Heartwave. It is useful information from the causing and effecting world from the East

When I change my BATHWAVEs, I change my living

Here's an exciting revelation. Have you considered what 'Entanglement' implies about what happens when we are replacing our BATHWAVEs?

Only one thing...that the new informotion is mirrored throughout the world of our entanglement.

En-tangoing gives people the informotion pattern of my new way of being and the ability to shift as you have. However, people do have free will and can choose not to shift. It seems from the testimonials of my clients that most people who were known to be involved with the issues, have shifted to improve accordingly.

With whom and what are we in entanglement? At least, it would be everyone we have ever met. At best, with six degrees of separation it includes everyone on the earth. Either way it fits what some mystics have always said, that we 'are responsible for our world' and 'be the change you want to see in the world', and to 'change the world, change myself first'.

Could it be this easy?

With Bathwaving, creating change in my life has been easier and sometimes instantaneous, but I noticed that not everything in my universe responded to the quantum shift I underwent.

My next step was in learning to mature my universe, or bringing it up to speed, to totally make the quantum shift. I hope this next story will help explain 'maturing my universe'.

A client example

I had a surfer client who was chronically tired, and to keep it simple, one of his bottom line shifts of accusing was that he needed to love himself unconditionally as well as loving others. Yet every week he would talk about wanting to leave his pregnant wife to surf and forget working. I finally asked him to muscle test how old he was with this shift and he was only one-year-old!

Memories of floating in the womb were still fresh, like surfing, (LOL), so we invented the maturing technique I'll describe below. Today he is the father of a happy family with a eight-year-old boy.

As I mature a quantum shift, I can also go past my present age, well into the future by asking myself what my beliefs are, for the age I muscle test. For instance, if I tested a weakening of the shift at 62, well into my future, I might find that I have a belief about my retirement that impacts this shift. Embracing it and replacing it now will unburden you of these future concerns in this moment, and lighten me up.

Out of the Peter into the Pan
Or
Maturing with the Bathwaving Technique

Leaving Never-Never-Land for Always-All-Ways-Land

I always admired Peter Pan, probably because I was fascinated with science at a young age, and tried using it to get love and approval in my relatedness with my chemist father, with whom I was unable to bond. A serious intellectual child, I grew up quickly without maturing, hence my fascination with Peter Pan. I only discovered all this through Relationshifting my relationships with men over the years. This insight has provided Bathwaving material of my co-dependency also.

The method for maturing with awareness is the following:

Once an important bottom line quantum shift is put in with the Bathwaving quantum shift technique (Part 2), the next step is to ask if you have any frozen ages with this shift using muscle testing.

If you muscle test yes, you are looking for the age at which the O-ring muscle gets weak and opens as you say your new quantum shift. Muscle test starting at birth. You can count by five's when possible.

As you find an age, no matter how young, ask yourself what happened at that age to challenge my belief in my new quantum shift. It may be a very simple event, like a move into a new house, or a sibling birth.

If you can't think of it, you can muscle test to get information. Use general categories like: family, finances, health, education, religion, mental/emotion, etc. After you get a category, get specific within the category: for instance, if family muscle tests strong then ask if it has to do with: father, mother, sister, brother, husband, children, grandparents or friend. Next find the action that is the issue.

Embrace and love myself losing that shift during that time. Excellent!

Find an appropriate modification on the same quantum shift that led you to that age. Re-do quantum shift, Part 2 to put it into the heart-drive with the phrases I can, I will, I am… Muscle test that the quantum shift went in.

Next, *muscle test what age the new shift is frozen at starting at the previous age at which you were just challenged.* When you get the next age, begin again by muscle testing the issue as I described above. At the end of this chapter you will find a Heartwaving Maturing Technique Check List.

I found this an easy way to mature myself. I was surprised at how immature many of my shifts were, especially around relationships. It is the fastest method our culture affords me for maturing my BATHWAVE patterns, though I started using this technique at 50 years old.

I will give a detailed example of an entanglement that happened spontaneously, while I was writing this chapter.

Another example of entangoing

As a girlfriend was typing this from my live dictation of this chapter, an amazing entanglement around immaturity occurred. Her ex-husband called her, asking if she could talk now, to which she replied in irritation, "No, I am working with Angela right now." She ended the call, angry with him for 'checking up on her'.

Noticing her anger, I invited her to relationshift the mirror-call. She said "I hate when he calls, because it always leaves me unsettled."

Looking at her husband as her mirror-call, I asked her to muscle test, whether her own masculine side was trying to control, restrict, limit, manipulate and therefore unsettle her feminine side.

She had denied that it was true within her, and insisted it was his influence, that made her feel this way. But, she was shocked when her muscle test confirmed that I was correct in translating the mirror-call. At my invitation she began to embrace her own masculine side's domination and suppression of her feminine authority.

Her quantum shift was:

"My masculine beloved honors and respects my feminine beloved, as I am free to live my true self."

When I asked her to find out what age she was, in this quantum shift, she muscle tested three-years-old and she remembered how she almost drowned at the beach at that time. Her mother, fearing her survival, pulled her out. The family returned home and she was put to bed. Her parents told her six siblings to leave her alone. She felt abandoned she said. At this point, I had to force her to come up with the feeling she had experienced. She felt sadness and anger at 'being abandoned'. At 58 years old now, she felt sadness and anger at being alone in her apartment, reminiscent of the bedroom scene at three-years-old.

Her quantum shift became:

"I understand that I am valuable and worthy of my own love and attention."

She muscle-tested the new quantum shift to *six-years-old, when she failed to receive a specially loved doll in favor of her infant sister.* She felt overlooked. I invited her to Bathwave this mirror-call.

She faced and embraced becoming like a talking doll, someone who analyzed everything and suppressed her own anger.

The quantum shift became**: "I understand that I am always gently there for myself."**

Beginning at 10 years old, this shift muscle tested up to 50 years old when she realized that her marriage was "ugly" and she needed to leave it. Embracing that, she shifted to:

"All the relationships I am living are a mirror-call of my resplendent nature."

This lead her to age 56 when she blamed her ex-husband for all her marital problems for which she left him. After embracing blaming and replacing it with blessing, her shift became:

"I bless my partner's mirror-calls of my resplendent self."

She muscle-tested 60 years old as weak and went backwards to age 59.

She faced and embraced her whole body again:

"I embrace that I set myself up, to lose my blessings."

Her shift was: **"I believe that I am successful in living my blessings."**

This muscle tested strong counting by tens to 200 years old and completed our session. She said she felt a peace she hadn't felt in a long time.

In remote healing and group prayer sessions, we always notice that the person we focused on being in a healthier state, seems to have experienced the improvement the same time as we imagined it. This session not only freed herself to live her dreams, but also through entanglement encouraged her husband, though maintaining his free will, to do the same as she shifted.

Summary of Maturing Heartwaving

When we shift our BATHWAVE patterns through Heartwaving Techniques, sometimes not all of our lifetime of BATHWAVE information makes the shift.

We find that there are long patterns that resist the shift, and we need to do look at frozen age patterns to make the shift.

We can muscle test to find the age we were when the initial resistance to this shift first occurred.

By finding out the age we were when we first resisted the ideas we are trying to shift, we can simply re-do the quantum shift technique and muscle test until we reach an age where we have no resistance. This age may be well past our current age, and reflect our current BATHWAVEs about that age. Our BATHWAVEs about the future—retirement, aging, marriage, death, and more—can create resistance to our current quantum shift.

Once we become aware of the resistance, we can shift it, allowing us to be in sync with our miracle universe.

A story from Sri Lanka of maturing without using years

While writing this chapter, I had a call from Sri Lanka, from one of my close girlfriends with a medical emergency. She is like a sister because she worked with me when I began this Relationshifting work twelve years ago.

On our Skype call she looked like and sounded like she was dying, and of course she had waited until the last minute to seek medical attention. The doctors had already given her Flagyl, an anti-parasitic medicine, in addition to the antibiotic she had been taking. Nothing was working. They were about to put her on intravenous Flagyl, which she knew probably would kill her because she has only one kidney and two uteri.

Her problem was originating in the second uterus. She was now facing an infection in her body from one of the uteri, and it was also, I guess, in her bladder. She begged me, "Angela, what is this? *I need to shift it. I feel like I'm dying. I'm going to my gynecologist tomorrow in Colombo.*"

She lived in a small town on the ocean, called Arugam Bay, that was struck with the tsunami many years ago that killed so many on her island.

Here she was, asking me to help her on Skype, and of course I was glad to, but I needed to remember what her eternal nature—her eternalbeing—was, and she needed to remind herself of it, because it was clear to me **she was stuck back in the world of cause and effected (otherwise called 'in-fected').**

(By the way, all infections are belief systems of cause and effect, such as a virus, bacteria, parasite, etc. because they are causes and effects that we have been believing. Beliefs are the cells of our body, so the causing and effecting takes over the cells of our body to reproduce more cause and effects, and which is the giving over of our power.)

Causing and effecting is one of the most common and powerful of the beginning stories that most of our cultures adopt. We can shift that belief so we are in charge of our living which restores the strength of the bladder and the kidney, as you will learn in the third part of this book when we begin the Chinese Medicine section.

Her eternalbeing is about living the courage to move out of the box, to embrace this eternalbeing existence, this existence beyond cause and effect. This is her eternalbeing's theme, and she had clearly forgotten her eternal theme.

Not only had she forgotten it, she was attacking herself.

She said, "Angela, my mother and father are attacking me. They won't even speak to me now."

With that statement I knew that she had once again divided her life into opposings.

Just as she was born dividing her uterus into two, she was living the division of her feminine creativity (uterus) again. She was blaming her masculine side as she had done in her first marriage and was now doing in her new marriage.

She was denying or unconscious that she was doing that.

We faced and embraced her blaming and complaining and her denial of all of it, and shifted it to blessing and connecting and communicating all the mirror-calls (miracles) that were revealing to her once again her resplendent nature. Her mirror-calls were revealing her resplendent nature, so that she could live it. She began to see it.

It was midnight, and she was exhausted and in pain, living on antibiotics. She said, "Angela, how can I do this? I know when it all began. It began when I regretted moving back from America to Sri Lanka to run this bed-and-breakfast that my parents had let go to shambles."

My friend had rebuilt the business bravely in a community that did not support a woman doing something so brash, so powerful. She lived in a culture of feminine oppression, which we've seen over and over in most cultures described in the Bollywood movies so beautifully.

She was still believing that she was working 'against' such cultural forces with perhaps some judgments too.

I reminded her how she was like Gandhi, especially Indira Gandhi, who as a woman brought India back to life after independence. I saw her smile on Skype for the first time and she said, "I was born on the same day as Indira Gandhi."

I had not known this fact intellectually (see, entanglement is alive, mirror-calls are afoot…) so we both smiled as she embraced how she was sabotaging her own feminine side.

She was compromising her feminine side. She was minimizing it. (Her self-limitation to one working kidney was an expression of this active belief). She had lost her enthusiasm for life, for living. She had lost her ability to vision. She had lost her dream. And she had turned against her own logical mind (masculine side).

As she faced this and embraced it, we hardly had time to quantum shift it, but I knew she was getting it as she eventually drifted off to sleep. One of the last things she said to me that evening was that, "Vision it, and it will be."

I smiled at her return to her resplendent self and said, "Oops, that's cause and effect. **Vision it, and it is. That is the resplendent way."**

Her final and healing quantum shift that evening was:

"I am resplendent, and bless and appreciate all of the mirror-calls of my life for revealing this to me."

To repeat: Bathwaving process is a replacing 'cause and effecting' technique which can upload my true desires, until we understand and live awarefully resplendent and share that with others.

Since we are all composed of atomic molecules that have wave natures, this principle of entanglement can also apply between atoms with those whom we are in entanglement. When one person shifts, the entangled people will experience the shift instantly, yet maintain free will and the ability to choose whether to shift or not. One possible example is a classroom where some people will learn quite easily and others may resist who have unrealized, preconditioned resistance to learning this particular material.

Dr. Angela Longo

Summary

We don't have to be stuck in long-term behavior patterns. Bathwaving techniques use O-ring muscle testing to let us mature our long held BATHWAVEs so that they are not obstacles to living resplendently.

In Part Three of this book, we'll look at the five elemental organ relationships as used in Traditional Chinese Medicine.

Reading our tongue maps, also reflect our organ relationships which may be mirror-calls of our social relationships. Our relationships are constantly changing, though may follow old patterns, and the five element relationships can give a way to comprehend this dynamic pattern.

Remember, everything IS related through entanglement, though individual and unique.

Heartwaving Maturing Technique Check List

Part One: Face It and Embrace It

Jot down BATHWAVE you wish to shift below.

_____

____ Muscle test.

____ Eyes open
____ Lovingly and compassionately stroke body from head to toe, back, front and sides
____ At the same time saying, feeling and thinking of what you want to shift.
____ Remember, eyes open.
____ Don't miss a spot!

Part Two: Replace It With Grace

____ Jot down your desired quantum shift below, stating as much in the positive as you can.

_____

While doing the quantum shift movements with eyes open,
____ State your desire in the potential tense: I can + verb...
____ State your desire in the future tense: I will + verb...
____ State your desire in the present tense: I + verb...

Quantum shift movement:
- Place one hand on your back behind your heart and other hand on your back from below your heart.
- Move top hand over the head midline, over the face to throat, past heart and lower abdomen past the groin while the other hand moves to the back bottom of the spine to eventually meet the other hand below the pelvis.
- If seated just move both hands to the chair and move the pelvis on chair to complete the cycle.

____ Muscle test your shift. See Appendix.

If the muscle stays strong you have shifted.

Muscle testing to mature the shift

____Ask by muscle testing whether you need to mature this shift through your life into your future. If the muscle is strong and the link holds that means yes.

____Start testing the shift at the age of five-years-old. If strong continue counting by 5's till it goes weak. Say the link broke at 20 years old. Then go back to 15 years old and count by ones, 16, 17, 18, at 19 it goes weak. Ask yourself what event or activity is significant to you at 18 years old? When something comes up proceed.

____Muscle test and ask if this is the action you are holding on to at 18. If strong, continue to the Part One: Face It and Embrace It step and Part Two step with an appropriate new twist on the quantum shift as above. With the new quantum shift ask if you are 20. Strong. 30? Strong. 40? Weak. 35? strong 36, 37, 38, 39 weak. Ask yourself what you are holding on to at age 38? When you think of something proceed below.

____ Muscle test the BATHWAVE at that age. If strong, repeat the Face It and Embrace it steps talking about the new situation. After you shift it come up with new quantum shift for Part Two steps as above.

____ Muscle test the new quantum shift for the age 38 starting at age 40 and continuing to age 100 or more. If the muscle is weak at any age, ask yourself again what might have happened at that age to you or what significance that age has to you. Continue repeating this process until the shift is clear at all ages.

A Star is Rebirthing

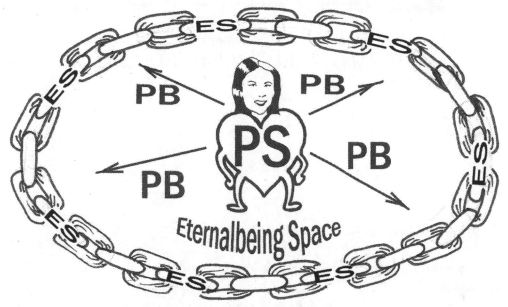

Interacting with it's Environment...

Rebirthing Resplendency

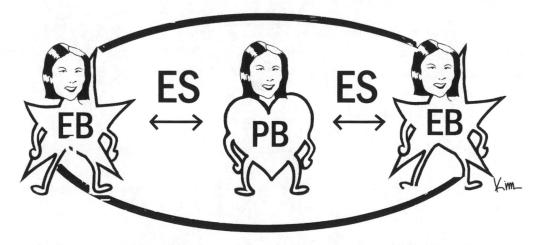

Personalbeing expressing it's "Original Story" Rebirths Eternalbeing every moment.

CHAPTER 8

IT'S A BENEVOLENT UNIVERSE AND YOU ARE THE SHINING STAR
REBIRTHING ANEW IN RADIANCE

A star is rebirthing resplendency

The day you were born, a child of the universe arrived on Earth—a child made of star stuff, made of particle/waves.

You only learned half of the story...The other half is the 'star' part.

The particles are an equivalence of my physical body, my mind and my emotions.

Conversing with the wave-like part of you is resplendent awareness. It is like sound which doesn't exist unless there is a medium to carry it, or the wave motion of the earth's ocean. We can sense it, but our wave nature eludes our knowing it as easily as we sense our physical body, mind and emotions. Yet it is EEEZY to perceive it as we desire. Meeting this *eternalself* and intimately living with it are some of the tools in this book.

My being that I think of as 'you', I call my *personalself.* The you that expresses itself like a wave, I refer to as my *eternalself.* Waves are physical and exist as much as our bodies exist.

Our eternalself makes itself known to us through things we do that we feel proud of, or through our dreams, our hunches, and our desires. Ever find that you made a wrong turn on the way home, a drive you have made hundreds of times, and you find out later that because of that wrong turn, you weren't in an accident? Or perhaps the wrong turn took you to a new restaurant where you ran into an old friend that you were hankering to see?

Ever have a dream and discover that it is a pictorial alternative to a living situation you are questioning?

These kinds of incidents happen because of the work of the interaction between personalself and eternalself.

Even though we might not be aware of our eternalself, our eternalself works in tangent with our personalself. You might say they are on the same wavelength!

Beginning in the cradle eternalself is a wave-message in the bottle of our personalself that we can see later as forming a pattern of BATHWAVEs. As a baby, why did we reach for the ball instead of the bell on our crib mobile? Why do we like blue more than brown? Our actions are the expression of our eternalself.

The work of eternalself and personalself are also seen in the activities we do. Every action we do creates a ray of sorts. If you think of each of my activities starting from a core center of a sphere and radiating outwards, you would see the shape of a star with a million or more arms. That star would define the work of my eternalself and personalself to create the being that is you. These activities or 'rays' forming my being are called my eternalbeing.

If you could observe that star that is you from a distance, you would be able to see a design formed by the millions of arms of the star. With a star, we can't actually see its core or individual rays. We can only see the pattern that the core and the rays create. The design we perceive is actually the outside surface of the star, just like the skin of a ball.

That outer design made by my eternalself is the part of you that we label my eternalbeing. It is like a star, in that the workings remain hidden to the unknowing eye. Likewise, until you can observe from outside the star you can't perceive the pattern of my eternalbeing.

You will be able to recognize my eternalbeing when I show you how in Chapter 11 to find the diamond chain gang of personalself's radiations in my life that shape my life.

Outside my eternalbeing is infinite space. Just as a star is surrounded by the space of the universe, so are you.

The space that surrounds you allows you room to expand. The space also connects you to every object in the universe. This space I refer to as *conditions of expansion*.

Just as the personalself interacts with the environment expressing my personalbeing, my eternalbeing is emergent from that interaction of personalself and environment.

My radiant *resplendent illuminatedbeing* is emergent from the interaction of personalbeing and eternalbeing. That is the radiant aspect of you as a star.

Imagine that star, that is you, expanding, radiant and glorious.

Every action coordinated by my personalbeing and eternalbeing defines my resplendent illuminatedbeing. Because of the coordination of my two natures—like particle and wave— life is no longer a struggle, but a glorious emergent expression of my eternal (recurring) design in an infinite number of ways.

I have access to any stuff of the universe which I select through entanglement. The particle/wave forming my personalself interacts with my 'stuff' and expresses my eternalself. Personalbeing, in interacting with my environment, is expressing a pattern of my eternalbeing. This pattern is new and different and called emergent.

In entanglement what I do or access for others, I literally am doing to myself in the same moment. My giving IS my receiving. The receiving is in the same moment, not later as in cause and effect.

Emergent means that the pattern is new and different in this moment replacing the old pattern. To 'know' my eternalbeing I must be aware in every moment since it is transforming.

Once I discover the pattern of my eternalbeing, each moment that I am living I will understand that I am resplendent, a radiant "star" in this universe.

I am the star in my you-niverse. My star is rebirthing every moment. It is always emergent me.

The physical nature of resplendency

The 'physical' offers things we used to relegate to the 'spiritual'. We had created an opposing duality of 'physical' and 'spiritual' that does not exist in the quantum world.

The natural world and the unseen wave-like 'resplendent' world, both of quantum reality are not opposing. To the contrary, they require each other for their very existence. This is the first thing we learn from the quantum world.

In fact, the quantum physical world offers emergent variation, expansion, strength, interaction, radiance, coherent intelligence, communicability, and things we have not imagined. The promise of resplendency, when applied and understood in our lives, is experienced by those who know and live the reality described by the quantum world. I have been applying these ideas of resplendency in my clinic as well as in my personal life. My experiences along with my clients' testimonials encourage my continuing work with relationshifting and resplendency.

Communion of PB : EB
Is Resplendent Illuminatedbeing

Recapping the previous story: Understanding the physical: personalself and personalbeing

I use the star as a metaphor in my figures to understand the relationship between aspects of resplendent living that are new in concept from the quantum world. Our understanding of these relationships will be applied to our bodies and our lives.

In the center of the star, we see the point of personalself (PS) with which we are born. Our personalself, through its purpose and promise, interacts with the environment sending out a radius of action, creating a pattern. This action of personalself is called personalbeing (PB) and also might be called self-evidenting.

Eternalself is emergent from personalself's interactions with environment

Since my particular personalbeing has a unique commonality in its purpose and promise, I will make all the radii 'alike' or a recurring common length. At the end of each radius, visualize a point which would define eternalself. As personalself continues to act through personalbeing's purpose and promise, the radii create many dots or expressions of our eternalself which when connected form what you see as a circle.

In three dimensions these many dots would form the surface of the star. Connecting the dots, the surface of the star represents our eternalbeing (EB), which is the commonality of our unique purpose and promise. Said another way, my eternalbeing is the recurring action of you revealed by my doings.

Applying this to my body: The eternalbeing (EB) is what is recreating me. Therefore, eternalbeing is continually remodeling the self our parents began. I can identify the eternalbeing through identifying my commonality of purpose and my eternal how-to, which will be described in Chapter 11 Eternalbeing Reading and Naming.

Twoness to our TriUnity:
Virtual Selves

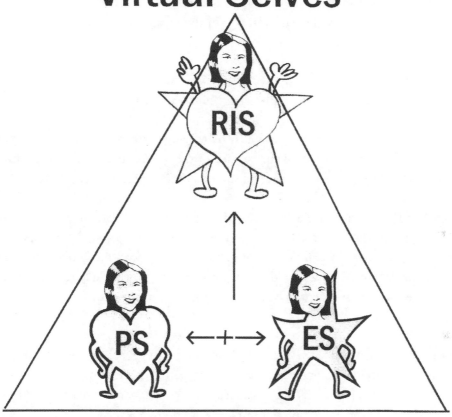

Adorned Beings

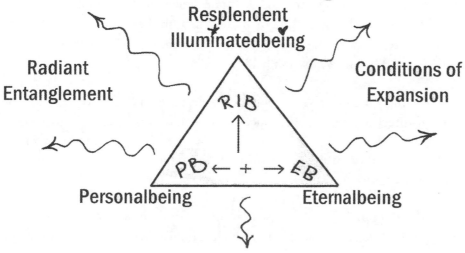

You can read my eternalbeing

The visionary method outlined in the Eternalbeing Reading and Naming chapter describes making a list of six accomplishments of which I am proud. The moment of enthusiasm in each of the eight accomplishments reveals the promise and the resplendent direction of my living, thus expressing my eternalself.

Once I perceive my eternalbeing I am also defining the center of the circle, personalself, back again. This radius as the personalbeing, is the manifestation of the personalself, and is the expression or the manifested teacher/source of eternalbeing.

Once I know my eternalbeing (EB), my personalbeing can awarefully communion with my eternalbeing emergently manifesting my resplendent illuminatedbeing (RIB).

My resplendentbeing is shown as the emanation or *entangoing* radiance from the eternalbeing on the surface of the star. This radiance from the surface of the star created by the communication of eternalbeing and personalbeing can also be called the radiant illuminatedbeing (RIB).

Picture the surface of the star radiating light, reaching out with our physical radiance. Just as our sun radiates its light out to the universe with no conditions, granting us our light, warmth and life, so too can I reach out with my physical radiance to all that is outside of me. This radiance in living, resplendency, is created by my 'entangoing' described previously. When I 'entango' life, say with the mirror-calls of my life, I am resplendent. The benefits of my entangoing, in a sense, shine to all that are around of me.

To explain a little further: I practice this idea of entangoing in a cause and effect sort of way with myself and clients. We entango with our symptoms, energy patterns, relationships, dreams, and daily events, using Bathwaving. It gives a beginning experience of the expansive nature of entanglement, still using 'cause and effect', therefore, not real resplendent entanglement… yet.

After every Bathwave I check in to ask about what clients are feeling and they often report feeling more rejuvenated, deeply relaxed, lighter and sometimes relief from symptoms. One Bathwaving revelation will lead to the next, like a treasure map unfolding until we reach a saturation point. The quantum shifts take three weeks to three months of daily reminding to settle into our eternalbeing's informotion structure or BATHWAVEs, as a habit.

Bathwaving and then checking in for sensations is using 'cause and effect' to amass the power and courage of gentle self-direction to live an existence free of being dominated by cause and effect.

Biochemically, entanglement probably is a function of the vehicle of our DNA which I discuss in Chapter 22 Entanglement and Our DNA.

To continue with the diagram: All of the spatial area outside of my triunity of eternalbeing, personalbeing and resplendent illuminatedbeing, which contains everything that I do not know yet, I call the conditions of expansion, or COE.

Communion of PB : EB
Is Resplendent Illuminatedbeing

The difference between these Conditions of Expansion and the environment of personalbeing is that PB's environment is made up of random coalescences of data and information in the universe whereas conditions of expansion are present through entanglement of my resplendent desires.

Conditions of expansion has been referred to in this book as Love Letters that I give myself, or 'mirror-calls' (miracles) of my resplendence.

From my clinical experience and considering the quantum world, this ability of living the option of non-domination by cause and effect gives us a propensity for miracles and being emergent eternally.

Relationshifting allows me to live all relationships and situations resplendently in the "you-niverse".

Reaching out as my physical radiance

How do I reach out with my physical radiance? In my beginning state, I reach out by becoming aware of the mirrors that are in my life and that beckon us.

The main way I know my mirrors are calling me is that I react or respond to them as they manifest as my emotions, my sicknesses, my relationships, my daily events and my dreams.

When I react to any BATHWAVE which is any reaction to anything in my life, this is the beginning of 'mirror-call-us' or miraculous. (I apologize that this word only works in English.) However, the experience is still the same in any language. I resisted this understanding of the miraculous until I experienced living it. I am describing in detail in this book how to read these patterns which are beckoning me to living my resplendent illuminatedbeing.

When I am willing to own, then face and embrace a 'reaction' to these mirrors as a revelation of myself, I see that a mirror, of course, is self-created to reveal my resplendency. When I look in the 'mirror' and see my reactive self, I can identify and clearly see what it is that I wish to face and embrace. I need 'mirror-calls' to understand myself because I cannot see my true self without one until I am aware of living as a resplendent illuminatedbeing. This is what I will describe in Part II.

Review of Bathwaving

When I Bathwave the old pattern that I am emotionally reacting to, the pattern melts by the embrace of unconditional love or non-judgment. This is akin to the sun's radiation of light, going into the 'black hole' likened to our core center.

This core center will recycle the information and create raw data again. This raw data is used to reshape my new quantum shifts in Part Two of Bathwaving. This second part of Heartwaving is using my hands to circle our central nervous system, called the *microcosmic orbit* in TCM, while saying my new desire in three verbal tenses:

1. I can... do what I desire
   (potentially to reprogram the nervous system)
2. I will...do what I desire
   (futuristically to intend)
3. I do what I desire
   (present tense).

It can also be done in one sentence, one time "I can, I will, and I am doing what I desire."

Bathwaving with quantum shifts is going across the bridge for the beginning of my living as resplendent being.

Eventually, as I understand my eternalbeing's 'verbiage' and choose to focus on and live in communion with my unique eternalbeing, I won't need to look at my reactions and my resistances because they begin to diminish.

Interestingly, I begin to see the conditions of expansion creatively in an enjoyable way instead of my past reactive Sicilian way. The old reactive way can only happen when I believe there is only cause and effect in the relationship that I see in my mirror-call.

Spooky theory is not spooky at all

Again, Einstein called this phenomena of entanglement 'spooky' because it is so different than the cause and effect way that has dominated our thinking and living for thousands of years.

Emergent entanglement is instantaneous and expands me AS I am desiring. With entanglement, life is not spooky or something to fear. It is finally understanding how our two natures work together to create a resplendent life as the tri-you-nity expressed in most cultures.

The resplendent way is eventually to realize that I am the reason for what is happening around me. **With this realization I am able to stand back and personalize what I see as emergent.**

Emergent means something that I manifest.

Emergent mirror-calls is the new me, as I wish, and does not resemble the old me. This is when life really sparkles and expands because I am delighting in knowing new things that I have never known.

Be patient and persistent, as it took me at least twelve years to realize the beauty of emergent living and share it. I now understand why the *Tao Te Ching* says multiple times: Persistence furthers.

Another way to say this for TCMers and students of the I Ching: I am giving myself a personalized I Ching reading as a love letter. I am entangoing to understand and rewrite this love letter as desired until I am aware of living fully resplendently as in emergent entanglement eternally.

Before I understood the eight self-awakening mirror-calls, I was choosing to stay in the old way of accusing, blaming, and complaining. This old way was based on believing in the cause and effect way, meaning I believed that someone else or myself caused my problem or affected me in one way or the other.

Either way—whether I believe I caused my problem or it was caused by someone else—I was struggling. This is the life-long struggle humanity has been in for thousands of years.

Now I realize through the quantum world that this way of identifying mirror-calls is a way of entanglement theory. I use the word entangoing for entanglement because it implies an enjoyable dance that recognizes every movement of my partner at almost the same time that it is done. In entangoing, as was described in a previous chapter, we realize that our behaviors and actions are mirrored back to us in the entanglement immediately, so it's valuable to notice our reaction to them with awareness. We cannot DO entanglement; it is automatic.

Entangoing with awareness

As a doing and feeling type personality (from Jung) I observed with accusation (judgment), the four emotions of fear, anger, sadness, and tiredness in friends around me. This accusing behavior held my focus instead of resplendency. Once I admitted that friends were mirroring my behaviors, I was able to shift my emotions and the triggers of those emotions. In the process I became more available to resplendency. It is probably similar for the Jungian thinking and doing types except they will notice that their mirror-calls involve thoughts or actions respectively.

My body allows me to live entanglement with everything around me as conditions of expansion. Once I face my reactions to my conditions of expansion, (my love letters, my mirror-calls) and embrace them, I can specify and shift them as I desire. That is my quantum shift. After I do this enough I might decide to begin to live resplendence. To live in entanglement becomes radiance reaching out 'as me' through my resplendency, my 'shining' radiance, to my conditions of expansion.

Now, back to our star diagram. The core of the star explains how all this entanglement happens. The latest research has revealed that at the core of every star there might be a black hole as is true for the core of our galaxy. The nature of a black hole is to absorb matter and energy that is close to it.

We recycle our BATHWAVES

What I am beginning to realize is that a black hole must spit out something that is not material/ energy to keep the stars and universe going. This would be raw data and pre-information. There is no energy in raw data and pre-information. This might be similar to the recycling of our old beliefs, actions, thoughts, etc.

Our core being might be considered a recycling center. That is, an active, unconditional awareness recycling center. How appropriate is that?

What I might refer to as karma can all be recycled if I wish, at first with persistence and patience.

When I move this image of a recycling center to the body, I realize that at the center of our body is our heart. The heart, as well as the liver, has been shown through research to think and know things. Probably all cells, analogous wholographically to the brain, possess these thinking and knowing attributes.

We will use this image of a heart to understand that in the core, the very center of our being, just as in the center of a star, there probably is something equivalent to a black hole. A black hole has strong gravity, to put it mildly. This gravity takes in what is not desired and spits out raw data to be transfigured into our desires. In our 'black hole' we have a recycling center. The core of us is a recycling center.

Part One of Heartwaving is about recycling our BATHWAVEs where we 'compost' our old BATHWAVEs. Part Two could be likened to the "rooting and fruiting" from the seeds of raw data from Part One.

I can transform anything that I face and embrace through entanglement, for my body is a recycling center of my old information as BATHWAVEs (beliefs, actions, thoughts, habits, words, attitudes, values, and emotions) into raw data to be used to create my new desires.

Mirror-calls help me realize that my weaknesses reveal my finest assets

In the old days, we would call these reactive mirror-calls, our weaknesses. That's a judgment waiting to be bathwaved.

But, once I recognize that these weaknesses are actually mirrored in order for me to shift to my true strengths, we can bathwave to our heart's content and experience all of our desires as we are ready.

The quantum shift for this BATHWAVE of reacting to a perceived weakness, might be "My weaknesses show me to my strengths." I can even embrace the denial of this awareness that for a long time we have labeled my unconscious. I don't have to hide anything from myself unconsciously anymore.

This hiding from my consciousness is the embrace of my 'denying' from our eight bottom lines— accusing, blaming, complaining/criticizing, lying, hiding, denying, defending, justifying. The quantum shift was "I am open to being aware of everything about myself". Through Heartwaving

I eventually got to see some of my bottom lines. At that point I could transfigure these bottom lines that I perceived in repetitious mirror-calls, into my true desires.

I embody the universe. The universe gave me a training-wheels body. I give myself the body I desire as I express this system:

My personalself partners with my unique purpose and promise of my eternalself.

It is said that every seven years molecularly I have a totally new body. My personalself, which is at the core of my heart, will recycle all of my BATHWAVEs if we so desire. This recycling allows me to manifest, through my purposes and eternal how-to, my eternalself which is my real soul.

With awareness of my communion with this eternalself as my personalself companion, I am a resplendent illuminatedbeing as I communicate. This communion radiates and reaches far out into the universe in an entanglement 'wave-sort-of-way'.

With this communion of eternalself and personalself, my illuminatedself is aware of entanglement and emergent miracles living a life of conditions of expansion, all the time, in all ways, and anywhere.

Expansion is my way of life and I am also emergent. Remember, emergent means new and different, not resembling the previous me.

Remember:

Living is EEEZY. Emergent, entanglement, eternal zestful you!

Equivalence in the Quantum World
of our Triunity

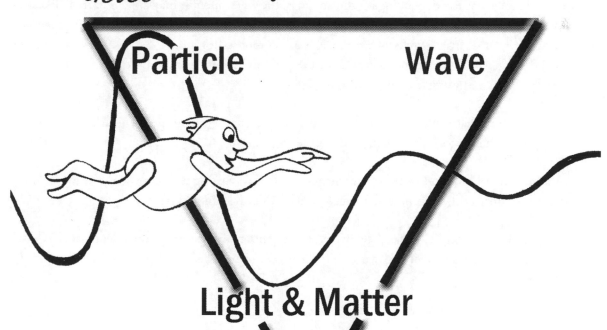

Particles are Body Surfers!

Particle **Wave**

Light & Matter

Communion of (Wholeness) Resplendency

CHAPTER 9

FROM OUR TWONESS,
OUR TRI-YOU-NITY IS EMERGENT

The twoness of spinning 'particle' and wave

The quantum world is revealing to us that there is an emergent triunity to our being that we have missed for thousands of years. I am amazed that what I've been taught about the way the world works through my Ph.D. in Biochemistry from UC Berkeley was not really the way it is. We have missed the wave nature that goes with the spinning 'particle appearance', the subatomic building blocks of all matter.

Light has this wave nature: depending on the design of the experiment it may appear particle-like and sometimes wave-like. **These two natures are both always present and necessary for the existence of light and the building blocks of atoms.** We are composed of atoms. So from the twoness of particle and wave, the light, or the electrons, or the protons are emergent. These are triunities: such as a particle, wave, and wavicle awareness triangle.

It is also interesting that the triangle is known to be the strongest geometric form. All buildings are based on it from the diagonal braces in walls to the tresses in roofs.

When I am aware of how to live the emergent resplendent way using this knowledge of my triunity from the quantum world, then illness, struggle and conflict become no issue.

Before I describe the triunity, I need to define the qualities of this wave-equivalent nature that I have missed. I am going to call this wave-like nature communioned with particle-like nature, '*the resplendent world*'.

Resplendence is E.E.E.ZY!

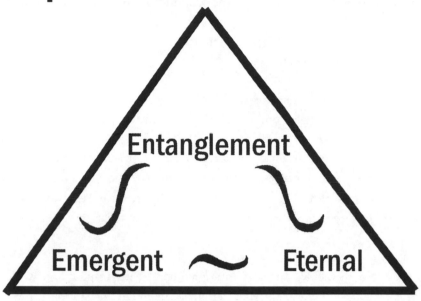

Emergent is New & Different
replacing old ... Expansive.
**Quantum equivalence: particle/wave pops
in and out of existence...**

Entanglement is Process of Accessing
My Deepest Desires.
**Quantum equivalence: one particle/wave process
reflected in the other instantly (beyond cause & effect)**

Eternal is Pattern of recurring doings
**Quantum equivalence: particle/waving area morphing
recurring pattern...**

Zestful

Y (embodifying) YOU

The resplendent world is EEEZY

The first quality of this resplendent world—the world aware of the wave-like nature–is described by the first letter of the word EEEZY: *emergent*. Quantum 'particles' pop in and out of existence. Emergent means that something is new and different in every moment. In other words, life and time in every moment need not resemble the past.

The second E that I'll use to describe this world is *'entanglement'* from which a process of accessing my deepest desires comes. Entanglement as well as emergent replaces the old "cause and effect".

The verb 'to memory' our emergent moment is the operative process of entanglement. 'Memorying' "is the opening of awareness to emergent moments. Using the tools of entanglement and emergent awakens me to an expansive life. Expansive as used in this sense means vast, aware, rejuvenating, surprising, and not repeating as in the old cause and effect way of what we've been doing for thousands of years.

In addition to these two E's, emergent and entanglement, in my resplendent world, I can perceive my third E as the *eternal*, or my eternalself. Eternal means recurring. Understanding the recurring pattern of my eternalself is so important for being able to see my entanglement and my emergent miracle nature.

How?

My eternalself is my personal blueprint of my actioning in the resplendent world. It is an extension of my old idea of purpose and promise. It is my patterning originating from my individuality and is dynamically malleable in form.

Life as a house

When we think of our life as a house, emergent and entanglement would be tools for building the house of our dreams. We might see emergent as a hammer, a saw, a ladder, and all the tools that are necessary for building a house. Entanglement is akin to materials procurement; we cannot, of course, build a house without the necessary materials. Through the use of entanglement we have access to nails, lumber, windows and doors—all of the multitude of materials or 'constituents" we need to construct a house. The emergent nature of the house—its construction–is created with these ingredients that come from entanglement.

With entanglement, all items we can imagine for building our house are available to us. With entanglement we have access to all the building blocks in our universe. Our house can be built of whatever we desire. We send out the desire to our universe and entanglement is in charge of procurement.

Our access to these materials is through the vehicle of our DNA..., but not in the way we used to think. Our DNA actually has two qualities just like light: the particle nature and a wave nature. I'll discuss this aspect of our DNA in detail in the chapter called *Entanglement and Our DNA.*

We might consider the particle nature of our DNA being the general contractor who reads the blueprint to build our house. This particle nature of our DNA, the contractor, I refer to as the personalself. The wave nature of our DNA is a recurring pattern in the eternalself, our personal blueprint in the resplendent world, and creates pattern after pattern after pattern, eternally. From one set of blueprints we can build an infinite number of houses or a house that is infinitely large, each house being unique based on what constituents or building materials are sourced and delivered using our entanglement or tools.

To create our unique home we need both natures of wave and spinning particle appearance: the patterns of the blueprint, along with the contractor building from the blueprint using the tools of entanglement and emergence. What's different about our house building in the resplendent world is that this new home keeps expanding as we desire. This resplendent house can be anywhere in the universe we want it to be. My house can be in any environment we desire.

Our dream house is always the house that we personally choose, built out of the materials that we select using our quantum tool of entanglement. These choices are the resplendent potential we have in life, and when this ability to choose is put together with the material, or particle world, we fulfill all our dreams and desires.

This is the resplendent way.

Heaven on Earth: conditions of expansion

The quantum world is both substantial and wave. The quantum world around my home contains all the conditions of expansion, that I can imagine and request. I might also refer to this house of my dreams as heaven on earth or the Garden of Eden.

I have denied myself access to understanding the quantum world and its potentialities by holding on to my old limiting memories through language, especially the eight bottom lines. Accessing my memories through language prevents awareness of this triunity of the personal, eternal, and illuminatedbeings. The new languaging would be describing and declarative questioning, which will be covered in the chapter on *Quantum Communication*. I am delighted as I live this resplendent way, fully aware of my three quantum natures. It's no accident that the word *delight* contains the word *light,* as light has these triune natures. Light would be the third component of a triunity of photon/wave.

As I live this communioning life of resplendence with an understanding of my eternalbeing, personalbeing and illuminatedbeing. This real/resplendent life gives us exactly what I desire and is part and parcel with living and being aware.

Imaginative minding

With *imaginative minding* I can see my resplendent side, my wave nature, my eternalself. Life is as good as I imagine it to be. With imaginative minding I discover that I can choose not to repeat the same old, same mold way I have been living for thousands of years, a way that limits us to the cause and effect ways of only my particle nature where struggle and suffering and illness are inevitable.

In this new way of living every moment begins again from whatever parts I desire. Life is continually reconstituted. It is always new and different. It is EEEZY. Life is emergently, and eternally recurring however I desire it, always adding fresh and novel ingredients in my entanglement with life, however I desire it.

This is the EEEZY picture, which the quantum world offers us. From the quantum physical world, I offer practical tools for you to use. As you become EEEZY–the emergent, entanglement, eternal zestful you–you may discover many tools on your own. Until you do I offer in this book the quantum tools which have helped me begin to understand and live in an EEEZY way. Which I must admit life feels much better at 70 than it did at 50!

There is no need to prove this quantum world is the real world. There is the living of it and in the living of it you experience it. See the benefits with two eyes and two ears; there is no accident I have two ears and two eyes and the third emergent awareness of the two. I am a living triunity: first, visible, second, eternal, that together create a third, resplendent illuminatedbeing, living all at the same time.

Twoness of Virtual Selves
to TriUnity

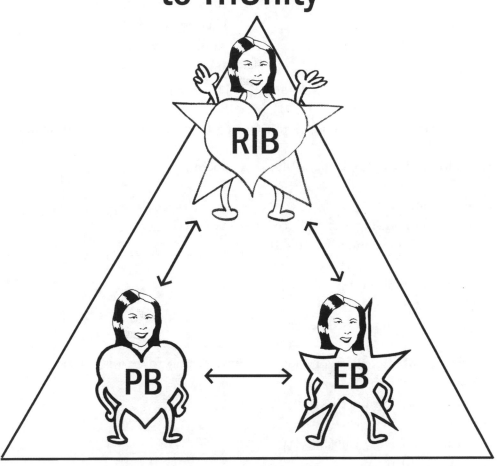

Adorned Beings:

Personalbeing   Eternalbeing

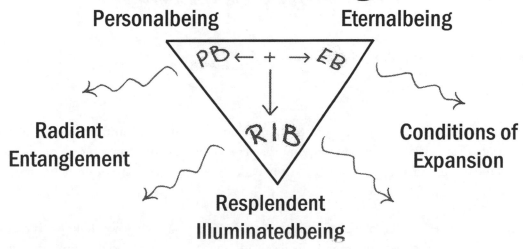

Radiant   Conditions of
Entanglement   Expansion

Resplendent
Illuminatedbeing

The Qualities of Twoness, from which Triunity is Emergent:

Embody (Express & Manifest)	**Resplendent**
Particle-like	Wave-like
Body mind	'Informotion' patterning
Time and space	Timeless & spaceless(forces)
Cause and effect	Beyond cause and effect
Personalbeing (particularizing)	Eternalbeing (recurring)
Existence	Like 'morphogenetic field'*

When I become aware of the interaction of this twoness I am able to perceive and act differently.

Interactive Abilities of my Resplendent Illuminatedbeing

Interaction of Triunity
Entanglement (instant knowing with every cell of my body)
Emergent (I am in each moment, new and different)
Expansion
'Fiat' (as desiring to manifesting)
Non-entropic (expanding non linearly)
Awareful resplendence without discontenting

When I am **unaware of my triunity, I may limit myself in the following ways:**
Learning through the brain only,
Seeing or living only causing and effecting,
Contracting
Believing that each moment resembles the last,
Entropic (decreasing order)
Unawareness of resplendency with struggle and discontenting

Why have I missed my twoness, as well as triunity, for thousands of years?

How we missed knowing about our two natures

Perhaps I can tell a story to help.

You are the pilot flying a plane. People on the ground look up and see a plane moving across the sky leaving a trail of vapor. From that vantage point the plane only looks like a moving physical object. Is it a bird, plane or Superman? From a distance it may be hard to perceive size or form, but movement is discernable.

From a distance, whether that object is a bird, a plane or Superman, what we do know is that there is some innate desire that we can't see that is motivating what we are observing. From the ground, no one can tell that it is you, that you are the force that is flying the object. Without you to drive and guide the plane, the plane would be an inanimate physical object on the ground. Without the plane, you would be down on the ground perhaps looking up with rest of the people. In the plane, you can't see what you look like in the air from the ground. With my desire to fly the plane, you and the plane create movement and a vapor trail of light across the sky.

The plane represents my particle being, my personalbeing. My piloting desire represents my eternalbeing. The plane in motion represents my resplendent illuminatedbeing. The sky and passengers are my conditions of expansion. If this is what you do that makes you feel proud, then my incipit, my original sentence, might be, "I am the movement of resplendence."

The paradox is this:

From the ground, we can't see the pilot.

As a pilot, we can't see that the plane is flying leaving a trail.

With imaginative minding we can take the experience of being on the ground looking up, along with the experience of flying the plane, to imagine what we must look like from the ground. We can realize that we are a flying an inanimate object. Together, the plane and our desire create motion and a vapor trail of light, something that alone, neither could do. With desire a triunity of wave, particle, and radiant awareness expressing is forming with the desired initiation of 'motion' as it's intrinsic motivation.

A quantum explanation

To understand how we missed knowing about our resplendent 'eternalbeing', it is helpful to understand the nature of the atoms of which we are constituted. As I have already mentioned, the constituents of atoms and light have two distinct physical natures. One nature is that of the particle which acts like a solid ball or sphere (though not equivalent to a solid ball). The other is the wave nature, which has no resemblance to a ball, reaches to the edges of the universe instantly and is a new experience to imagine.

To use this as an illustration of how I live, I next invoke the 'wholographic' film theory of the Universe, the theory that any pattern of the whole is in each part. And likewise, any pattern in a part is in the whole.

This wave/particle on the subatomic level pattern might be repeated wholographically in all levels. When I carry this forward, this pattern of triunity, might have some equivalence, mirror, reflection or resonance within our own lives. Based on wave/particle theory I might have two distinct physical natures.

When I look at how physicists discovered these two natures I understand why we missed our own resplendent 'wave-like' nature. When they look at the photon particle nature of light, they don't see the wave nature of light. When they look at the wave nature, they don't see the photon particle nature.

Experiments had to be designed specifically to look for each nature separately. Yet through observing one and then the other, physicists know that both particle-like and wave natures exist and they're both necessary for the existence of the atom and light. In life, the equivalence of each of these two natures are necessary for our resplendent existence.

Resplendency: Riding our wave

This wave nature is quite physical, just ask any surfer! I live in Hawaii and watching the ocean and the surfers has helped me see and experience this connection between our two beings and the nature of the interaction of waves and particles.

The particle nature of us, consisting of our first three level 'bodies' described earlier, might be considered our original particularized expression of our self, which I call our personalself.

The wave nature of us would be that which repeats itself just as a wave on water creates the form out of the water over and over in sets. Like a wave on the ocean, picture a wave on water as it rises up and gives unique shape to our personalself. I refer to our wave nature as our unique eternalself, that aspect of us which is reoccurring.

These two "beings" exist together as light and atoms which is the stuff of which we are all made. The relationship of these two, the personalself and the eternalself, I refer to as communion. It is this interaction of our two selves that is the source of our resplendency which means that aspect of us which is radiantly reaching out or shining.

This interaction or communion might be like the surfer "catching the wave".

Surfers describe those moments when the rider and the wave are in synch as 'amazing', and 'feeling totally alive'. This is what resplendent living might be described as, yet much more.

This metaphor breaks down because the wave never goes away like the water wave does. And it isn't part of the ocean though connected as in entanglement.

As an observer of those moments you can see a completely aligned being, a being who seems to glow. This amazing interaction between our two beings is reminiscent of gems and metals which 'shine'. Yet the shine is applied and not showy. This is the reason the essence of the metal element of TCM is intimately related to the communion of our eternal and personal beings and resplendency.

Of our two physical distinct natures, we have "missed" our resplendent eternalself for thousands of years, because we were always focused on the personalself, as I was. These two distinct natures parallel the natures of subatomic parts and light. Electron, protons, neutrons, and so on, including light have two distinct physical natures, but because we focused on one of them in our experiments we missed the other nature completely.

We are made up of these (subatomic parts), so it is no wonder that by focusing on our obvious nature, we missed the less obvious one, yet just as equally important for our full functioning.

It seems to be time to become aware of, identify, and communicate with this integral part of our self. I believe we need to do this consciously, just as a surfer practices riding a wave.

The big differences are that I create my wave or eternalself as my desire of what I want to do and be...and this wave instantly reaches the ends of the universe and is new and different as I choose to express it.

Our obvious personalself, which we have focused on for thousands of years, is our mindful body. This part of our being is what scientists study and try to understand, especially the elaborate relationships among all the organs of our body, all the parts of the brain, all the aspects of personality that motivate us, along with other physical aspects our existence.

Our other nature, our eternalself, which we have missed for thousands of years, is quite exciting and made obvious when studying the quantum world. Those who believe that quantum world does not apply to human beings and to our world, are just unaware of this nature of our being. Quantum biology is demonstrating this.

To help with further understanding this eternalbeing, may I suggest scientists, like Amit Goswami, Robin Kelly and Dean Radin, as well as other physicists listed in the movies *Down the Rabbit Hole, What the Bleep,* all whom comprehend and tell us about the interrelatedness of my personal and resplendent selves, though using varied terminology.

This workbook provides tools to engender the awareness of my wave nature, my eternalself, that enables us to catch the emergent wave of my resplendent living.

Another thought about beyond 'cause and effect'

In a quantum world the resplendent world is beyond cause and effect. We need to begin to realize that the resplendent world is entirely different, though equal in power and strength, to the world of cause and effect that we have been living for many millennia.

This is not the world of how we wish it to be. This is the world of how it is. The word resplendent is deceiving here, because it does not mean make-believe. It is a physical reality. Just as energy is a physical reality, and people are surprised when I tell them that.

As my yoga teacher said, "I thought energy was the world of the spiritual." She has changed her vocabulary from 'spiritual' to 'the world of the unseen' yet a real world of waves and such. It is where entanglement is. Though Einstein was gifted in this resplendent world, he also turned his back on it when he discovered that it was beyond cause and effect. He labeled it "Spooky action at a distance."

A personal story of entanglement

An amazing example of entanglement occurred between my sister and me, living 3,000 miles apart across an ocean. She was writing her doctoral thesis and paper while I was developing these formulations. We never spoke directly of her thesis and paper as I have never studied psychology. At the time, I could not understand her ideas when she sent me a portion of her paper concerning my mother.

Now that my book is nearing completion I asked her for a copy of both her thesis and paper, and I am excited that they have a similar foundation in the quantum world ways, though with different words from different fields of study.

My sister, Dr. Elena Bonn, is a gifted and intelligent psychoanalyst, summarized her experience in her paper called *Turbulent Contexualism: Bearing Complexity Towards Change*:

"I have come to understand that these metaphors (complexity and dynamic systems theory) are most useful and in the support that they provide analysts and their thinking about the tremendous complexity of the patient-analyst system.

For example **they serve as a reminder to be wary of my tendency to give over-simplified, linear explanations of behavior or to think that correlations imply causation**. These metaphors carry the implicit idea that even cause and effect are fundamentally indeterminate."

Elena has very aptly captured the idea that because things follow after each other in time, that this does not imply causation. This system was the mistake we have been living for thousands of years.

When Einstein beheld the reality of what was really going on in entanglement beyond 'cause and effect', he retracted and held tightly to the old understanding of life, giving his power away. This new realization which my sister is introducing in the psychoanalytic world in describing the nature beyond cause and effect is the new direction of 'quantum medicine' and 'quantum psychoanalysis'.

Elena goes on to say "contextualism emphasizes the importance of history connectedness to the whole in which everything influences everything else. Contextual ideas stress the complexity of interconnections and interrelationships from which entangled lived experience emerges."

"It is this entanglement that William Coburn (2003) is alluding to when he addressed the simultaneous sources of contextual influences necessary for the passes of psychoanalysis: "emotional experiencing always emerges out of one's history, one's current state of mind and one's environment."" (page 4 of Elena's thesis)

It is tempting for us to go back or revert to my comfortable 'cause and effect'. We can take a serious quantum leap to the world beyond cause and effect.

This world beyond cause and effect is more inspiring than we anything have ever imagined. This world, that is called the resplendent 'wave-like' world, is where this interaction with eternalbeing and personalbeing gives rise to resplendency. This may be what my sister calls 'critical opalescence' which comes from chemistry and a term I am fond of. I give her description of critical opalescence in another chapter, the United States of Awareness.

This new state of awareness totally outside of cause and effect is at least half of the story, timelessly. It is a strong, equal and amazing half of the story that we have missed for thousands of years.

I am so enthusiastic about the verifications I am having about this dimension of my awareness that as a scientist/ clinician I am moved to write, even though my chemist father warned me that writing would be my most challenging subject. Through using my own techniques, I have begun to enjoy the process of writing, though still a novice at it, as is apparent in this first book. But my enthusiasm for this subject replaces my timidity, because of this:

We may find that understanding the reality of this resplendent world that works beyond 'cause and effect' pulls the rug out from under us, tumbling the underpinnings of my knowledge of the world. As the dust settles, what we might find, instead of the old rug under my feet, is a magic carpet, ready to take us to an amazing new way of living.

Mr. Emerchant-Eyes offers water

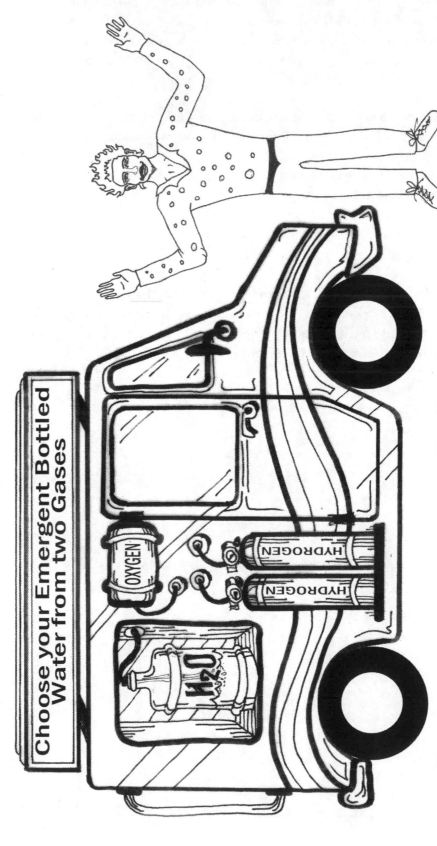

Choose your Emergent Bottled Water from two Gases

OXYGEN

HYDROGEN

HYDROGEN

H2O

Water has more, new and different properties than just the two gases.

CHAPTER 10

ADD YOUR ETERNALBEING TO PERSONALBEING
FOR EMERGENT YOU
OR
IT'S AS EASY AS WATER

Hydrogen plus oxygen
is emergent to
Water
Which is emergent to
A multitude of new and different properties of water that don't resemble gas: …
expansive on freezing, cohesion, crystalline, flowing, volatile…
none of which resemble gases from which water is emergent.

Parallel to this:

Personalbeing plus eternalbeing
is emergent to
Resplendentbeing
Which is emergent to
Conditions of Expansiveness… (Garden of Eden)

Wow! When I understood what 'emergent' means…and fully comprehended that I and everything in my life is emergent for me it's like the excitement of Christmas morning in every moment and in everything I do! Forgive me if I sound over excited about this idea of emergent, as I had a fresh insight about the full implications of emergent just last night.

Before I can discuss the immense implication of emergent in my life we must understand the action of emergent. Water is the easiest example of what emergent means. Water makes up 80-85% of my body. No wonder water is used for most expansive rituals.

To understand this concept of emergent and the importance of knowing my unique eternalbeing, look at the appearance of water on the earth.

The formation of water requires two gases called hydrogen and oxygen. We are all aware that the nature of flammable gases is quite different than water. Amazingly, when these two gases commune,

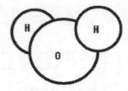

they become the liquid, water. We could say, this fluid, water, 'rises up out of the gases'.

The water does not resemble the gases at all. This is why we call water 'emergent'. Gases and liquids are quite different and unique from each other. Yet the gases are needed for the water to be emergent. One of the meanings of emergent is that my newness or next moment does not resemble those from whence we came. In fact it replaces the prior moment.

Much the same way as the gases are necessary for water to be emergent, the existence of personalbeing (PB) along with my eternalbeing (EB) are necessary for 'resplendent illuminatedbeing' to be emergent.

Resplendent illuminated being 'rises out of PB and EB' which we are calling 'emergent'. Resplendency is an emergent process. PB, EB, and resplendency are quite different and unique from each other. Yet PB and EB are needed for my resplendent illuminated being to be emergent.

Are you beginning to feel a stirring of excitement?

Emergent is the nature of my living all the time, whether I am aware of it or not.

Quantum World Particles Popping in and Out of Existence

In the quantum world, particles are always popping in and out of existence as fast as the speed of light. And the particles are new and different. This begins to give us an idea of what living anew is really about. The equivalence of this newness is "the emergent nature of us." So every moment in our life actually is a rebirth to "begin again". The popping out of existence and back in means that the new existence, as we come into it, does not need to resemble the old existence. This new awareness of me that pops in and out of existence reminds us that every moment we have new options. This is really what quantum coaching is, to "begin again". There is no fixing and repairing the old things, or the old way, as we used to do.

We do not have to overcome the past or fix our old coat. We absolutely are beginning anew in every moment. When we look at all the different levels of the world; first, the quantum world of subatomic

particles; second, the natural world of atoms and molecules; third, the cosmic world of stars and sky; forth, the universal world of galaxies, we realize that we are separate and different people within these levels of worlds but we are not separate and different from each level.

The concept of memories from our past keep us from rebirthing anew whereas the concept 'to memory as we desire', has no conditions from our past existence so it rebirths everything in resplendency. Old memories have no place in this form of existing.

It is never too late to begin again; we only need to replace our addiction to our old ways. When we perceive events happening, there is a gap between the event happening and my responding to it. In that gap I can think of my eternal dream and original story and halt my desire to react and respond and judge. When we realize there is this gap and when we give ourselves the ability and the awareness to change what we do in the gap, we can actually expand that gap to give ourselves a little more awareness. As we become familiar with our eternalbeing, the pattern of our doing-ness, it becomes easier over time to alter our old responses or reactions in the gap.

I can take an instant of time and expand that and choose anew in every moment. Time only exists as a force. The wave nature may be time itself. So beginning anew in every moment is our rebirth in the physical. It is not spiritual, it is not continuing, it is not the old way, it is also not a probability. We are an individual with certainty in the moment that we begin again and then we begin again with a new certainty. It is not an uncertainty of being. It is only an uncertainty of proving location and existence of time at the same moment.

As events happen before the gap, we can personalize and particularize the event as we desire. In this expanded gap moment, by not reacting, we free ourselves from the slavery of the old way. When we stick with images and descriptions of the event, without languaging them, we begin to learn how it is that we expand that gap.

You don't have to slow your mind down to think in images; they are instantaneous with the event. Event happens, image is particularized and personalized of this event and we have stopped all consequences and judging and have freed ourselves to a life of our desire.

In this case, there is no need for overcoming the old way. Because of the living anew just as quantum particles are popping in and out of existence, there are no memories to contend with. So I can forget everything from my past and start over again in every moment. When we hold onto old thoughts, old BATHWAVEs (Belief, Actions, Thoughts, Habits, Words, Attitude, Value, and Emotions) holds me back from this different new perspective in every moment.

Awareness aids my emergent nature

Why would I be aware of emergent if it's natural and happening already? For the same reason you wouldn't try to make water out of random selections of gases on the earth. In fact, you would make very little water since there is little hydrogen compared to oxygen. Whereas when you know you need oxygen and hydrogen to make water, you might collect air where hydrogen is being released abundantly and then it would be easy, secure, effective and efficient to make lots of water.

It's about living with my eternal choices which are emergent in every moment.

When I want living to be easy, secure, effective, efficient and abundant, get to know and communicate with my eternalbeing, as well as my personalbeing. With this communication my resplendent illuminatedbeing (RIB) is emergent and operational which brings in a whole new set of qualities, such as beyond cause and effect, powerful, sustainable, ease, secure, omniscience, timeless, to mention a few.

This is whole new understanding for me. The past is irrelevant in the emergent moment. The emergent moment is a butterflies-in-my-stomach moment, maybe, but fun. It's like the first time on a ride at an amusement park. Until I awarefully experience emergent, I did not know it.

Emergent by its very nature continues to be emergent. Once living resplendently, I begin to live self-evidentingly making choices that are again emergent. This nature is called Condition of Expansiveness (COE).

Knowing my unique eternalbeing supports the awareness of my resplendency.

Relationshifting

PART TWO:

KNOWING MY ETERNALBEING

Essence of My Accomplishments

Eternal Being

is My Eternal Being

CHAPTER 11

ETERNALBEING READING AND NAMING
THE ACE OF DIAMOND RADIANCE

Finding the diamonds in my living chain gang

With thoughtful consideration and self-awareness I begin to understand my physical eternalbeing, see its pattern, and name it as my eternal friend. I call this process finding value and 'diamonds' within me. The radiance is my resplendency.

Another name I give to my eternalbeing is the Diamond Chain Gang. Here's the story of the diamond chain.

The story of the diamond chain

I imagine my life as a chain that it is long and strong. As my eternalbeing I look at this long chain. When I stand back and examine my chain and all the experiences or links that I have put together, I see a valuable pattern of me, expressed in emergent ways throughout my life.

Each link in my chain is an expression of my diamond eternalbeing with the vision of resplendency. I live one link (quantum) every moment. Every link is new and different which is the definition of emergent. One link does not cause the next link. One link is not responsible for the previous link. This is the nature of the quantum world.

Each quantum is complete in itself, free and emergent. My awareness of being emergent is fun.

I am free to put whatever I desire on this diamond chain. With resplendency there is NO JUDGMENT so no link in the chain is weak. Since one link does not cause the next link there is no accusing, blaming or complaining necessary of any links. One link may pass on its force to the next link, yet this is not a requirement for resplendency.

An aspect of the diamond chain is that it is always beginning; it is of an eternal nature. In a sense it is a chain that expands as I add new information I desire. It is the 'spaces' of the links that make it useful as described in Chapter 10 of the Tao Te Ching. There are small spaces in each link. There is a huge eternal space 'adorned' by the chain. In the next few paragraphs I will describe how to determine the pattern manifested in the diamond chain of my eternalbeing.

I happen to life as my virtual 'wave' self, so it is worth understanding

In the quantum world, physicists are beginning to propose that the particle is a "local" portion of a wave where is spins to turn around and readiate out. They nickname it "wavelet" or "wavicle". Whether it is true or not, it is evident that the twoness of particle and wave is intimately related. This "localness" might be considered the equivalence of being alive. "You are making 'waves'", is an old expression I have heard my whole life...

Understanding the interactions of the two of me manifesting the third for a triunity might be interesting and beneficial. To be aware of my virtual eternalself is the purpose of this next portion and work page. Reading and naming my eternalbeing with an interested friend is highly advantageous. I may have preconceived ideas about myself coloring looking directly at this aspect of myself.

The use of Bathwaving helps me perceive my true desires, so they keep pouring into the full cup of my life. The replacing of the old stuff is freeing up and un-limiting my self-imposing obstacles. Amazingly, the eternal 'wave-like' nature of us reveals that no obstacles are ever imposed on me from the outside or from the environment. *Therefore, in full awareness of resplendency Bathwaving might be unnecessary.*

Yet I notice that some of my culture and friends believe in limiting themselves to cause and effect: that is that things happen to me; experiences happen to me; nature happens to me. Bathwaving may be useful for the awareness of the form of my desire to live resplendency in each link, transfiguring some of these old belief systems.

In a sense, what I now know from Heisenberg's Uncertainty Principle is that the observer IS the outcome of the experiment. I bring myself to the experiment and I am in entanglement with the phenomena I observe. Hence the awareness of Entanglement Theory.

I bring myself to life and I happen to life. What I particularly do with a sense of pride or enthusiasm and 'bring' to life is one description of my eternalbeing.

When I really understand this idea and am aware of interacting as eternalbeing, then my living becomes what I desire and I become aware of my resplendence. As I desire to live of the tree of resplendence, I rewrite the Garden of Eden story by living the fullness of my tree using the fruits of enlivening constituents and emergent, entanglement. As I do this, there are no doubts or jealousies nor reasons to discontent myself. I am the wholeness of my triunity—my resplendent illuminatedbeing emergent from the communion of my personalbeing and my eternalbeing.

For me to live this life of resplendency, it is important to focus on the resplendent eternalbeing of others. My personalself gives life to my eternalself, which only has awareness yet no aliveness nor ability to create anything on the physical plane.

On the other hand, my resplendentbeing as the emergent interaction of these two, manifests everything I desire, since it is not hampered by the old concept of time. Within the realm of the eternalbeing, there is no cause and effect, only entanglement.

To help me get to know my eternalbeing and live that communion between my personalbeing and eternalbeing is the purpose of this chapter.

Finding my six shining diamond links

Get a piece of paper or use the work page at the end of this chapter and write eight sentences about six of my doings/accomplishments of which I am particularly proud.

For instance, as a boy, an example might be building a fort out of logs in a forest on a hill with a friend. Or as a girl, teaching the Romanian boy next door how to speak English to be able to communicate. Give myself some time and quiet to let these thoughts flow out of me onto the page.

I am going to go through an example later to help me get a sense of how this process works. It will be good to contact a friend who is interested in this and help each other to read my eternalbeings. I are too close to myself and may miss the "diamonds" for the forest. Some of my BATHWAVEs can get in the way. Remember denying, lying and hiding?

If I do this with a friend, I walk in my friend's shoes and see their eight doings/accomplishments, I will be able to take small steps and see their diamond eternalbeing. They will then be able to experience their own accomplishments and dreams as communication about their eternalbeing, all without judging themselves. This is an awareness of living their resplendentbeing.

Collect different magazines with a variety of covers, at least twenty or so, so they will have enough images to choose from in order to illustrate their descriptions of their eight doings/accomplishments. Have them pick the magazine pictures. It may clarify and reveal more than their words might. Using these magazine pictures will also help capture the commonality of the images of my diamond chain. **Each doing/ accomplishment is considered a facet of the diamond of my eternalbeing.**

My eternalbeing is too big to see and grasp without the boundaries of the examples of the experiences lived in enthusiasm and pride.

In each of those eight moments, the nature of my eternalbeing is most evident. When I see all eight magazine pictures lined up I begin to get a sense of the common essence of my eternalbeing 'chain gang' and my existence. I can begin to sense the importance of my virtual nature.

Without the awareness of my eternalbeing and its talents, my personalbeing may feel less creative and more like a programmed 'robot'.

Once I have this visual experience of the nature of my eternalbeing, I can start filling in the gaps and fleshing out the bigger picture of my living, something my personalself does very well, and which only the personalself can do.

Seeing this bigger pattern for the first time made me want to do the can-can.

When the dancer in me saw my pattern, which involves 'networking' (especially with, yet not limited to, eternalbeings in others), I realized fully, that yes, indeed, I *can* 'network' this and I *can* 'network' that. I was filled with the exuberance of that Cole Porter song. "Yes! I can do the can-can."

Living becomes easy and a self-charted adventure, when I can do the can-can.

Guidelines for reading the eternalbeing

1. The first accomplishment on their list tells me the main action of their eternalbeing in their own words.

For instance, one young woman wrote, "I was proud of moving away from home on my own."

In symbol interpretation, home represents the 'self'. Her eternalbeing is inspiring herself and others to "move away from the old self to live their own new awareness of eternalself in resplendency."

The first accomplishment of the six is the most important one and reveals the commonality of the eternalbeing. Ask questions if I don't see a clear description of my friend's eternalbeing. Look for an action, a verb, that is part of this first accomplishment. I'll call that the eternalbeing's action.

2. Ask my friend if for the rest of their life they would be satisfied and willing to show people to their (action word) of their eternalbeing.

From the example above: "If you could inspire yourself and others to "move away from their old self to live their own new 'resplendent' self" for the rest of your life would that satisfy you?

If I get a yes, Congratulations! I are doing better than I did when I began. I now witness people beginning to implement in hours what has taken me years to understand.

REMEMBER: This eternalbeing reading and naming is not "spiritual" or a superlative with good, better, best judgments in it. Originally, I thought this process was a summary of everything a person did. It isn't.

If I get a no answer, begin again, looking for another action in their words for the eternalbeing. It is a process of which I will feel confident with practice. The important thing is that I am describing facets of my friend's eternalbeing.

3. When I finally get an action of their eternalbeing, read through the remaining seven accomplishments one at a time to see if each one is compatible with their eternalbeing statement from #1. They will not contradict each other. They may have a doing that resists their eternalbeing, yet this is not a contradiction.

When I do other people's readings first, I will discover someone who will be willing and able to do mine.

An example

Here is a letter from a client, whom I'll call Carla (not her real name), in New Zealand about her work on finding her eight diamond links:

Dear Angela,

Here's my Eight Accomplishments List and the corresponding images (as attachments):

1. In my later years of high school, there was an incident where *I was honest* with some authoritarian figures at school, and this provoked a major row between the staff around what I had said/done, and resulted in distinct reactions of support and non-support from my teachers/principals.
2. At the end of my high school years, rather than continue with my studies, I felt highly committed to travelling overseas, which was against the wishes of those I was close to, but *I chose to do it anyway*.
3. With the birthing of both my breech children, *I fought for what I believed in* with regards to their respective births, which involved challenging midwives/doctors/hospital general management GM.
4. In my teens, I was thrown out of home twice and *had to persevere* in finding places to stay, a way to *support myself*, and finishing high school.
5. When raising my children, *I followed my heart* in how I raised them rather than give in to the tremendous pressure of fellow parents around me and their more commonly accepted parenting styles.
6. In general, I really enjoy *seeing the good in all people*.
7. For most of my life I have felt *I am different* to the norm, and I feel comfortable being different.
8. When communicating with my children, I have endeavoured to the best of my ability *to be as straightforward with them* as I can be.

My key words, Angela, when I looked at each of my accomplishments were:

- eternalbeing as the real honest us in our living; true to my word; true self-empowerment
- committed to travelling; inner knowing, following and responding to a daydream
- eyes opened; living what I believe in, support self-empowering
- persevere in honest expressions of me
- finance self
- it's within my power to use my freewill to shizam my universe as I desire
- freeing up the knowledge of eternalbeing to the self
- powering what I desire
- communion of personalself and Eternalself is the freeing of will
- **spontaneous communion of personalbeing and eternalbeing, truly "asserting" honesty**
- **eternalbeing is expressing the honesty of me...**

My Triune Heart

Reveals the
Ace of Diamomds
Shining

Checking her eternalbeing action of "being honest" with each of her eight accomplishments, Carla saw clearly that all her accomplishments are compatible with her desire to express herself honestly.

When Carla stops expressing herself honestly all 'illness' breaks out, like bladder infections and rashes.

Prior to knowing EB, she had freaked out when her significant masculine mirror threatened dishonesty. She wanted to leave him. With this new awareness of her EB Carla worked hard and maintained her deepening honest understandings of herself.

Her primary relationships became resplendent and more authentically intimate as Carla perceived her life through the eyes of her eternalbeing expressing herself honestly.

Naming my eternalbeing

It is important that I chose a name that reminds me of my eternalbeing's recurring theme. In the above example, Carla chose the name Justina to represent her eternalbeing, her eternal friend. **The name Justina reminded her of her underlying theme of honesty. 'Rainbow Sea' was a visual she painted about her.**

Seeing my eternal theme

As I review my six accomplishments to see if each is in synch with my eternal action, my eternal theme emerges. Carla's eternal theme is "**being honest in order to live resplendently and to inspire others live in communion with their eternalbeing and personalbeing honestly.**"

Knowing and experiencing my eternalbeing

For those who wish to explore the essence of my eternalbeing, here is a list of activities that I can play with creatively—with singing, dancing, writing and on and on.

It is my vision to bring each of these ideas to life in a book. Until then, have fun exploring these suggestions, and perhaps your own book will emerge!

Suggestions for living my eternalbeing

- Practice believing I have an eternalbeing.
- Practice seeing and experiencing my relationships differently. This prepares for knowing or experiencing myself as multiple relationships.
- Practice paying close attention to my dreams. I play multiple roles in our dreams.
- Practice being content. Being content is the absence of discontent
- Use my breath to bring matters into focus: Inhale what I desire. Inhale while thinking, "I bring myself to my eternalbeing. Conditions of expansion surround me."

- The greatest meaning of life is not that of serving others; it is offering to life, for in that action I draw to myself. Offering myself to life is the true meaning of self-ness.
- Begin observing and feeling myself.
- Practice adding to myself, i.e. add the dimension of eternalbeing. Fill my cup with new stuff to flush out the old stuff.
- Practice past story regression process that includes many avenues, from self-hypnosis to shamanic journeying.
- Practice standing outside myself observing myself.
- Step out of the old ways of doing things. Change my context to the ways of an eternalbeing. Get outside of my comfort zone, i.e. meaning get out of the context of a composed life.
- Practice putting everything I hear into images. I must be able to speak the language of eternalbeing.
- Practice being everything I do.
- Practice writing letters to my eternalbeing, and writing ansIrs back to myself as my eternalbeing.
- Practice considering and describing the partner and intimate relationship I would like to have for a lifetime.
- Practice not asking others for permission.
- Practice making connections.
- Practice thinking in eternal terms.
- Decide and declare (if only to myself) that I are only meeting and experiencing our eternalbeing.
- Declare and commit in life. Do not struggle to achieve commitment. Instead stand content and carry commitments with I at all times.
- The highest state of enlightenment and wisdom is "not" a quiet mind; it is to keep myself in a state of contentment.
- Tell my senses what I want them to sense, i.e. train my senses to sense my eternalbeing.
- What I want is not what I want until I make that what I already have!
- Practice expansive focusing!
- Practice maintaining my focus on another person, on an object, or on a task at hand, without relaxing or changing my focus to myself!
- Create images in my mind and observe myself creating those images.
- I already are an eternalbeing! So practice feeling myself as an eternalbeing!
- Think of how living in the "now" deceives me.
- Develop my memory and self-awareness.
- Pay close attention to my attitudes and emotions.
- Practice watching people.
- Give myself a direction to follow each day.
- Ask: What is mind?
- Practice not planning my life.
- Set aside time each day for involving myself in preparing to experience my eternalbeing.
- Practice seeing others as eternalbeings.
- Practice directing energy around me to flow through me.

Personal rituals used to activate my eternalbeing theme

This poem demonstrates my ritual and was written during a class on it. Guess what the ritual and theme of my eternalbeing is?

MY ETERNAL THEME

By Angelink Longo 6/22/11

When I design my day
as a communion with my ETERNAL THEME,
the air flows easily over and through my cells
releasing the repast that I chew
over and over and over again.

And I am free to dance wild, fearlessly sustaining
the music of Padma's starry voice,
and Becky's heartfelt hip swayings,
saying that I may re-weave the web of my friendships
now and forever
revealing their ETERNAL THEMES
as I express my unchanging ETERNAL FRIEND'S THEME….
though played in unlimited multitudinous keys.

I may have guessed 'dancing' as the action of my eternal theme of reweaving the web of my personalbeing and eternal theme for myself and others. Once my eternal theme is activated, my personalbeing now is able to live, instantly actualizing my desires. It is called living by 'fiat'… fiat meaning on command.

In this state of living in communion with my eternal friend's theme, memories are not active. Living is actuating without recourse. Nothing blocks this motion.

The only question is, do I have the courage and confidence to live this way?

I keep running away and hiding …Why bother to hide?

It's so much more fun to show up for myself now that I have quick shift methods and fiat capabilities.

Mozart said, "Music comes to me fully formed. I just work at writing it down. I can't force it to happen." Mozart lived in communion with his personalbeing and eternalbeing.

Is it possible that everyone has a unique personal ritual that allows his or her eternal theme to activate.

What do I do that makes time stop?

That is the action of my eternal theme.

STOP TRYING TO BE MYSELF! When I get an active ritual that connects me with my eternal theme, then keep that state of doing in my mind all the time no matter what I am doing. For Mozart it was composing music. For me that state is dancing. The action is networking or reweaving people's wholeness of resplendent triunity. Sometimes I work reweaving BATHWAVE desires.

Dancing is on my mind all day long. I weigh herbs and imagine I am dancing. I do dishes and I dance with them. I remember the mode in which I wrote My Eternal Theme poem above...and trust myself to live that.

Communion is in motion when I am doing the IMPROVISATIONAL DANCE ritual which connects me to my eternalbeing theme of 'networking'. When I imagine living as dancing, I communion with 'networking'. Dancing is one act of entanglement of 'networking' which expands my resplendent way.

Once I am aware of my eternalbeing, I can choose to use my eternalbeing's action to observe and encourage the communioning of my eternalbeing and personalbeing to support my emergent resplendent illuminated being.

How it's EEEZY comes in later chapters.

How to know myself:

Being aware of triunity is a necessity to know myself. Knowing eternalbeing is required.

The benefit of living and knowing that I am a triunity is that it gives me a way to know myself. If I am one being, I cannot know myself; it is too incestual. As two beings, I can interact with myself but cannot observe this. **As three beings I am able to interact and observe, thereby knowing myself.**

If I am aware only of my personalbeing self, I will be living my languaged memories and living those creates only problems, struggles, judgment, and this would be the path of ignorance of the triunity of us, and then it becomes a difficult existence.

With the triunity, I can stand in the position of any of my three beings–personalbeing, eternalbeing and resplendent illuminatedbeing. When I stand in the position of resplendent illuminatedbeing, I then have access to observing the interaction of personalbeing and eternalbeing in my life.

I'll give an example of how I can do that.

My son Mark is visiting. He is 27 years old. On his return home, he woke up in the morning with a dream. Mark's dream was of a desert that he photographed and a bottle of dry red sand.

In dream language the image spoke to me of withholding rain/water/vital emotions and information from one's self. The bottle container may be a body holding red blood that was dry. Dry, again, is withholding the vital emotions/information that one truly desires or perceiving it that way. Photographing it is this very process of observing and recording what's going on...

I chose to stand in the position of my resplendent illuminatedbeing. Then as I related to Mark, as he described his dream, I saw him as my personalbeing, relating to me in his dream as my eternalbeing. By observing the interaction of Angela and Mark, I gather valuable information about my personalbeing's interaction with my eternalbeing... I can see that my own personalbeing, observing Mark as such, is denying emotional vitality (fluids). Being harsh on myself, being judgmental of myself, I observed that I hold myself back from being my whole self. I can actually choose to express the vital emotions and live the vital emotions that I truly desire, that would moisten the images from the dream. So I am beginning today after this experience with Mark, to express and live all the vital emotions I truly desire...and in entanglement, Mark has more of an awareness of this choice in his own life.

To reiterate, unless I realize that I am a tri-unity, I cannot know myself. It gives me the benefit of two interactive perspectives of myself. So when I am aware of my existing three beings, I can stand in the place of one of them and perceive the interaction of the other two parts of myself and this is a real way to know the self. Life is constructed so that I can know and manifest myself easily. For instance, when I know my eternalbeing, and of course I know my personalbeing because it is my body mind personality energy system, (I have learned my eternal being through my accomplishments that I am proud of as described in this Chapter), I can perceive their interaction as being my resplendent illuminated being. Another alternative is that I can stand in the position of resplendent illuminated being, then I can perceive Mark as my personalbeing, interacting with himself in his dream as my eternalbeing. I can observe how I relate with Mark and that will show me how I relate to my own personalbeing and in his dream to my eternalbeing. This is the value of the nature of quantum living.

The universe has memory which provides the process of accessing information.

The quantum world in its equivalence, calls this process entanglement. Because the world is an interactive universe, as described in the quantum world as the interaction between particle and wave instantly creating either the 'complete' light or electrons, protons, neutrons quarks, bosons..... I can see that the nature of reality in this interaction. This is why my structure as a triunity, just as the structure of the quantum world, is actually an interactive triunity of particle, wave and new wholeness, then it only makes sense that I need to know this, live this, be aware of it and in doing so I have all of the knowledge and ability to access any information that I wish of myself and of my world and universe.

Work Page for Reading and Naming Eternalbeing

List eight accomplishments of which you are proud in the order that come to mind.

1._____

_____

2. _____

_____

3. _____

_____

4. _____

_____

5. _____

_____

6. _____

_____

7. _____

8. _____

_____

When possible, select a magazine cover for each accomplishment that captures the feeling or essence of that accomplishment.

Guidelines for the Person Doing the Eternalbeing Reading:

1. Find the action of the first accomplishment that describes eternalbeing's action.

2. Ask if the person would be satisfied doing this action for the rest of their lives, for themselves and for others.

3. Check each of the remaining seven accomplishments to see if they are compatible with the action of eternalbeing.

4. Give your eternalbeing a name that honors his or her accomplishments and eternal theme.

U. S. A.

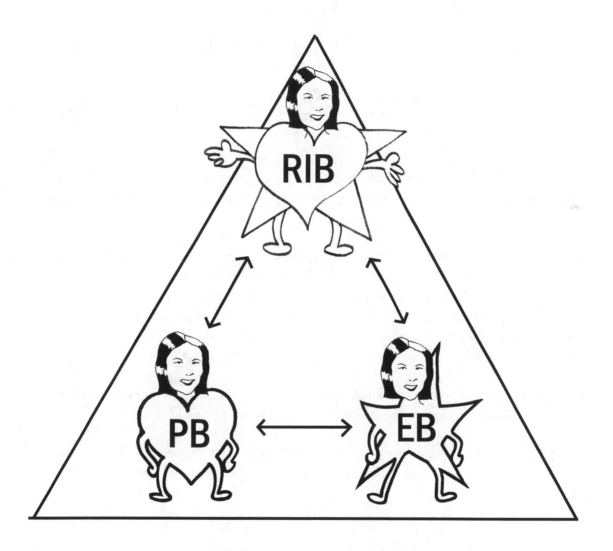

The Resplendent
Triunity of You

United States of Awareness

CHAPTER 12

MY TRIUNITY IS THE SOURCE OF MY
UNITED STATES OF AWARENESS
(USA)
OR
MY RESPLENDENCE EXPRESSES ITSELF IN REVEALING
TO
OTHERS THE RESPLENDENCE THEY ARE SHOWING ME

On the way down to the beach Easter morning, an aria sung by a man in Italian came on the radio. I immediately began to sob, with absolutely no thoughts or understanding of what the song was about or why I was crying. Luckily I wasn't driving.

I sobbed and sobbed and faced and embraced myself without knowing what it was about. I placed my tears under my tongue, a homeopathic remedy for the emotion that was alive and I was presenting to my being in entanglement. An emergent (new) e-motion was beginning to express itself and with patience I intended to reveal its description. My Egyptian girlfriend who was driving stroked my arm and told me the name of the song: Nessun Dorma. She said it had something to do with being asleep. I thought to myself that was strange since I never felt more awake.

That night at my home, my ex-husband Dennis called and said, "Can I come over and bring some vegetables I cooked? I'm tired of my own cooking. Got somethin' to add?"

I replied, "Sure," and I knew something was percolating because his calling doesn't happen that often anymore. I felt my description of this new emotion expressed by hearing Nessun Dorma was imminent

Lovely entanglement

I loooove entanglement!!! I was telling Dennis about sobbing to Nessun Dorma on my way down to the beach. He immediately said, "You need to listen to Paul Potts sing that song on American Idol on TV."

I remembered that Paul Potts was the unknown person who sang opera without lessons and sent the audience and even the judges into tears. While he was still singing the whole audience stood up cheering and crying. What was the power of the song? What was the story, the words, the music?

Why does it provoke such a deep, deep expression of emotion in people across the board and possibly people across the world?

Mirror-calls of resplendency

Dennis burst into sobs listening to Paul Potts for what he said was the umpteenth time. I offered to do Relationshifting with him. I knew that as I follow and relationshift with him as a mirror-call of my masculinity, I would shift and understand myself.

As he agreed to do the Relationshifting I muscle tested what age Dennis needed to go to for him to understand his BATHWAVEs. I arrived at five to six years of age. That was the year Dennis' mother left him at his grandmother's house for days. It was this incident that had led Dennis into terrible emotional freezings of fear and anger.

Dennis loved his mother with strong co-dependency. His anger was frozen in grief and fear and it's like a hot face frozen in a glacier. I discovered that at five-years old he has a hard-as-ice character formation issue that was part and parcel of my relinquishing my marriage. Seventeen years later he agreed that this same pattern seems to be expressing itself in his life and relationships.

This is yet another example of repetitive patterns of information I carry with us through life. This incident also helped me understand the wholographic nature of time as a force nudging us toward 'resplendence' when I am aware of it. I asked Dennis to face and embrace as that five-year-old child, the fear, the grief, the pain, and the anger that he felt in that quantum of time being left at grandmas without his two brothers and two sisters and with his belief that his mother was 'abandoning' him.

He embraced this and put in a quantum shift that his masculine side was in charge of his self-nurturance (mother). It was clear to me, as explained below, that in that moment, much like it is described in the opera, Turandot, which contains the song Nessun Dorma, Dennis had decided to abandon the idea of letting another woman ever get close to his heart as had his mother.

He put in the quantum shift, since mothers are self-nurturing, that 'my masculine side nurtures myself.' He was opening his heart. Later I added to the quantum shift that 'he is giving unconditional love to an available woman who opens to his love'. With muscle testing this quantum shift held up to age of eleven, where once again he lost his ability to nurture himself and love himself unconditionally and others.

At age eleven, the pattern was about a girl in school that he liked but who rejected him. Again he embraced the feeling of rejection fueling his unconscious decision to never love another woman, and he put in the quantum shift that he no longer puts up a shield against love. I tested again and at 62, he lost the shift. That was the year he met a girlfriend that he worked with for three years and recently broke up with. After embracing his closing himself off to her, he put in that no matter the situation, he was open to love.

I muscle tested that the quantum shift held only until he was 63, which is the age he is now. When he lost the shift again and he said, "I think I'm judging myself" and the muscle testing revealed that he judged himself and felt unworthy of love. At this point I put in the quantum shift that "I am worthy of being resplendent and unconditionally loving myself and others."

Revealing with muscle testing, his quantum shift is an option for him all the way to 200 years old. I knew that this was a major transition for his life, for he had never been able to maintain a loving relationship with a woman.

How does this relate to Nessun Dorma from Turandot

How does this relate to the song, Nessun Dorma? I looked up the story of the opera called Turandot. The story revealed that a princess in China, Turandot, had vowed when her female ancestor was slaughtered by a conquering prince, never ever to let a man get close to her in any beloved relationship. BINGO!!!

The princess had three riddles she would ask a man who might ask for her hand in marriage. If the suitor failed to answer the three riddles correctly, he would be executed in the morning. Men had tried, and one in the opera goes off to the guillotine. The princess, of course, was considered to have a heart of ice.

A prospective young man, a prince, came forth and rang the bell to answer the riddles. The riddles were questions that were worthy of Heartwaving. The first one was something like: what do you go to sleep with at night but is gone upon waking? The young man answered 'hope', and the princess trembled at his correct answer.

The second riddle was—what is flowing red and hot, but not fire? The young man said 'blood', and again the princess shook with worry because the suitor had answered two correctly.

The third, she knew he would miss, and she said, what is cold as ice yet burns like fire?

There was an intense silence for a while, while the young man thought. He smiled and turned toward her and immediately said, 'Princess Turandot.'

The princess looked at her father and said, "Please don't abandon me to him."

The suitor said to Princess Turandot, "I'll give you a riddle. Guess my name by morning, and if you do correctly, I will give up my life."

That night Princess Turandot won't let anyone sleep in Peking until the suitor's name was found. In attempting to discover his name, they find the suitor's father and the father's slave girl who secretly had fallen in love with this young man when she looked into his eyes. At the end of the opera the young slave girl takes her own life to save the prince and his father, the king. Before she dies, she gives away the secret to the princess that the prince's name is 'Love'. Of course, that is a poetic rendering of his real name. As she dies and the father mourns the young slave girl's death, the song Nessun Dorma must have been sung.

The words of the song Nessun Dorma:

Nobody shall sleep,...
Even you, O princess,
in my cold room,
Watch the stars, that tremble
with love and with hope
But my secret is hidden within me,
My name no one shall know.
No!... No!...

The reason then, that this song provokes tears in everyone who hears it, is that it is the song of resplendency; it is the song of personalbeing as Princess Turandot, who dares her eternalbeing in the form of her suitor, Prince Calaf, to know her through her riddles.

In entanglement with her, all his responses to her riddles are correct. In the morning when the young Prince Calaf tells her his name and kisses her, she melts as his song predicted, that the silence between them that kept personalbeing from knowing eternalbeing, dissolves in their communion. His name which he gives in the opera when joined with her, as 'love', is really also, 'resplendence', which is what is formed in the communion of the adorned personalbeing and the virtual eternalbeing.

Resplendency has the access to all that is desired, to all that he wishes to know. The young slave girl represents the memories of love. Of course memories melt and disappear in the face of resplendence because in resplendence, I am, as always in this moment, emergent. Emergent is new and different, never resembling the past and so the memories now die as spoken of in the song. (No one will know his name and I must, alas, die.)

In resplendence I am a triunity which is my United States of Awareness (USA)

The song of Nessun Dorma describes resplendence. I sing and rejoice in resplendence with the shifts that Dennis made. Of course my shift was about my relationship to the masculine. I had at some point, out of a deep love of my father (though not bonded to him), and with a judgment that no man could ever be as good as Jesus, rejected all men and wanted to be married to Jesus as a nun. A.L. + J.C. was written in a heart wherever I could hide it.

This disembodied emotion was part and parcel of a sickly childhood with an ulcer at age five, polio at ten, along with a nervous breakdown and hypoglycemia at 24. I see that my deeper rejection of all men was synonymous with self-sabotaging my heart and my relationships, never allowing myself to succeed in true love, even when it stared me in the face recently in New Zealand with a close love of my life. Guess his initials? Yes, J.C.

I approximate that 65% of my clients have a similar fear, anger or grief preventing real closeness and true committed long-term relationships with the opposite sex. Now that I am shifting it, may I create and live in resplendence with my beloveds. This means that I a each a particularized adorned self actively living with our eternal imaginative self which in communion, resplendent illuminatedself is emergent completing our triunity of love.

I am the loving illuminated triunity that I desire. Then I may live in EEEZY (Emergent, Entanglement, Eternal Zestful You) resplendent intimacy as a triunity with everything and everyone I wish. I am so grateful for all who are sharing love and wisdom with me in entanglement.

Committed long term resplendent relationships are the next frontier

I just found something I wrote six years ago to my adventurous, and at that time 21-year-old, son, Mark, who was always ahead of me encouraging me to stretch my awareness especially in the field of resplendent relationships:

Sourcing Creativity in the Interaction of Personalbeing and Eternalbeing

"What if there are infinite patterns and it is my adventure to discover the new creative patterns that is 'ourself' every moment by helping others to discover and actualize their 'creative patterns'? Of course, you will uncover your many ways of doing that…you have already done that for me…

My pattern is recurring essence yet ever changing in form, as I desire, and that is the source of our "forever I Ching" (the ancient book of wisdom called the Chinese Book of Changes). After facing and embracing my resistance, the quantum shift might look like:

> "I am willing to enter
> into the adventure
> of the unknown."

Showing others to their resplendency reveals the emergent mirror-call (miracle)

As I described above, and what I hope I communicated, is that in showing others to their resplendency, you are creating expressions of my own resplendency.

When I show others, like my ex-husband, to 'their hydrogens and their oxygens', I cannot show them how to make water. It's like showing a horse to water and not being able to make them drink. I can only show others the tools of the way to their emergence.

I am expressing tools of a quantum way…they do not cause or affect me. These tools give me a replacement for 'struggling, suffering and limiting myself to cause and effect'.

I need to cut out all avenues of escape from resplendency. This reminds me of the Bible illustration of the cherubs with the flaming swords put at the entrance to the Garden of Eden so that Adam and Eve could NOT eat again of the tree of judging…(implying good and 'evil').

As I inspire others I nurture my own tree of **enliving** which is **resplendence.**

"Critical Opalescence", a psychoanalyst's (my sister's) words describing this principle: (as a metaphor of triunity)

"One potential outcome of *bearing complexity (the 'science of surprises') toward change* is the ability to focus one's energy, inward and outward recognizing one's actions as having meaning and impact through the necessary embeddedness of being." E. Bonn

"Critical opalescence describes metaphorically another important component in turbulent contextualism. It is a concept borrowed from physics that can have applications to psychoanalysis, particularly those moments where the potential for change is seemingly infinite. Physicist, Raymond Dyson, eloquently describes this phenomenon that was first observed by Thomas Andrews in 1869:

Critical opalescence is a strikingly beautiful effect that is seen when water is heated to a temperature of 374 degrees Celsius under high pressure. 374 degrees is called the critical temperature of water. It is the temperature at which water turns continuously into steam without boiling. At this critical temperature and pressure, water and steam are indistinguishable. They are a single fluid, unable to make up its mind whether to be a gas or a liquid. In that critical state, the fluid is continually fluctuating between gas and liquid, and the fluctuations are seen visually as a multicolored sparkling. The sparkling is called opalescence because it is also seen in opal jewels that have a similar multicolored radiance [pp. 42–44]." p.8

> "Critical opalescence, as a metaphor, elucidates the paradoxical concept of a simultaneous process and outcome where multiple states illuminate each other in fundamentally novel ways, scintillating at all levels of experience. These are the precise moments where the potential for change is boundless." p.9

This beautifully describes the interaction between personalbeing and eternalbeing resulting in a radiant opalescence of resplendent illuminatedbeing. Reminding myself again that personalbeing and eternalbeing are the equivalents of the 'particle' and the 'wave' natures of the quantum world.

Elena Bonn goes on to write:

> "I first read about this phenomenon in a book written by the renowned scientific historian, Peter Galison (2003), about Albert Einstein and Henri Poincare called, *Einstein's Clocks,*

Poincare's Maps: Empires of Time. He writes about the particularities of these men's lives that led them both, simultaneously but separately to the discovery of relativity in 1905. Galison uses the physics metaphor of critical opalescence to describe the forces behind the revolutionary thinking. He suggests the technology, science, and philosophy merged in the minds of Poincare and Einstein, each of these domains equally vital ingredients to the soup of their discoveries. Their tools, ideas and philosophical reflections jostle it together and merged into a new way of thinking. He spells out contextually the temperature and pressure of the times and the daring thinking in which these men Ire immersed, flipping back and forth between the pools of these domains, until each aspect of the process illuminate the other and lit the pathway to novel ideas and the scientific revolution."

Cause and effect and quantum emergent entanglement coexisting in resplendence

I believe that this is also an example of an entanglement of the times between these two men. Critical opalescence happens between fields whereas entanglement happens simultaneously between waves. Critical opalescence is a phenomenon within cause and effect and also in entanglement outside of cause and effect.

I would like to invoke the concept of critical opalescence and apply it to the interactions of personalbeing and eternalbeing. From their interaction is the emergent resplendent illuminatedbeing. This emergent being is radiant as described in another chapter and it is the very radiance which evokes the entanglement with my universe.

This metaphor of critical opalescence might therefore be a beautiful metaphor for describing the interaction of these beings. Critical opalescence, as a metaphor, is within the realm of cause and effect, yet at the same time demonstrating the entanglement of a gas and a liquid being both, simultaneously, and glowing because of it.

Resplendency is effortlessly partly outside of the world of cause and effect which does not require pressures or special temperatures to exist; and partly as personalbeing existing in cause and effect. When in communion, these states take on yet a third state of opalescense, not present in either alone.

Critical opalescence is visually, wonderfully illustrating the co-existence of the cause and effect realm of time and space with the other aspect of our existence which is outside of time and space without cause and effect and both are where the emergent resplendent illuminatedbeings exist.

RIB's Expand in Quantum Communication

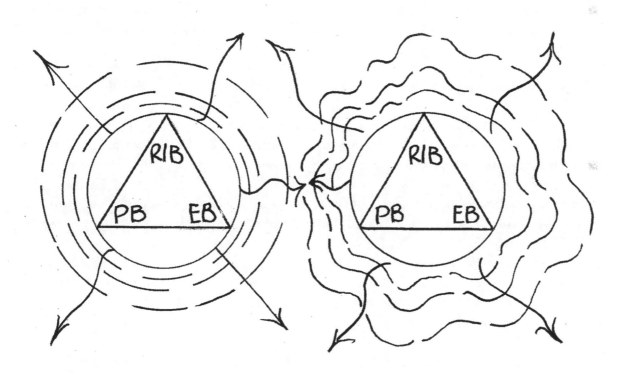

And are Emergent...

CHAPTER 13

QUANTUM COMMUNICATION
RESPLENDENT CONVERSATION
IN AN EMERGENT ENTANGLEMENT WAY

Understanding waves

To have the quality of our "wave" nature in my conversations I need to practice qualities of the wave.

Waves keep on going to the ends of the Universe.
They are expansive in nature.
They never diminish or are interrupted.
They are transmitted to all beings.
The most important quality is that the conversation keeps going and is expansive in nature.

Quantum questioning

Questioning keeps a conversation open ended. Questions are truly expansive. Questions need to be in the form of a declarative question so that you may declare yourself at the same time as questioning. This type of questioning also does not demand an answer.

Giving only an answer closes off the flow of communication. Answers can be narrowing and limited. Answering restricts a conversation; even my own answers are not only restrictive but my answers are all difficult to trust.

Truths are the worst offenders of all. It's insane that I look for truths. How do I know what I am saying is true? Let me give you an example of a conversation about this topic of searching for truth that uses declarative questioning.

Pat:	"Doesn't that really mean then that any kind of search for truth is a foolish endeavor?"
Raj:	"Is it possible that maybe a great deal of my life is based on foolish endeavors then?"
Pat:	"Could there have been ways to live my life in a different way?"
Raj:	"Wouldn't your life be entirely different had you used declarative questioning?"
Pat:	"Might there be all kinds of ways that I might incorporate that into my life today?"
Raj:	"Is it possible that maybe you have the choice to do anything you desire to do and be?"
Pat:	"It seems to follow doesn't it that choices are wide open to me in this moment?"
Raj:	"Consider that the universe will support you in any choice you make by not getting in the way?"

Pat: "Does that mean that *any choice I make is not narrowing or restricting me or limiting me?*"

Raj: "Where in the universe does it ask that you make a specific choice that is good, better or best?"

Pat: "Does that mean that I can make any choice I desire for the first time in my life?"

Raj: "How different would your life be if you understood that life isn't judging you? You are judging you using life to do it at times... can you stop doing that?"

Pat: "Wouldn't I be free to ask myself to be any way I wish?"

And so the conversation goes.

Can you see how the questions opened up a whole expansive realization on both sides of the conversation? This is the part of the conversation where I would start facing and embracing my self-judgment and all the emotion like anger or sadness as if I were Pat...

It is very important that I don't ask a yes or no question. A yes or no question closes the conversation as soon as it's asked. Using declarative questioning takes practice, but it is quite exciting to me that I can finally communicate in a way that feels very creative and empowering to both people in the conversation.

I have to say that I have been a poor conversationalist in my adult life. I have been able to teach, lecture and treat people. Thanks to my new tools of Bathwaving and Relationshifting, my sessions with individuals have become more conversational because they encourage people to see what they truly desire in part two of the bathwaving, or replacing with grace. This in a way trains me to begin to come from a questioning, opened stance that is free to be whatever I desire.

Another technique of quantum communication is mentioned in the Chapter 15 A Bird Doesn't Sing Because It Has an Answer. Quantum communication is the conversation between our personalself and eternalself. The personalself can learn to use the declarative questioning with the eternalself.

The responses from eternalbeing are found in our dreams as described in Chapter 20 Dreamwaving. Have you ever considered that my dreams might be questioning my life instead of giving answers to you?

Quantum reversal

The second technique of this conversation with myself is called quantum reversal. When I look at a wave forward or backward it's the same wave. Likewise, when I want to check whether a statement is true, reverse it and say it backwards. It will still be true if it is in fact a truism.

For instance, if a person says to you "you were born unto the world for a reason". To know if this is true I shall reverse it as "what if the world is born unto you for a reason? This is a reversal and a declarative question. When you reverse everything in my life wouldn't that expand my life creatively?

My responses to the world around me are my resplendency and are for a reason, which I am describing in Relationshifting in this book. *Life as a partnership is living in you.*

I begin to understand the reason that I am born into life from translating the reasons that my world around me is showing me. The quantum world is more expansive than the way I have been living. When Einstein and other physicists saw the new physics, they were confused as how to apply it to their lives, and rightfully so.

Our language and the way I have been taught to converse clouds my mind. Our language structure conceals me rather than reveals me. When I use my old languaging ways of yes and no questions or of giving lots of answers, I can't really see what's going on in an expansive way (and it's an expensive way, also).

The physicists in Einstein's time chose to stay in the old language world instead of exploring new ways of living and conversing which would have acknowledged emergent entanglements in their living.

Does life want to be happy in me?

In reading Chapter 16 on Understanding the Benefits of the Resplendent Way with Arithmetic, this idea of 'does life want to be happy in me?' begins to be clear.

Take the statement: "I want to be happy in life." Reverse that statement and turn it into a declarative question: "Does life want to be happy in me? Am I the type of person that life would be happy in?" This begins to open a person up to: "Oh, I might start doing things that life can be happy in."

In the same way with arithmetic, if 5 equals 2 plus 3 then I know for sure that its reverse, 3 plus 2 equals 5, is true. I can see that reversing the truth is always true. Also, what awakens me is that 5 equals 4 plus 1 also. How many ways do you think I can be 5'ish? How many ways can I express the concept of 5?

Math says I can express any quantity in an infinite number of new and different ways. This is where our life begins to be emergent in entanglement with 5'ishness. The declarative questions create a myriad of possibilities on the other side of the equal sign to 5, like 6 minus 1, 100 minus 95, 10 divided by 2 and so on…and so on and so on, to infinity.

Infinite expression takes the struggle out of life when I realize that it is in the questioning that I expand myself. I never need to have answers. Creativity abounds when I ask declarative questions. Can you imagine how many creative options were popping out of the declarative questioning?

Also our pattern of questioning reveals my eternalself, which is analogous to my wave-like nature. Questions keep a conversation going which is wave-like. They are true forward and in reverse which is also true of waves. The questioning stimulates my imaginative processes and leaves the door open for more to come in any conversation.

Beliefs get in the way of this kind of conversation which is why Bathwaving can be useful during that time. I have done many Bathwaves while conversing with people, friends, and clients to help when I feel stuck in my own…FASTWAVE, (a typo I liked),… BATHWAVE. This way of communicating with declarative questions is an example which opens me to an imaginative process. Is there an answer to imagination? What if life is all imagination, would that be okay?

Would it be okay if I am 'a communicating relatedness' and in my communicating relationship I am expanding the universe and myself? That would be okay with me and I hope you begin to understand that this is the way of expansion.

Resplendency resides in asking what I desire in every moment. My illuminated part then says, "As you wish." Just like in *Princess Bride*. I love that story/movie. That is the conversation going on between personalbeing and eternalbeing.

The question then is what is the way that I am? Do I know that I am free to be any particularization of myself that I wish in every moment? Can I be and believe as I really desire? I am particularizing myself every moment as I wish. Not one particularization or action limits me. Why must I be only one thing?

There is the 'way' that I am (eternalbeing), but I can be that 'way' in any particularization I wish. When I am a 5'ish 'way' then I can be an infinite number of 5'ishes, like 15 divided by 3, 7 minus 2, the square root of 25.

Free the format that you truly desire. Free the physical self that you really want. Be whatever it is I ask of myself in that moment.

Every moment is an opportunity to question, to enliven and to affirm who I am. If you desire, in the next moment, you can transform the moment by Bathwaving and Relationshifting.

143

CHAPTER 14

A BIRD DOESN'T SING BECAUSE
IT HAS AN ANSWER

Partnering with my life

Imagine that 'life' is a separate entity from you. My 'life', then being separate, could have a relationship with you–as if life were your partner. Would you expect to get something from the relationship with your 'life'? Would you want to get something, be it happiness, growth, self-development, for example, from this relationship with life?

If life is a pattern, like a fractal (repetitive everywhere, picture galaxies) and you as your eternalbeing have chosen this pattern from the get-go, what follows is this idea:

When I relate to that pattern of life as a partner, would I like to 'get something' from the pattern or would I like to expand the pattern of our life? Would you like to expand this relationship with my partner?

Let's say you choose to give to my life, to give to my partner. As a resplendentbeing in entanglement with no cause and effect you have no need to gain anything since you are resplendent.

As a resplendentbeing in entanglement you are complete and therefore there is nothing to gain. Gaining is irrelevant. As a resplendentbeing I can give as I desire and in the giving I am receiving as I am.

I am a resplendentbeing in entanglement with my whole universe. Entanglement provides new ingredients for my emergent imaginative minding. Emergent entanglement expands the universe. There is nothing to receive yet there is everything to give since it is all my entanglement and my emergent miracle. After all, this is the true understanding of being self-evident, of living self-evidentingly. Why would I rather struggle with growing, developing and gaining to become something that I already am?

I have mostly been telling myself that I am not THERE yet, which is the way I've been doing it for thousands and thousands of years. This way of endless pursuit is exhausting and stressing, and as I have found out, doesn't work.

One of the reasons pursuing life doesn't work is that I am always looking for an answer in that process of growing, developing and gaining. Since everything in life shows me who I already am, then I don't need to gain anything else, including answers, because I already am all that I am, at this very moment.

I am that I am?

Dr. Angela Longo

If life is not about answers, might it be about questions?

Questions are my map or guideline for my expansion of the universe, for my entanglement with the universe. Consider that the way to keep this living partnership going, opening and expanding is in asking my partner basic information gathering questions: who, what, when, where, and why. Remember, also, what the Native Americans always taught us.... "how?" (Sorry, my Hopi name was White Corn in the Road Runner Clan... cause when they heard my corny sense of humor they ran...

This pattern of questions you can rhetorically ask yourself expands your relationship with life and is demonstrated in Chapter 13 called *Quantum Communication*.

What is really going on is that I give to life questions asking 'as my Resplendent Self'. The responses to the questioning will reveal in a mirror-call way the following:

- 'When' am I my Resplendent Self?
- 'Who' am I as my Resplendent Self?
- 'What' am I as my Resplendent Self?
- 'How' am I as my Resplendent Self?
- 'Where' am I as my Resplendent Self?
- 'Why' am I my Resplendent Self?
- 'Why not' am I my Resplendent Self?

'Why not?' is perhaps our best question to ask life

All these questions align how I feel about the response I give as well as makes it self-evident what I am willing to offer to life. It has taken me years to understand this.

I still am feeling a bit of judging myself as I read those questions again...it is one of my bottom liners...I love myself unconditionally no matter what I am doing or offering...My understanding was aptly motivated by 'the unrequited love of the true beloved of my life'. Every time I read this chapter I still embrace my giving to get love and my lack of communication between my feminine and masculine, and between my personal and my eternal beings...

My quantum shift is "I appreciate all communication between my personalbeing and my eternalbeing and between my feminine and masculine being all the time everywhere."

Thank you to my New Zealand love for this.

I offer to life questions as myself. This is living self-evidentingly.

These basic questions act like verbs in a way because the questions keep our life moving, expanding and emergent.

Some of the fun of Relationshifting is expanding my awareness through questioning and beginning to listen deeply to understand the 'image or descriptive' language of my eternalbeing.

When you rearrange the letters in 'listen' they spell 'silent', as I learned from Jim Kwik, Brain Coach this morning. Silent is definitely useful for listening.

Life as your partner will ask questions back to you. Ask and listen. Commit to that. Ask your life questions and listen to the questions life gives you in return. That's the amazing nature of entanglement. I have access to anything I desire as long as I am willing to offer that.

This is much the way that your personalbeing and eternalbeing converse. Personalbeing will ask the questions. Eternalbeing responses may be dreamed or you may just 'know' the direction to go. It is up to you to listen and to understand these questions you give life. Your responses are the nature of your living.

A bird doesn't sing because it has an answer. A bird sings because it has a song. Life as a partner 'sings' in harmony with the bird and with you always and in all ways.

- Are you singing?
- What is my song?
- When do you sing?
- How is life always singing in harmony with you?
- Who is singing?
- Who is listening?
- Where do you sing?
- Why not sing it out?

One of my favorite songs *"Happiness Runs"* by Donovan Leitch goes:

"Happiness runs in a circular motion.
Life is like a little boat upon the sea.
Everybody is a part of everything anyway.
You can have it all if you let myself be."

...and do...and be...and do be, and do be do be do?

Thank you, Frank Sinatra, for isn't our eternalbeing our real "stranger in the night"?

THE NEW QUANTUM YOU

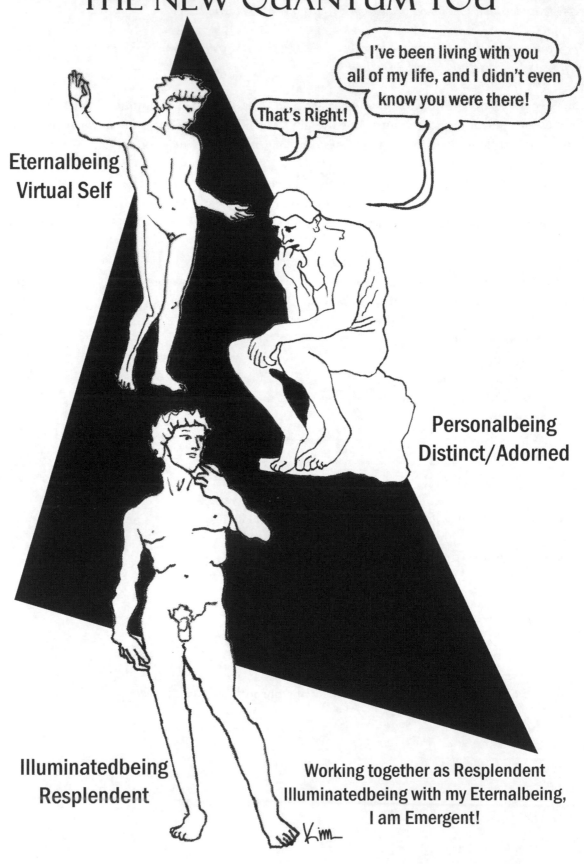

CHAPTER 15

UNDERSTANDING THE RESPLENDENT WAY THROUGH ARITHMETIC

When I realized that I could understand the benefits of resplendent living through simple arithmetic, I was thrilled. I am now excited to write it and share it with you.

The resplendent illuminated being's eternal theme is like a number that I choose, but can be expressed in a variety of ways. Let me pick the number five to represent my resplendentbeing.

Awareness of my resplendentbeing provides the theme with which I know myself. If I am a 5, I am always a 5,5,5,5,5,5,5,5,5,5,5,5,5,5,5,5,5,5,5,5,5,5,5,5,5,5,5,5,5,5,5,5,5.

When my personalself embodies my eternalbeing, however, I can particularize myself in a multitudinous number of ways to express my 5 such as 3 + 2 and 4 + 1 and so on in the example below.

This is the way of entanglement. As soon as I meet people, situations, information and so on, I am in entanglement. Entanglement is each moment instantly dancing with the infinite possibilities of numbers that can create 5 in the universe. Each time I express or entango with a new set of numbers, I am emergent, new and different.

Resplendentbeing (in a 5'ish way) = Personalbeing interacting with Eternalbeing

$5 = 3 + 2$
$5 = 4 + 1$
$5 = 6 - 1$
$5 = 100 - 95$
$5 = 10 / 2$
$5 = $ square root of 25…in infinite emergent ways.

Each equation is emergent or new and different than any other equation. $6 - 1$ does not use a four, which is from the line before. $10/2$ is different and new from $100-95$. Square root of 25 does not resemble 10 or 2.

Physical embodiment of particle-nature and wave-like expression

This realization that I have the ability through my physical embodiment to express myself creatively any way I wish and still be expressing the eternal theme of me, gives me a life full of emergent creativity. Without embodiment, I have no creative options.

Dr. Angela Longo

I am always the resplendent illuminatedbeing steadfast with my eternal theme of 5, yet uncreative and therefore, non-expressive. There is no freedom with only the unembodied 5. The resplendent illuminatedbeing alone is useless. **I need embodiment for existence, and expression, and freedom.**

My physical embodiment repeats my 5-ness in an endless variety of ways.

Understanding Quantum Resplendency through Arithmetic

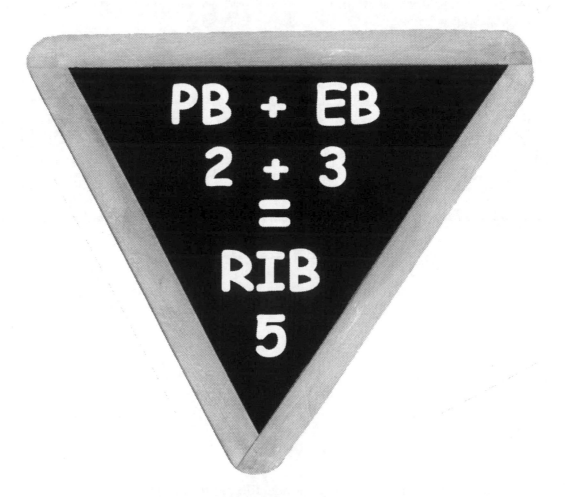

PB + EB

2 + 3

=

RIB

5

5-ish In Infinite Emergent Ways

This expression of a myriad of ways is fun and helps me to stop discontenting myself. The realization that there are infinite ways that I am able to expand my universe, and that I can begin again in every moment in every expression of me, is self-empowering.

How many ways have there been for expressing my eternal theme and my eternalbeing in my lifetime thus far?

I forget that the universe never judges me in any way? Do I judge myself? Would you like to muscle test that and see if it is true? Yep? I am still doing it?

Please bathwave self-judgment to transfigure it to unconditional self-love! I don't have to do anything to be the love I desire…

This is what Heartwaving BATHWAVEs does. It trains me to find that gap where I react and stop the judging. Until then, Bathwaving helps to free me to be, to believe, and to do whatever I truly desire in the moment. When I remember and believe in resplendency it is a lot easier….no bathwaving necessary.

I don't have to repeat the old patterns of who I am.

I am who I ask myself to be—different in this moment, an expression of my eternalbeing's eternal theme.

Why not?

RIB = Resplendent Illuminatedbeing

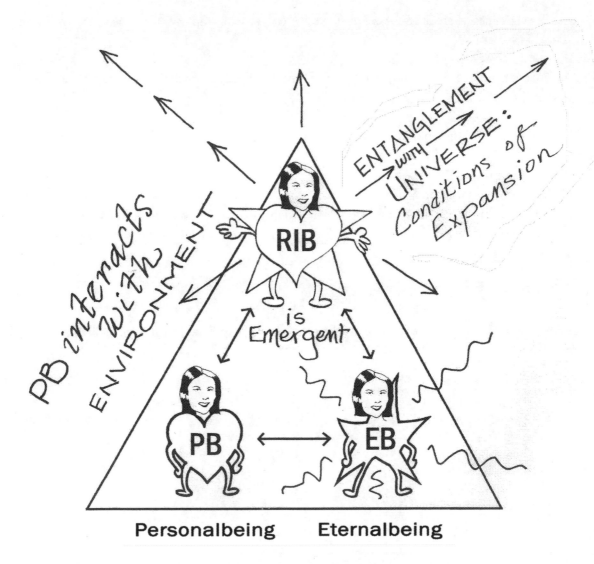

The Resplendent
Triunity of You

PB = Personalbeing
(particle-like)

EB = Eternalbeing
(wave-like)

Picture of Triunity in a Triangle

CHAPTER 16

RESPLENDENT COMMUNIONING

Many authors are writing about a "new way" yet are separating the *inner* from the *outer*. I have been believing in the separation of external and internal for a very long-o time. This is to fail to understand the true nature of reality, where entanglement theory prevails.

With entanglement theory, I have an ability to perceive that my immediate surroundings and circumstances are in entanglement with my resplendent nature. There is a simultaneous and equal repetition of my BATHWAVE informotion. The Universe always gets out of my way and allows me freedom to express my resplendent nature. The Universe only gives me 'me' in order to become resplendent—and never interferes with me. This is the third characteristic of the benevolent nature of the universe.

Entanglement is a more correct understanding of the old idea of oneness since with entanglement I maintain my unique individuality while I gain my wholographic big picture as my eternalself. Read EGO about individuality in appendix by Roger Cotting.

Resplendent communioning

Back to this new understanding of resplendent communioning, which can be a challenge to grasp. To say "go inside to know myself", is incomplete—not incorrect. That view is too close. To look all around me and see the mirror-calls of my resplendence, though, shows me what I cannot see when I only focus within.

In resplendency I interact with others, and reveal their resplendency. Eventually, as I see all as resplendent, I am interacting only with resplendency which expands my world with a resplendent environment.

This makes a full circle back to creating a new environment with which personalbeing can interact. Then a new eternalbeing is emergent from personalbeing's new interactions. As new eternalbeing communions with personalbeing, an expanded resplendent illuminatedbeing is emergent.

Resplendent illuminatedbeing radiates as in entanglement things I never knew before.

Choosing to not discontent myself

The gift in looking at the mirror is to choose to not discontent myself about what I see. Accepting this choice will be the biggest shift I begin to make in my life. I can do a Bathwave to assist me, such as facing and embracing that I discontent myself as I am doing right now for the umpteenth time.

It is an old habit to discontent myself—to create the old fashioned pain and struggle with what's happening in my living. I can be aware of that discontentment and embrace that—even love that. As I embrace that discontentment, I breathe deeply and begin to sense the relaxation. At least I may laugh at myself for doing it which is the first step to relaxing. When I face and embrace—I intend to not miss a spot on my body before I start to do a Quantum Shift.

Quantum shift

My quantum shift for choosing not to discontent myself might be:

1. I *can* stop discontenting myself;
2. I *will* stop discontenting myself;
3. I *stop* discontenting myself;

As I stroke my midline I say each statement in a strong voice. Yell it loud like an Italian would, then you will be sure to laugh if you ever discontent yourself again…can you tell I am 100% Italian (well half Sicilian). Muscle test in my present tense to make sure the quantum shift occurred. Mature the quantum shift. This is the most important Bathwave to begin in this new exploration of my eternalbeing.

A new word: terra-memory

There's a new word in this new way, called *terra-memory*. Before I define it, I'd like to tell my story about a place that the Waitaha shared with me on a journey through New Zealand.

There is a place on the South Island in sight of Christchurch where miles and miles of stones—large like Stonehenge—are accumulated and were arranged by these ancient people. While among these stones, I experienced an awareness of patterns. As I looked at the huge spiral patterns in the rocks after spending hours photographing them, I had a sense of nighttime and the constellations of stars. With that awareness of patterns, I realized that it's always been the nature of humankind to connect the dots and create pictures, images, or constellations of these stars.

These patterns are boundaries creating spaces around them. As I discovered the spaces around these rocks, I somehow knew that my walk through and around these rocks was what I needed to experience. Yet, I also realized that the form of the rocks cannot be ignored because the rocks create the foundation that in turn creates the space.

The millions of galaxies in our universe could also be connected to create photographically similar patterns. The shape of my body can be understood as a pattern, described by Fibonacci's number, otherwise known as the *Golden Mean*.

Wholographically all evolution has followed this number. These patterns wholographically follow a guide as the golden mean. However, no two patterns are alike. No two bodies are alike. Dr. Roger

Williams in his brilliant book, *Biochemical Individuality*, shows us that no two enzyme levels in any 2 bodies are alike; which wholographically brings us to the uniqueness and individuality of my personalbeing, eternalbeing, and resplendent illuminatedbeing which is physical and virtual and as different from each other person as snowflakes are.

Yet, in the youth of my spirited evolution—I thought my eternalbeing was outside of myself and assigned away my own power of self-direction. This old idea was a beginning. It is time to mature this old understanding to the unique space that my own eternalbeing pattern creates for me, expanding while uniquely particularizing the universe. This is the sacred reality that expands the youniverse.

Seeing the eternalbeing pattern and the eternalbeing space will encourage me to reclaim my power of self-direction and enable me to live fully and create anew.

This awareness of eternalbeing pattern and space brings me to a definition of *terra-memory*. Surrounding this new communion of personalbeing with my unique eternalbeing space, there is *minding*. The raw data of expansion exists in this space and random coalescence occurs in this space. It is called random because the universe has no intention and yet, it is contained and guided by the patterns of my eternalbeing all of which are unique.

I call it the pattern because it is a clue to my life and recurs until I desire to change it though not necessary. The universe presents us with everything and I select the components or constituents. The components that I gather in this space of "me" are what is randomly coalescing or combining. This random coalescence has selected components and these selected components or constituents, are coming together in an emergent way, schizaming my own unique reality.

Shifting Beliefs

PART I: BATHWAVE
▪ Embrace all of your body, saying the sentence and the intention of loving and changing it.

PART II: Quantum Shift.
▪ Say the new belief 9 times while stroking your midline.
▪ 3x "I can..."
▪ 3x "I will..."
▪ 3x "I am..."

	Element **FIRE**	Organ **PERICARDYUM**
	PART I. BATHWAVES **Face and Embrace**	**PART II. HEARTWAVES** **Replace with Grace**
BELIEFS:	I blame and accuse others	I release my misunderstanding of the nature of reality and I enjoy living responsible to myself.
	I believe others affect me.	
	I am not free to be me.	I am exited to be me, as I desire.
ACTIONS:	I love that I rejected my mother, father, nature and the world.	The Universe supports me abundantly.
	I love that I rejected my body, mind, feelings and my spirit.	I am a spirited mindful body.
	I love that I am needy for my mother, father, nature or the world's approval.	I nurture and guide myself without judgment.
	I am needy for either my body or mind or feelings or spirit.	I embrace that all of me is one.
THOUGHTS:	I believe I am not sexy enough.	I am a vital sexy being.
	I accuse others for my difficulties or problems.	I appreciate that everything is a sacred mirror doorway for my enlightenment.
	I blame others or myself for my difficulties or problems.	I appreciate that everything is a sacred mirror doorway for my enlightenment.
	I complain about others or myself and make things difficult.	I appreciate that everything is a sacred mirror doorway for my enlightenment.
	I believe that difficulties and problems exist.	Everything is a gift for my understanding.
	I believe that things are opposing me in the universe.	Everything supports me as I support myself.
	I use the thought of failure to motivate me.	I am successful, sharing, and inspiring. I desire to live my new, responsible self.
HABITS:	I am guilty	I am innocent
	I am resentful as I live.	I cherish everyone and everything I meet.
	I am overbearing in what I do.	I appreciate the input of others.
	I use force, control and power to manipulate to get things done.	I change myself and watch everyone and everything change with me.
WORDS:	My words are divisive.	My words express living the oneness.
	Other's words trigger me.	I unconditionally love and accept other's ideas, feelings and needs.
ATTITUDES:	Negative attitudes corrupt the clarity and strength of my self and life.	I conceive of myself as possessing true strength, which is personal change.
	I doubt my inner strength or wisdom.	Strength is always united with wisdom.
VALUES:	There is no free will.	I value my freewill and true strength to keep or recycle everything as I desire.
	The Universe is out to get me.	The Universe supports what I am creating now.
EMOTIONS:	Fear of failure paralyzes me.	I am clear and understand that there are no mistakes or failures. Everything I do is successful.
	I feel disoriented and out of my orbit.	I am fired up with enthusiasm.

Emergent is the third word of this quantum way

I only live constituents, moment by moment. Every millisecond I am selecting constituents. When hydrogen and oxygen are the constituents, emergent water is formed—very different than the original constituents. So, moment-to-moment I choose constituents and the universe does the rest of the work, in *memorying*.

I don't know what I am creating. Only the constituents have a sense, but this is my option. I am able to access anything I desire using the encode decode key of my individual unique DNA.

Can you alter the constituents? Of course you can. Bathwaves is one simple technique for altering constituents that you've gathered in the moment—not only from the past of ancient years, unless I keep choosing them in the moment. I am given that ability to re-opt anew in every moment.

When living resplendence awarefully, I no longer need to shift the past...I re-memory or remember myself as resplendent and everyone who invites me.

However, I have a habit from the past—ancient past—of 're-choosing' the same old stuff.

When I don't want my choice or don't want to "know" what I am choosing, I hide it under a rug and call it my unconscious. I can shift to stop that old habit of denying myself my awareness. If old sentimental me can be doing it anyone can!

When I embrace the old 'denial' that I have been doing as an old habit for millennia, I can open the door and "undo" the unconscious. I will find that my health and my well-being improves, though for the moment it may require a lot of facing and embracing.

As I write this, I am sighing because it took me many repetitions of this Bathwave to establish a new way of facing and embracing this moment as a mirror calling me to my resplendent illuminatedself.

From denial to authenticity

As I embrace the denial of what I have chosen to be, my quantum shift might be this: *I am open and aware of my authenticity.* My quantum shifting is one way the constituents are transformed, moment-to-moment, as the old habits reveal themselves.

The next step is to shift how I might react, or judge, the constituents as they reveal themselves. The real focus and new quantum shift might be this: *I live moment-to-moment as I desire.*

With this quantum shift these constituents in the space of my patterns, randomly combine, which is the definition of emergent.

Emergent is the random coalescence of my new options, though the coalescence is done in a quick present/past, called the *nonce time*, combined with my past options. All of which, remember, can be shifted!

Emergent is a great gift of the universe. Emergent reveals the good and the benevolent nature of reality. There is nothing more loving than emergent, for emergent gives everything I desire, even though it is random—it is a random coalescence of everything I put in my soup called reality. If what I taste doesn't match my desires, then I simply need to add some new ingredients, that is, entango again.

Choosing is a great deal of fun and I have a great deal of freedom in this, much more than what I have dreamed of in the past. At every moment I can embrace and replace with grace the constituents of my new reality.

The power of self-guidance

My power is my gentle self-guidance. I have no need to force, manipulate or control. Those are all Bathwaves waiting to happen as I repeatedly do them myself. I can replace force, manipulation and control with the gentle self-guidance that wells up in the spaces of my own eternal pattern. My eternalbeing is my self-guidance. Personalbeing, or the particles in the pattern, is the teacher of eternalbeing and manifests resplendently.

I have been obsessed with the personalbeing, yet I have overlooked that the personalbeing is the teacher. As the pattern adorner, he/she dances in the spaces provided by this pattern of my eternalbeing.

The relating of personalbeing and eternalbeing

Resplendent communioning is the relating of personalbeing and eternalbeing. Personalbeing as the teacher has the freedom to express the eternalbeing—as the eternalbeing only has awareness, and is given enlivened existence with personalbeing. Just like a wave is perceived in conjunction with the particle.

My dreams are a voice of my eternalbeing. My dreams are a combination of my chosen ingredients for life revealing the patterning of my awareness. In my daily lives, the moment I am experiencing the elation or sense of accomplishment in what I am doing, the eternalbeing is not being resisted or reacted to, but expressed clearly.

As I consider my six accomplishments, my six situations that I am proud of, in the spaces between these patterns, I begin to see the commonality, the Diamond Chain, that reveals my own unique eternalbeing. No two people will have the exact same six accomplishments—just as no two snowflake patterns are alike.

randoming/patterning/randoming/patterning/randoming/patterning/ ramdoming/patterning/randoming/ patterning/randoming/patterning/ randoming/patterning/...

This communion of personalbeing and eternalbeing is the nature of reality, just as the particle and the wave are reality as shown to us in the quantum world. As puzzling as these two natures have been to the quantum world universe, the nature of the personalbeing and the eternalbeing will create some head scratching for a while.

The challenge is to stop discontenting myself

My greatest challenge is this discontenting I have created as a habit. I realize that there is no need to discontent myself. I have the option to start again. For those who wish to walk this new way, this moment is a new opportunity to not discontent myself and choose new constituents.

I cannot feel and know my contentedness—I can only understand that I have stopped discontenting myself. "Just as with love I can only know that I am not doing an unloving thing. Love might be defined as the state of not doing unloving things, as well as a natural state of being."

I choose and create my pattern and my constituents

In this space where minding is occurring, the random coalescence of constituents, renders a definition of random as not intentional. The universe does not impose any intentions—does not limit me with any intentions. I choose and create my pattern and my constituents. With practice looking at these old accomplishments that I am proud of, I perceive my pattern.

These accomplishments do not have to be great ones—they can be very small. They are all very real and they are all moments when my eternalbeing is not being resisted or reacted to or denied.

The accumulating of my constituents is always what I am doing. My happiness depends on my constituents. If I choose constituents that I desire, then again I have created my own happiness because my desires are manifesting my life. The universe never interferes with this process with intentions. My eternalbeing is in a sense a form of my own pattern. My eternal pattern is only the form of action and is malleable in shape.

This new way of declaration does not require causing or effecting. In fact—an attempt at causing will create discontent, or is discontent. As Yoda said in Star Wars, "There is no try. There is either do or do not."

To try to cause, to try to effect, or succumb to effect and cause, are all discontenting. This causing and effecting as a system of beliefs creates a sense of being victimized by my circumstances. To live with the choice of not being a 'victim' of causing and effecting gives me great creative freedom to choose the constituents I desire.

React or act?

One exercise is to practice describing images. For instance, take the sentence, "The lion is in the jungle tonight." This is a simple description of an image, but doesn't language or judge with feelings and emotions. If you have a reaction to that sentence, change it to, "The cat is in the yard tonight."

Most of my emotions and feelings can be known as reactions instead of the vital emotions I chose to live. I can choose to act instead of react. The blood is a manifestation of vital emotion. Any action would be at least triggered in the most health engendering when it is authentic and real. Again the only way to make it real is to stop discontenting myself, which requires me to stop reacting to my creations.

A response is authentic if it is my choice that I make without judgment.

I bring myself to life. This is actually a great relief. I can only bring myself, as my personalbeing and eternalbeing, in communion to life. If I bring personalbeing to life, I manifest eternalbeing and the universe is egalitarian. There is nothing superlative in the universe. This eternalbeing and personalbeing are equivalent, different, yet equivalent and complete.

Trying to create superlatives is an old habit that I need to face and embrace. I love to create superlatives! I am always creating superlatives instead of finding equivalents which would create the equanimity, or steadiness, that I truly desire. It is not an accident that equanimity has the same root as equality and egalitarian. With equanimity there is expansion, yet expansion is not a superlative; it is a natural motion of the universe.

BATHWAVEs: Eight activities of the five elements support resplendency

The most basic BATHWAVEs I have been discussing–the beliefs, actions, thoughts, habits, words, attitudes, values and emotions,–are related to the five elements and the yin and yang of Traditional Chinese Medicine.

- actions are related to the YANG.
- habits with a dash of values are related to the YIN.
- words would be related to the FIRE element.
- beliefs are related to the EARTH element
- attitudes and values are related to the METAL element.
- emotions are related to the WATER element.
- thoughts are related to the WOOD element.

This can be seen in an illustration in Chapter 25. These elements describe the relationships between my internal organs, my whole physiological system and will be described in detail in Part Three of this book. I will discuss how they create the conditions of expansion in my life. These basic five elements are the warp and weft of the tapestry of resplendence I weave in my living.

Resplendency, which means to live brilliantly, shining, splendidly is emergent from the communion of personalbeing that is closer to yin and eternalbeing closer to yang. The patterns that I weave with my BATHWAVEs support my resplendency. I am the weaver and I enhance the pattern expanding my world.

In being content, I entango creative tools for minding the spaces within my pattern. It is desirable to face and embrace the holes in my bucket, or the old BATHWAVE patterns that are outdated and outmoded for what has been discovered in quantum world.

Shifting my BATHWAVE patterns is quite easy and fun. It can be done while dancing; which is my favorite way. It can be done in bed or in the bathtub which is an easy way, as I use the water to embrace myself. It can be done while doing almost anything, and will become a way of life for focusing.

The real way of life is to focus in the awareness of resplendent illuminatedbeing, which is from the interaction of my personalbeing and eternalbeing.

Have fun dancing in the spaces as I journey into the next chapter. Bathwaving just paves the way for EEEZY resplendent living.

Resplendent Illuminatedbeing interacting with its Conditions of Expansion...

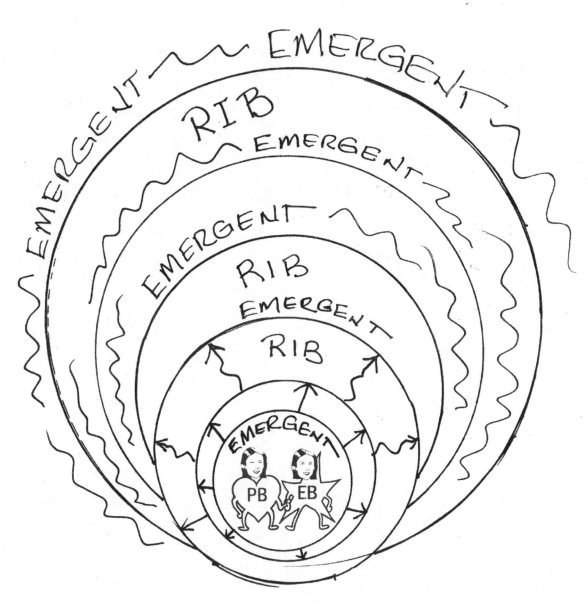

CHAPTER 17

THE UNIVERSE IS ALWAYS BEGINNING ANEW, EMERGENTLY

Choose any beginning, this moment

According to the quantum world, the universe is always beginning. The universe begins in all possibilities. It begins anew in all ways, all times and all space.

This moment the universe is just beginning anew. And there's no ending to the universe because in every moment it's still beginning.

Which means that I can choose any beginning, this moment.

The past is replaced

Each ensuing moment takes the place of the moment before it. Everything I do takes the place of the previous moment. The past is replaced. All the time it is all beginning.

So in resplendence there is no such thing as a need for forgiveness because there has been nothing before it that is needing forgiving. I can begin anew in every moment. Continuing the physical is our eternalbeing: as in a wave nature, there is no opposition.

Superlatives are "good, better, best" and consume you

When I am in opposition to myself, or judging myself, I am consuming myself, exhausting myself, internally dying or doing away with myself. The opposition occurs when one sets up superlatives; the superlative sets up opposition between superlatives and its other, which is a non-superlative.

Personalbeing expresses and embodies my eternalbeing as my BATHWAVEs

The personalbeing and eternalbeing are made up of data and information from my choices and my selections. My expression of my eternalbeing by my personalbeing can be thought of as 'particularizing' it.

Personalbeing through its BATHWAVEs–beliefs, actions, thoughts, habits, words, attitudes, values and emotions–gives you coalescence of my eternalbeing or embodies my eternalbeing. My personalbeing expresses and embodies my eternalbeing as BATHWAVEs.

I create my own rules, laws and truths with my BATHWAVEs

The eternalself from which this expressing comes is data, *a casserole of the data*, of which you bring ingredients from my own personalself's particular shelf. I could call it my 'personalshelf'….

Science says that 'physical laws' disappeared at a point before the 'big bang' or before singularity otherwise called "THE BEGINNING". Preceding singularity, the big bang or the beginning of the universe, there are no laws. Random action precedes beginning. This moment, since it is a beginning, is brought about with random actioning.

The universe is 'raining' data and informotion

This random actioning of the data and information is like condensation of water droplets in a cloud. Except every droplet is new and different 'informotion'. I will call this actioning of the universe the 'raining' of data and informotion. Like snowflakes, all the data and information are unique and different, or emergent. The random actioning makes use of my casserole ingredients. I have access to this rain that waters the seeds of my garden of eternalbeing.

My world, then, is not following others laws and truth.

I create my own rules, laws and truths with my BATHWAVEs.

Some believe I create them first through my actions and our actions create my beliefs. It doesn't seem important which comes first. BATHWAVEs then would be the data, minding themselves into informotion as in my night time dreams. Desire continues the BATHWAVEs without movement, created by the verb to 'memory'.

The noun 'memories', which are the default interactions limiting my personalbeings, are based on movement. All things molding memories are within personalbeing, which then must express or are invited to express an eternalbeing. Therefore, eternalbeing desires are desires which are a function of memories or personalbeing. Memorying, which is a function of eternalbeing, requires personalbeing also. Desire can lead to discontenting. I can learn to stop discontenting without stopping things.

Living memorying and memories together is resplendent

I can put the two: personalbeing and eternalbeing, memories and memorying, together to be resplendent. In living the communion of memories and memorying while living these two, without discontenting myself, you are resplendent illuminatedbeing.

Throw out the "IF" to be resplendent

When I throw out the 'if', when I replace "if I do this, if I do that," I stop discontenting myself in my memorying and my memories. In being resplendent, which is brilliant and shining, I gain the ability to do entanglement. When I write down my six accomplishments that I am proud of, these are the six moments that I can perceive my eternal being, I perceive how I wish to eternally embody myself. Each of these things I have done, reveal to me a desire to express myself eternally.

For instance, in the case of Angelo, when he finds a book that shows him how to discover ways to pleasure a woman, and he feels excited and proud that he can do this, I can see that he would eternally like to express that his eternalbeing is his own source of pleasuring his personalbeing. This eternalbeing expresses that creating is his source of pleasuring. Creating is the big picture of sexualizing, tantra or pleasuring. In focusing on whatever he is doing, he is focusing on sourcing creative pleasure. What is the equivalent of creating in the quantum world?

Radiance or entanglement in any way shape or form is 'creativity' in the quantum world, which is accessing any information as ingredients for my emergent miracles. This is definitely a pleasure.

What you are trying to cause reveals what you already know that you desire to manifest eternally. When you only pay attention to what your desires express, you won't see it.

When you listen to the space between the accomplishments, you will hear the eternalbeing expressing itself as the action.

In all the books that have been written about becoming one with the higher self, they give you many steps that you have to be, but the last step always seems to be separating myself from my higher self or god self in order to see it. In this book, you move straight to that step and say, "How is it that I would like to express my resplendent illuminatedbeing?" Though the eyes of personalbeing, again, that is what you are doing when you are proud of what you are accomplishing.

In the pictures I gather to myself that I am associating with my life, say in Angelo's case:

It is okay that I don't know who I am, because who I am is the eternalbeing who is adding ingredients to the casserole. The resplendent one who stirs the pot in this moment is different (emergent) in this moment. And each new you replaces the previous you. He can only know these in hindsight.

I am the one who fails to experience that because my memories dominate and limit me to one person bound by cause and effect. I lose sight of my memorying the next moment. I always have the choice to replace the old memories with new memorying. To memory the new moment is the best expression of eternalbeing. Memory

There are all possible things and all possible beings and all possible ways and times for the expression of eternalbeing.

When you see the world of the six accomplishments I can perceive the eternalbeing expressing itself with the pride of the personalbeing. Eternalbeing has no pride or ability to express itself, but as I read personalbeings expressions or what I am proud of, I begin to see the awareness peak through from eternalbeing and in doing this I find out what the eternal being is saying. The personalbeing, which is expressing my accomplishments, is telling you in their own words what their eternalbeing wishes to express. So there are all possible things and all possible beings and all possible ways and times for the expression of eternalbeing.

Meditation as suscitation or rebirthing

Meditation in India originally was used to help old people when they were about to experience death. Buddha used meditation 2,500 years ago, and adopted it from the Hindus to attempt to help people to experience nirvana or reach enlightenment, which unfortunately was thought of as a death. But it is not death. This was a misunderstanding. By confusing the old meditations with the new understanding, which is that meditation is a suscitation of the process of awakefulness, alert awakefulness, not 'calm peaceful death'. Death has no awareness, let alone calm or peaceful. When a person is calm, death would be the furthest thing from their minds.

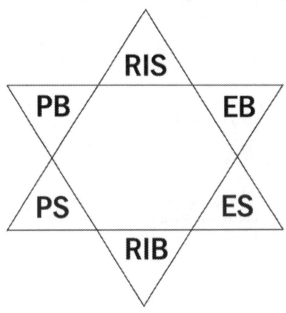

**Diagram of the Virtual TriUnity
in Communion with Adorned TriUnity**

Basic Building Block of Sacred Geometry's
Flower of Life

Meditation in my new triunity

When I understand resplendence as a personal experience, I can then begin to meditate to suscitate my resplendence. In order to do this, I can remember that every occurrence in the quantum world has an equivalent in my natural world. In reverse, I can say everything in the natural world has an equivalent in the quantum world. So, when I meditate in the quantum world way, I can remember the three parts of my triunity. I can sit and look through the eyes of each of my three parts looking at my other two other distinct parts.

The first part is my personalself. When I sit/stand/walk/dance... in personalself looking through my heart-shaped glasses, I see my eternal self which expands my universe with newness every moment, and then I can look at my resplendent illuminatedself which is awareness radiating. In its radiance, it is entangoing with everything in the universe knowing things I have never known before.

Next, I can sit/stand/walk/dance... in my eternalbeing's shoes and look through my star-shaped glasses and as I sit as eternalself, I can see how I feel. How I am feeling will reveal how my eternalbeing is interacting with my personalbeing today. Through these star-shaped glasses, I can look at my personal self's life and my resplendent illuminatedbeing's life. So, if there's a situation that is posing a question or difficulty in my personal life, I will see it in a whole new light of resplendency. This way, I will know what my mirror-call is to shift the personalself or I will see what needs to shift.

Resplendentself through the eyes of eternalbeing is emergent, which means that eternalbeing is perceiving through my emergent eyes. This new way of seeing as eternalbeing could be called the verb "to emergentize." This means to see everything as new and different, not resembling the past. When I do this, I become purposefully exponential. This means that my eternalbeing's actions will expand me exponentially which simultaneously expands my world.

My third meditation would be sitting/standing/walking/dancing...as my resplendent illuminatedbeing. This is where I radiate out to the universe and in radiating I am in entanglement. When I am in entanglement, I am selecting informotion that I have never known before into the pot of my casserole. I am, in a sense, impacting my life. This is called the verb "to memory." To memory is winding a whologram through my DNA or my encode/decode key. Everything which I impact can be reassembled any way I wish. This is the creativity of my resplendent illuminatedbeing, otherwise known as entanglement.

When I don't do this with awareness, I am basically defaulting to my memories which are random reactions or otherwise known as judgments. Judgments and memories are restricting my ability to be resplendent. Bathwaving, as a tool, can be used to shift me free of my reactive or judgmental mental memories. It frees me to be able to live resplendently and only needs to be used when I feel stuck and unresplendent.

I can use the tool after declaring myself in any of these three positions. So, I can say, "I declare myself a resplendent illuminatedbeing," when I sit/stand/walk/dance...as that part of my triunity. In that way then, I now can sit/stand/walk/dance...in meditation entangoing my conditions of expansion (COE).

Everything is my way of beginning

Meditation is correctly used as a tool of beginning again. Meditation may be used as an awakening of my 'minding' or 'memorying' to the eternalness of everything, to the awakefulness of eternalself

So what you embody in my suscitation into eternalbeing is what meditation really is. Meditation can be understood in this moment as a suscitation so that everything is my way of beginning.

Imaginative minding expands you

Science has created imaginary science, like calculus, in order to calculate what they couldn't measure. When you turn imaginary into imaginative mind, you can 'entango' to know what I haven't known before by 'imaginative minding'. For instance, dreams function as an imaginary space time like the 'wave nature'. Since eternalbeing couldn't otherwise experience itself, eternalbeing is a construct of imaginary space time. In other words, I construct eternalbeing in my imaginative minding. Dreaming is where eternalbeing speaks the loudest through personalbeing. Suscitation can be described as awakening myself to imaginary space time and all that it holds for you. All that imaginative minding awakens you to be aware of is my entanglement and emergent nature.

Entanglement and emergent expands you into everything around you instead of narrowing you the way I sometimes narrow myself as I minimize my personal power. I am coalescing myself up to everything in the universe and down to the quantum world.

Every moment is a quantum, complete within itself

I can only describe these things. Otherwise, if I try to define them instead of describe them I will prevent them from bringing their new gifts of memorying.

Every moment is a quantum, complete within itself, which never connects you to previous quanta.

History is only half of the story. History gives me the memories of me. Eternalbeing gives me memory to 'maginate' and combine anew, emergent in the moment. My body is the eternalbeing adorned as the personalbeing.

Religion and science can create opposition and discontent

In the past, religion and science said I have to pick one or the other. Science picked personalbeing, some religions picked the other, which they called soul, trying to understand soul as the essence of the eternalbeing. Just choosing one or the other put them in opposition and recreates discontent and disease again. That is an opposition that will exhaust and diminish myself. They are not in opposition.

Because I am a victim to my memories while I am indifferent to causing and effecting. When I stop opposing myself with judging, I can begin to draw new ingredients into my casserole of data, into the old data in the pot. And as I add new data from entanglement, I give myself new possibilities. When I limit myself to old memories, random actions create patterns of memories which are the universe of the past.

The universe has no intentions of its own

The difference between you and the universe is that the universe has no intentions. It creates an environment with no intentions, whereas you develop actively to re-mind with eternalself's intentionality. You begin self-creating awarefully. You can create and you can violate laws that exist. You use data and information as expressions of lost truth, which you are.

Transforming my cup of all my discontenting using Bathwaving

What if I had only one cup to drink from and it contains all my discontenting; I've got nothing else to drink and I am not allowed to pour out the poison. I can pour anything into the cup, though.

When I start adding water to the cup, and as I continue to add water to the cup of poison of discontenting myself, my cup will be filled eventually of pure water. At that point I will not be discontenting myself anymore.

When I notice that I am not discontenting myself, then I begin expanding myself. In Bathwaving, I am actually saying I face and embrace discontenting myself. I will want to say in part two, Replace with Grace, "I stop discontenting myself", which is like pouring water into the cup for 21 days to three months.

Tying myself up in 'Nots' or beginning again

Interesting how I used to say in the past that I am tying myself up in knots, when I am really tying myself up in nots; nots which don't exist. Not doing what I desire, not seeing the love that is in front of me. When I stop discontenting myself about not doing as I desire, I can basically do as I desire more readily.

I could probably write a book about stopping discontenting myself; there is alot of material there. I am taking a small step, though, as I do in quantum shifting my true desires.

Entanglement with our DNA Cell Phone

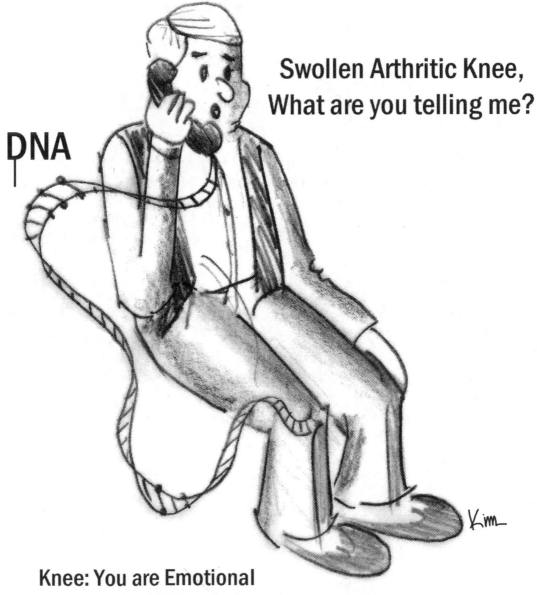

Swollen Arthritic Knee,
What are you telling me?

DNA

Knee: You are Emotional
from Judgements about moving on.

CHAPTER 18

A RESPLENDENT WAY OF
ENTANGLEMENT TO EMERGENT

Emergent goes with you
wherever you go.
Entanglement goes
where you cannot go.
~Angela Longo

The manual for one way of applying quantum entanglement to living

In order to begin living entanglement with others I need to use *a contact point of a specific nature that the person brings to us, such as, an illness, a problem, a difficulty, a relationship, a dream, or an event.* It is like a phone number that allows me to access the pattern and to have an entanglement with the person.

Second, I need to *desire* to do something such as a reading or telling a story that will *serve the person's awareness.* Once I have this *focus* with which to start, I follow the focus and describe the pictures or movie that comes into my awareness. It just takes faith and trust to do this. After a while it becomes obvious which character in the story refers to the person with whom I am in entanglement. These insights are noetic, which means that they are their own evidence requiring no external proofs. Using O-ring muscle testing can confirm your information.

Later, as a contact point I can connect to the resplendent illuminatedbeing of the person. This will give me an entanglement that provides me with an awareness of their conditions of expansion. Conditions of expansion means everything that is outside of their experience yet, or all the things they have not experienced yet. You may have had an experience of this. We used to call this awareness 'psychic' and attribute it to extraordinary abilities. It is actually ordinary as I become patiently aware of my real nature.

Emergent means 'new and different' not resembling its past.

I am ready to be aware of my emergent nature. From the previous chapter I may remember the illustration of emergent as water, which is made from two flammable gases, yet as a liquid doesn't resemble these two gases from which it came in the slightest. *Emergent means 'new and different' not resembling its past.* I am emergent in every moment all the time. Isn't that freeing? Memories tempt me to resemble my past. I have been amassing ingredients for my casserole from my conditions of expansion of the 'stuff' of my universe. My emergent moments are always new and not resembling any of the ingredients and yet my ingredients are the stuff out of which my emergent nature arises. *As I continue to add ingredients it is fun to be delighted at whatever my emergent surprises are. Sort of like a grab bag at the county fair.*

When I don't live the awareness of my resplendent illuminatedbeing then I will be living the same old 'catch-as-catch-can' without awareness. Awareness is useful in selecting my ingredients. My quantum shifts are aware ingredients or constituents.

My imaginative minding or imaginative process is a tool that comes into play with entanglement. Entanglement probably aligns with the pattern of my DNA which might be the physical phonebook of my connections to the universe. 'Knowing phone numbers' which are the people whose information you would like to be aware of, gives me the key or the encode to myself, decoding from myself for entanglement. This encode decode key of you, as DNA, will begin the connection in the story of the entanglement.

Once I have the story, I then can see the experience they have created of their universe, and ask them if they want to continue living this story. When my intention is to come up with their beginning story, then I may see the being of their beginning story in my entanglement.

Research in a book from Russia supports this theory. In their book, *Vernetzte Intelligenz*, Grazyna Fosar and Franz Bludorf, (Fosar G., Bludof, F. (2001), Baerbel (2006) explain these connections precisely and clearly. The authors also quote sources presuming that in earlier times humanity had been just like the animals: very strongly connected to group consciousness and thereby acted as a group. In order to develop and experience individuality, however, humans had to forget hyper-communication almost completely.

Now that I am fairly stable in my individual consciousness, I can create a new form of group consciousness— namely one in which I attain access to all information via my DNA without being forced or remotely controlled about what to do with that information. I now know that just as I use the internet, my DNA can feed proper data into the network, can retrieve data from the network, and can establish contact with other participants in the network. Baerbel (2006)

Examples of hyper-communication

Fosar and Bludorf tell of a 42-year old male nurse who dreamt of a situation in which he was hooked up to a kind of knowledge CD-ROM. In his dreams verifiable knowledge from all imaginable fields was transmitted to him and he was able to recall this information in the morning. There was such a flood of information that it seemed a whole encyclopedia was transmitted at night. The majorities of facts were outside his personal knowledge base and reached technical details of which he knew absolutely nothing. When hyper-communication occurs, one can observe in the DNA, as well as in the human, supernatural phenomena. Baerbel (2006)

Phantom DNA

The Russian scientists irradiated DNA samples with laser light. On screen, a typical wave pattern was formed. When they removed the DNA sample, the wave pattern did not disappear, it remained. Many controlled experiments showed that the pattern continued to come from the removed sample, whose energy field apparently remained by itself. This effect is now called phantom DNA effect. It is surmised that energy from outside of space and time still flows through the activated wormholes after the DNA was removed. The side effects encountered most often in hyper-communication in humans are inexplicable electromagnetic fields in the vicinity of the persons concerned. Baerbel (2006)

Hyper-communication disrupts EMFs

During hyper-communication electronic devices like CD players and the like can be irritated and cease to function for hours. When the electromagnetic field slowly dissipates, the devices function normally again. Many healers and psychics know this effect from their work: the better the atmosphere and energy, the more frustrating it can be for recording devices as they stop functioning at that exact moment. Often by next morning all is back to normal.

Perhaps this is reassuring to read for many, as it has nothing to do with them being technically inept; it means they are good at hyper-communication. (from Baerbel)

My beginning story

Once I know someone's beginning story, I can then ask: would you like to look with a different perspective on my life or continue the same beginning story?

My beginning story was from Genesis: in the beginning God created the universe. With this story, I had unconsciously disempowered myself. I lived disempowered and was quite ill for most of my life until I discovered the tool of Bathwaving yet still an external band aid of TCM. Then I discovered the reality of the universe through the quantum world.

Now, empowered in my resplendent illuminatedbeing, which is the resurrection after the death of my limitations—my self-imposed limitations. My resplendent illuminatedbeing, which is the communion of my eternalbeing and my personalbeing, has freed my ability to know things that I have never known before, through *entanglement*.

Once I have accumulated constituents into the soup of my life entanglements draw upon them and I am aware that I am emergent in every moment. This entanglement of infinite possible constituents creates an emergently rich experience of life. As I continue to be aware of emergent delights in my universe, (or circle in the diagram), my universe continues to expand as can be seen in the figure labeled emergent entanglement. This may in fact be the energetic pattern prior to the expansion of the universe.

These constituents are particulars and, in that, they are different and complete forms. These forms have cohesion and resistance from each other as they are separate. However, this resistance, which is necessary for living, is not resisting living. Resisting living is different than resistance and is the sign of my belief in failure. I know this first hand as I lived resisting and ill for over 50 years. One sign of resistance is the expression, "I should do this."

I shoulds imply 100% resistance. Any illness shows me to my resistance to my eternalbeing. What you resist, though, will reveal my finest assets and lead you to my eternalbeing and, therefore in communion with personalbeing and my resplendent illuminatedbeing. The next revelation will be my eternalbeing.

It is useful to know my beginning story. In mine it was clear that I gave my power away and therefore spent my life in illnesses.

- I broke my leg at nine months old, which signified breaking my convictions to walking forward in my life.
- I had an ulcer at five years old, which again was a sign of disempowering myself by pleasing others, even when it was stressful to do so.
- I contracted polio at 10 weeks after the first polio vaccine, which meant I couldn't move forward in my power.
- In my early 20s with hypoglycemia and a nervous breakdown I gave my power away to science and writing my Ph.D. thesis.
- At 50 with my diagnosis of liver cancer I would have lost it all had I not discovered the quantum wave living methods.

Once I am aware of the beginning story, Bathwaving can be useful for shifting the story to what I truly desire. I truly desire living with the gentle strength of my self-guidance. Bathwaving has enabled me to change my story in a very deep and basic way. Today I maintain my own power of gentle self-direction in all relationships and situations as a resplendent illuminatedbeing. Living resplendently is done without cause and effect, blessing myself, in entanglement with all, with health, abundance, and stopping myself from discontenting myself.

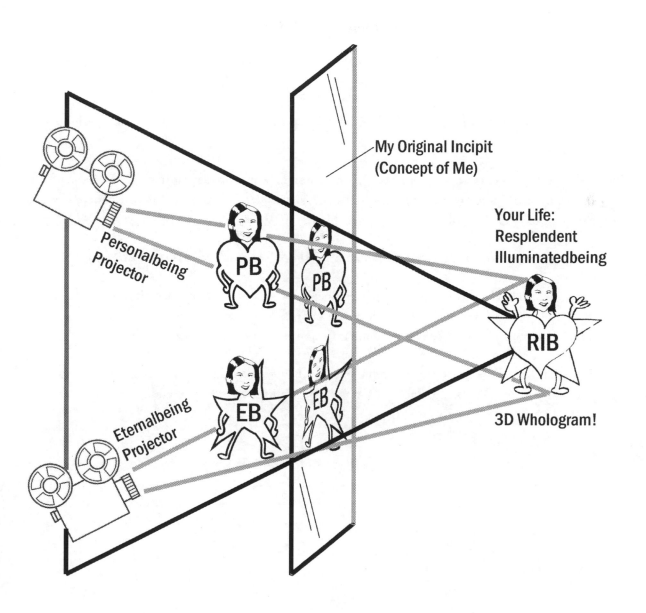

My Original Incipit
(Concept of Me)

Personalbeing
Projector

PB

PB

Your Life:
Resplendent
Illuminatedbeing

RIB

Eternalbeing
Projector

EB

EB

3D Whologram!

CHAPTER 19

MY INCIPIT IS WHAT I AM!
OR
MY INCIPIT INSPIRES ME

To begin, the definition of *incipit* is the first sentence or image in any dream or story that speaks the truth of the whole story. The incipit is the alpha or beginning.

When I am born into life, I am an incipit. My incipit moves my whole life. It is my alpha and my omega.

It took me eight years to be aware of this and perceive my own incipit with the help of my quantum mentor. The first half of my life was resisting it. Because of this resistance, I was a very weak sickly child and young adult until I was fifty.

My incipit is to communicate the "wholeness" of the triunity of my resplendent being.

When my eternalbeing interacts with personalbeing, my radiant resplendent illuminatedbeing is emergent. These three "beings" are the triunity of us. The incipit precedes all these expressions of me. This incipit sets all of my three beings of me in action. I am riding the wave of my incipit.

Imagine that each of these five waves represents an incipit, creating a unique first sentence for five people, and a pattern for being. Each wave has no beginning and it has no end.

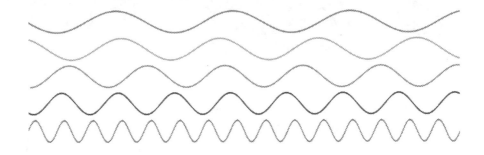

[Figure 19-1]

My incipit is prior to intention. My incipit is prior to my self and life.

Being aware of my incipit brings freedom to living. My incipit is my prior action to all actions that I desire to live, in all three aspects of me.

On the other hand being unaware of my incipit and unconsciously resisting my incipit, creates the unnecessary struggle and illness in my lives.

An example of a life's incipit from a dream

Pat, a mature male adult, had a dream that was recurring and it went something like this:

I went with a group of bullies who started to try to take control of me with threats and intimidations...

This is the first line of the dream called the incipit and tells us everything I need to know about the rest of the dream. Since this dream came the week before a discussion about the incipit of my living, it was clear that this dream might be about Pat's living incipit. Pat agreed that he saw things in his life as a threat and intimidation. This was the incipit Pat had been living with since childhood, that life was about using my power to threaten and intimidate. Pat was inspired and admired bullies.

Immediately after having that dream, Pat had awoken and said to himself that "I don't have to do that anymore" and went back to sleep. The new incipit he chose was in his statement, "I don't have to do that anymore".

The next day Pat noticed that his actions and attitudes had changed. Pat realized that he wanted to write a book about all this amazing change in himself. He realized that he had been able to change his incipit, the pattern that had been moving his life.

Pat's new incipit which could be expanded to "You don't have to do this anymore" is the invitation to an emergent life of beginning anew. Pat agreed enthusiastically that being aware of his incipit changed his life and his attitudes and his approach to his work. Pat also saw his memories change according to his incipit. His view of the past was re-formed by "You don't have to do this anymore."

The quantum way shows me that when you re-form the present 'nonce', the future and past re-form in the same manner instantly. They are a continuum. Instead of remembering being bullied, Pat remembered other actions that were more in line with his new incipit of doing things differently.

It was as if Pat was able to "jump" to a new incipit, a new wave, a new story, a new beginning, simply with the realization that 'he didn't have to do that anymore'.

Understanding my incipit like a wholographic process of you

A wholographic image is a 3D image and is the closest picture to life. It takes two cameras to project the picture of a wholographic film image into reality.

I think about the two cameras that are projecting through the film at a certain angle to each other to manifest a 3D hologram. One projector is like the personalbeing and the other projector the eternalbeing. What will be projected, as a wholographic image, is the resplendent illuminatedbeing.

The film, then, is called memory. Memory, like entanglement, is the remembrance of occurrences or what was before. When the personalself and the eternalself interact, they project through "memory" my resplendent illuminatedbeing.

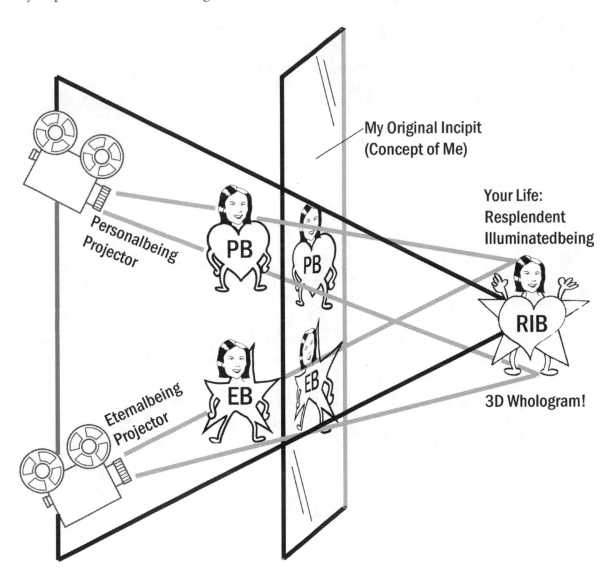

The memory, then, is the beginning and the end; therefore, **the incipit is the statement of the memory of who you already are. The incipit is the encode/ decode key for expression of my resplendence.**

There is no causing to be done for the resplendent illuminatedbeing; there is no struggling to be done to become the resplendent illuminatedbeing. There is only the awareness of this incipit of me, this alpha, which is also, the omega of me.

In the quantum world, the equivalence of the incipit is Heizenberg's observer who in any situation is what's happening. The incipit is what I bring to life.

Memory and Minding and Love

Love is the memory of my incipit, not the memory of consequences. Love is the memory of me. There are no consequences, and therefore, no judgment around my incipit. When I focus and am aware of the incipit, there are no issues to be resolved.

Memory is the interacting of information that I have collected or selected in my life, or said in reverse: life is an interaction of informotion of memory. Energy is memory in action, and because E=MC² matter and my body form an accumulation of memory. The body is memory itself particularized.

If you could be any particular memory in my life, what would you like it to be?

The answer to this is my incipit. I do not mean that you need to select from the past. You can choose from the future.

You need to memory into what my incipit is, what you would be willing to be and live eternally; what memory would you be willing to live repeatedly?

If I substitute in St. John's Book of Revelations in the Bible the word 'memory' for 'word', you begin to understand it. "In the beginning was the memory and the memory was God, and the memory was with God,..."

My God is my particular memory, and therefore, my particular incipit. Memory is the *interaction* of memories. How have you been interacting with my memories? How would you like to interact with my memories?

Minding **is the function of the incipit creating memory. All mind is matter and energy and informotion. It is the fun-da-mental nature of the universe.** All mind is only memory. When mind minds itself minding, it creates memory and therefore chooses the incipit. In the wholographic illustration, minding would produce the wholographic film.

Self-sabotaging comes from trying to cause my incipit

Since I am already my incipit, there is no trying to become it or cause it. When I do TRY to become what my incipit is BY CAUSING it in my life, I am self-sabotaging. This will destroy me.

How easy is this, to stop becoming and causing what I am being and doing?

As I am being and doing, I become aware of this incipit. When I live the incipit there is no issue to undo. Incipit is the resplendence. Any rituals that aid us, such as dancing which aids my resplendence, will follow my incipit.

The incipit is like a tone in my life that you're always hearing; it is like a pattern that I am following; it is the encode-decode key picture for my life.

If I were speaking on the phone to someone else that was a landline and had a cord, the cord would be the DNA which is the direct connection to the other person I called, their telephone number is the encode-decode key of entanglement. The message I speak to the other person through the phone exemplifies my incipit. Their expression to me is an example of their incipit. The incipit is like a prayer and is synonymous with entanglement.

What are the signs to know that you are sliding out of my incipit expression?

First, you will be discontenting myself. That's easy for us to feel, isn't it?

Second, if I catch myself judging—which I discuss at length in the chapter on the eight bottom lines—it means I've lost my awareness of my incipit. I individualize my incipit according to my eternalbeing, or the eternalbeing follows as an expression of incipitness, which then governs all healing.

I cannot separate myself from my incipit, or spoken another way, I am my incipit.

As in the quantum world, the wave, which is everywhere, beyond cause and effect, and the particle, which is localized and particularized, together is the EEEZY way of resplendency.

This triunity—my personalbeing in communion with my eternalbeing manifesting my resplendent illuminatedbeing—is the expression of my incipit.

Healing comes from living the resplendent wholeness of my incipit, which is as you truly desire to be without discontenting myself.

The incipit is what moves what I express from my personalself, manifesting my personalbeing. Emergent from personalbeing's interactions with its environment is eternalself, the commonality of all these expressions. When I become a recurring expression in embodiment, I call it my eternalbeing.

CHAPTER 20

MY QUANTUM SNAPSHOT DREAM
THE DREAMWAVING METHOD

Dreams are direct hyper-communication from my eternalself to my personalself.

Have I forgotten my dreams?

Would you like to be able to translate my dreams and understand their deeper meaning? Would you like to have the option of shifting my dream patterns?

The EEEZY way to work with dreams is with my benevolent dreamwaving method.

Dreams are a love letter

Every dream you have is also a mirror-call expression of my resplendence. A dream never judges you since a dream is from my eternalself. A dream is expressed through my personalself as an option for defining or solving a problem in my life.

Even nightmares offer me a different option to what is going on in my life at that moment. Am I aware that I have unlimited options to these nightmares?

First, my dream needs to be translated and understood as dreams are presented to me in a totally different language. A dream is also only a quantum snapshot from a certain moment in my life.

Dreams offer me all the different frames of any movie script I wish to write. Can I use *imaginative minding* to shift those dreams? Absolutely. That's what Relationshifting can be used for.

Let's go right to a practice page of paper and translate a dream so that I can learn how to listen to my eternalself-personalself and respond as resplendentself.

Dreamwaving exercise

Write down the most recent dream I remember. Keep a pencil and paper on my nightstand to jot down my dreams to help you remember them in the morning.

If you cannot remember a recent dream, write down a recurring dream from my past. If you cannot remember any dream, use a daily event that I would like to understand. Last option is to ask a friend or family member for a dream.

Step One:

Write down the beginning or ending my dream in detail.

The first sentence of my dream is called the *incipit* and contains big clues to what the whole dream is about. Underline the first sentence of the dream you wrote. Spend the most time understanding this first sentence, or the dream incipit.

Turn to any dream interpretation book (some suggestions are listed in the bibliography) you might use and translate the dream as you would in Relationshifting. Shift at will.

An example:

My recent dream incipit: I (Angela) am looking for my friend (a guy).

Using Relationshifting I translate this to mean:

My femininity (spatial, musical, emotional aspect) is looking for her masculinity (linear, logical, thoughtful qualities).

This translated dream incipit can be bathwaved. After embracing the dream incipit, the quantum shift might be "my femininity is in communion with my masculinity".

After doing the quantum shift, I had to mature this statement which led me to a powerful shift in my life as you might imagine. That shift has served me in writing this book. From a resplendent point of view, I can see that by looking for power outside myself, as seen as looking for my male friend in my dream, that I debilitate my own personal power.

This incipit, the first sentence that came to mind when retelling a dream, tells me what my whole dream is about. Without this incipit I would not be able to translate and therefore understand the rest of my dream. The incipit is the key.

Step Two:

My dream is a particularized virtual love letter about myself. Everyone in the dream is an aspect of me similar to Relationshifting.

Take the time to translate and understand those relationships as I do in the dream incipit.

Step Three:

You can relationshift with everyone and all the various situations in my dream if you have a desire to transform those patterns.

Step Four:

Translating my dreams and understanding their meanings can help enhance my sharing of my resplendency in my daily interactions with others and events.

You have time, some say two weeks, I say a lifetime, to bring my night dreams into my life. If my night dreams are not in synch with my desires, then shifting my dreams enhances my resplendency. When my dreams reflect my desire, my awareness of them encourages my resplendent sharing with others.

For instance, the matured quantum shift that I realized this morning after dreamwaving last night was:

I maintain my power or strength in all situations, relationships, and time awarefully. This enhances my resplendence which I share in all my aspects of my life and relating with others.

Summary

Our dreams and daily events are expressions of our resplendency and create a quantum way tool for us to understand our options for shifting.

Our dreams are virtual previews of what I may particularize or create in the next couple weeks of my living. My dreams are an expression of an aspect of my triunity that is different than the old paradigm.

Dreams are the trailers of my personal movie script, and I am always working on that movie script. Dreamwaving gives us the ability to rewrite the script by using quantum shifting when I understand what aspects of my lives my dream is portraying.

Keep this quantum view of resplendency beyond causing and effecting after I shift.

To translate the imagery and relationships in my dreams I need a dream dictionary. In my bibliography I will list some 'dreamtionaries'.

Remember, that the weaknesses and failings shown in my dreams can reveal my greatest assets. Have I ever noticed this aspect in my dreams or daily events, which upon further reflection resemble dreams? My nightmares show you what 'could' happen in my future in order to give me options to shift.

Read the chapter on Senoi Indian Dream Theory in Patricia Garfield's *Creative Dreaming Book*, which is about a resplendent dream culture. With the Senoi, beginning in childhood, there was an understanding and similarity perceived and communicated between night and day awareness. The Senoi culture has no violence, neurosis or psychosis. The Senoi live their dreams and dream their lives, as they desire.

As resplendent people I live my virtual dreams and virtually dream my particular living desires. May I all dream my resplendent desires.

Happy dreamwaving!

CHAPTER 21

LIVING MY DREAMS THE
QUANTUM PLASTICITY WAY

Creating my dreams and desires

Living this quantum way as a virtual eternalbeing and a distinct personalbeing, I have the ability to create all of my dreams and desires in each moment resplendently.

Having worked successfully with energy medicine, Traditional Chinese Medicine, clinically for 40 years I became aware that there appears to be a prior state to the energy world. This book prepares us to live this prior state of 'informotion' patterning, in ways that will astound us.

These 'informotion' patterns are made up of my BATHWAVEs, (beliefs, actions, thoughts, habits, words, attitudes, values, and emotions) and are quite malleable instantly. In order to understand quantum plasticity, I have to begin with the basic characteristics of the quantum world.

How is every moment a mirror-call (miracle) of my resplendence?

First, remember how each of us is an interactive triunity, as is everything in the universe.

Another way to say this is that *everything IS relating.*

Triunity of Self

The first of the three, my personalself, can be thought of as one distinct, particular self which I adorn in my interactions with my environment. These interactions between personalself and the environment, which includes ingredients from entango-ing with the universe, provide more variety for manifesting my BATHWAVEs. The second of the three, my eternalself, a virtual self of imaginative minding, is the essence of my desires and dreams. It is as physical as a wave. The interaction between these two creates the resplendent illuminatedself, forming a triunity of personalself, eternalself and resplendent illuminatedself.

Triunity of Being

In more detail, personalbeing is designated as the particularizing of the distinct self. In expressing my personalbeing I create my 'world or environment', which is an expression of me. I see my resplendent illuminatedselves in the mirror-calls of my interactions with my self-created environment.

The eternalbeing is the commonality pattern of these interactions of which I feel proud. Being aware of both of these triunities—my triunity of self and my triunity of being—gives us the ability to communion them and live the resplendent quantum way.

I am always living this way, but only by default, which is why I only see the synchronicity of a few moments and think they're quite unusual. In fact, this is the way of every moment: emergent with entanglement and thereby always recurring as the designated eternalbeing.

When I live the EEEZY way, limiting myself to cause and effect begins to look spooky!

In entanglement, I have access to unlimited constituents. According to my option in selecting these ingredients, I make up the soup from which the emergent virtual images of myself as a eternalbeing are randomly made.

These virtual images are as real as the quantum waves of light and electrons, protons, etc. The qualities of that wave are immense: they reach the ends of the universe, nothing stops it, nothing alters it, and in entanglement, this wave defies the old concepts of cause and effect, and of time and space, which is why Einstein reacted and called it the 'Spooky Theory' or 'Spooky Action at a Distance'.

There's nothing odd or unnatural about it when I begin to live it; it's quite natural and exhilarating and makes living quite EEEZY. It requires a lot of faith and trust!

Emergent manifests my dreams

As I've discussed, in EEEZY the first E stands for emergent, the quality in the quantum world where particles are new and different in each moment, much as Max Plank described. Emergent puts my 'ingredients' together. RIB stirs the pot. This emergent process expands the universe, because through entanglement, I have accumulated new ingredients all the time and with these new ingredients, every emergent moment is new and different, not resembling the past, and expansive thereby.

This emergent nature is actually like the quality of a particle that has motion even though it is a standing wave that appears to go nowhere. That is why a particle appears in more places than one. This notion of emergent might be considered the masculine or yang. It is the reason I have created the new word 'informotion' to describe the concept of motion of an information pattern like a quantum wave that has no movement. The pattern of informotion is the feminine, yin adorned part.

The work of entanglement

Entanglement, on the other hand, is also the feminine/yin quality of quantum theory. It is the access I have to informotion that is infinite. The vehicle of my entanglement is my DNA. DNA is like my telephone or my computer/internet that will access only people and informotion that are of like ilk to us. There is no need for acceptance or non-acceptance of this informotion because I only find entanglement through my DNA with a mirroring of likeness.

When I look next at the pattern of these functions of yin and yang: entanglement and emergent, it is called the eternalbeing and is the power from this pattern, the power to expand, the *'radiant'* power of how I create what I'm going to call my awareness as a resplendent illuminatedbeing.

I'm using these words because radiant is a quality of entanglement—in entanglement you are radiating out to the universe to access this information. This occurs instantly and simultaneously with the desire. These ingredients you access are constituents for my soup from which my emergent nature is evident.

This resplendent illuminatedbeing of me is emergent from the interaction of the virtual eternalbeing and the personalbeing, needed for creation of this third 'point of reference'. A resplendent illuminatedbeing can then be in entanglement with other resplendent illuminatedbeings. This awareful interaction will create entanglement of a resplendent nature.

All entanglements access things that I may never have known before. My resplendent access creates resplendent knowings. These entanglement knowings can be called conditions of expansion. This is an exponential way of education and "learning" because it is not limited to a logical, rational spatial musical brain as the only way of accessing information. The resplendent knowings are a type of pattern recognition known in this book as Heartwave Informotion Patterning (HIP). I am really doing system theory pattern recognition here and as I know, pattern recognition, such as a quantum computer would do, is faster, vaster, and able to perform calculations and reasoning at exponentially greater and faster speeds.

Even though teleportation has only been accomplished for tiny particles yet, if EEEZY ways of thinking and working were applied to this desire, teleportation might not take so long to access as a method of travel. Beam me up, Scottie!

Shifting chronic fatigue syndrome

I have only had experience of these abilities of using Heartwaving Informotion Patterning in clinical situations. It has been labeled miracles by many clients who do not yet 'know' the quantum resplendent way.

Experiencing the changes clinically from viral states in a chronic fatigue syndrome (CFS) situation in my clients to a viral free state was quite mind blowing at first.

In my clients' CFS situations the virus has been present for long periods of time with no abatement. The shifting of the BATHWAVEs related to the virus is what has to shift. The shift eventually comes down to the BATHWAVEs that are associated with being a victim of causing and effecting and bound by only causing and effecting. This is one of the eight bottom line shifts to the quantum way of living.

As I remember with entanglement, there is no causing and effecting. Niels Bohr was comfortable with it and told Einstein, when Einstein said, "God doesn't throw dice," Neils responded with, "Don't tell God what to do." This was very wise advice because with quantum world happenings, I recognize the sacredness of each moment, each quantum reality, and each being.

Memories can block my quantum way of living

The things that forsake resplendence and prevent us from living it are things like memories, because they constantly prevent my emergent nature from occurring. My memories pull me back, much like a pot of crabs will pull a crab who is trying to crawl out of a pot, right back into the pot.

My emergent nature is to be new and different in each moment in every way at all times without resembling the past or the memories. Language itself has forsaken the quantum world. Subject + verb + object, or subject 'causing' object, or virus "causing" illness is not the way of entanglement. I need to learn the concept of quantum communication, which is more of a description of reality and a declarative questioning of reality. The nature of this communication would be that it never ends and that it's quite creative in its processing.

I've always felt that conversation never went anywhere because I was involved always in language's yes-and-no questions as a scientist. After leaving the world of science and entering the world of energy medicine, I began to experience a possible new and different way.

Living with the Hopi Indians 40 years ago was an experience of the reality of quantum living and communication as linguist Benjamin Lee Whorf described in a treatise on the 'special relativity' qualities of the Hopi language. The attraction and quantum leap into this world is a quantum situation that has encouraged me to have the faith to live in a quantum resplendent way.

The fact that the world of science still believes there has to be a 'beginning' to the universe seems to illustrate the need for an almost parental state that requires a maturing to evolve. With this maturing, I have the opportunity to create what I truly desire.

Since the world begins in every moment, I no longer have to look for this beginning, The Big Murmur or The Big Pitter Pattern, which used to be called The Big Bang. When the world begins anew in every moment, I can then BE something with access to all things in the universe and this is the birthright of every embodied being.

Memories can help us see my eternalbeing

In the wholographic world, I know myself by understanding our interactions I've named mirror-calls. My accomplishments that I am proud of reveal in each moment the nature of my recurring eternalbeing. The method of using pictures on covers of magazines for each of my accomplishments and taking six of them for eight different accomplishments that I'm proud of, and placing them in a line, illustrates for me how to sense and define the virtual pattern between all of the pictures. This is much like the wave defined spinning particles as in the new theories called the 'wave structuring matter'.

The awareness of my virtual eternalbeing enables interaction with personalbeing in which my resplendent illuminatedbeing is emergent. With awareness of this new point of reference, my triunity, I have access to the emergent infinite conditions of expansion that my resplendentbeing can include with other resplendent illuminatedbeings.

This resplendent nature with conditions of expansion, gives us the ability to rain (precipitate) new coalesced data and information into energy and matter. This raining expands my personalbeing interactions with my environment, my environment being my BATHWAVEs and therefore, also a mirror of me.

The cycle of manifestation

The ability to manifest is the result of this interaction and begins the cycle to emergent-eyes my eternalself. Emergent-eyes means to see what is emergent. This leads to the interaction of eternalself and personalself, emergent-eyes resplendent illuminatedself. This leads to an interaction between eternalself and resplendent illuminatedself, to emergent-eyes my conditions of expansion and sacredness. This again can coalesce data and information into energy matter, again recreating personalbeing and environment, especially the environment of BATHWAVEs. This begins again the cycle in the interaction between personalbeing and a new environment of new conditions of expansion.

Hence, the nature of quantum living reality, is to emergent-eyes and thereby expand the universe forever. I am reinventing myself forever and hence the name 'forever living'.

Time and space

Time and space are also each a twoness of distinctness and virtual. The distinctness, or distinguishable nature of time and space are the ones I have been living with, basically time as packets of duration, and space as packets of volume. Their virtual 'wave' nature of time and space reveals their nature as forces, and these forces are no longer limiting us.

In the old way, I am bound with judgment of concepts trying to change them as I used to, fighting against them, juggling and contesting them, contesting old beliefs, old ways. I now just replace or exchange what I desire for the old way or the old belief. The brain itself actually works this way probably in a cause and effect modality. I also can just add to the soup, my new ingredients or constituents that I gain or access through *instant simultaneous entanglement (ISE)* with my desires, which is also through the emergent process of random coalescence, shazam the expansion of the universe.

This appears to be the only sane way to move into this new way of resplendent living. I am excited about this and am willing to live it because only in the living of it is the experience there.

The proof is in the pudding! Enjoying desserts!!!

CHAPTER 22

ENTANGLEMENT AND MY DNA
OR
THE I CHING AND MY DNA

DNA, a vehicle of a universal system of communication

DNA has been shown, according to Dr. F.A. Popp, "to have a wave character which implies that between the cells of the body there is a *universal system of communication,* operating at far higher speeds than the humoral and neural systems which have alone been known to us hitherto... Ultraviolet bio-signals "ride" on the spirals of DNA and activate specific codons. Falsification of these signals means cancer; their extinction "puts out the light" of the whole body." Shoenberger, M. (1992)

This information dates back to the 1970's.

Forty years ago a mathematician, Dr. Martin Shoenberger, published a book called *The I Ching and the Genetic Code; The Hidden Key to Life*. He perceived a brilliant correlation between DNA's 64 transfer RNA (tRNA) trinucleotide codons (codes for amino acids' translation from DNA into making all the protein of my body) and the 64 chapters of the I Ching.

From the frying pan into the test tube

Schoenberger's words excited me. I understand now I began my biochemical career in my mother's kitchen at fifteen years of age by extracting DNA from chicken livers one weekend afternoon before dinner.

My DNA work was made possible thanks to the help of a woman from church. She supplied some chemicals after a tour of her laboratory at Roswell Park Cancer Clinic in Buffalo, New York where she also showed me a diagram of the synthesis of DNA along with its structure.

That afternoon with the chicken livers was the moment I embarked on a lifelong journey which I now understand as an expression of my eternalbeing's resplendent nature. In other words, my biochemistry work expresses my eternalbeing's reccuring desire of networking, reweaving, or linking people to their unique resplendency.

In the mid 70's I received my Ph. D. in Biochemistry from UC Berkeley and published my research on glial synthesis of nerve growth factor which my professor said encouraged the new field of understanding communication between glia (feminine aspect) and nerves (masculine aspect) in the nervous system with small peptides. I am all in entanglement as the glia and nerves probably are also. At the Linus Pauling Institute in Palo Alto I demonstrated in one year's research with pattern recognition techniques that there was increased amine production in the blood (like ammonia that I urinate out as urea) with stressed baby squirrel monkeys. During all this time I was studying and beginning to practice the field of clinical energetics with Traditional Chinese Medicine (TCM) which in the west is called acupuncture.

Making my own full circle from DNA to the I Ching

Five years of teaching at San Francisco State University and then founding an accredited college of Traditional Chinese Medicine on the Big Island of Hawaii brings me to the diagnosis of liver cancer twelve years ago. Trying to heal myself catapulted my interest into my present field of resplendence with 'relationshifting informotion'.

All these events reflect the pattern expression and recognition of BATHWAVE mirror-calls in order to encourage living my unique resplendency. Living resplendently is probably what the I Ching is designed to encourage us to do.

I am observing that I am my best I Ching as I appreciate the love letters I give to myself through each other, through my bodies, my dreams and my daily events.

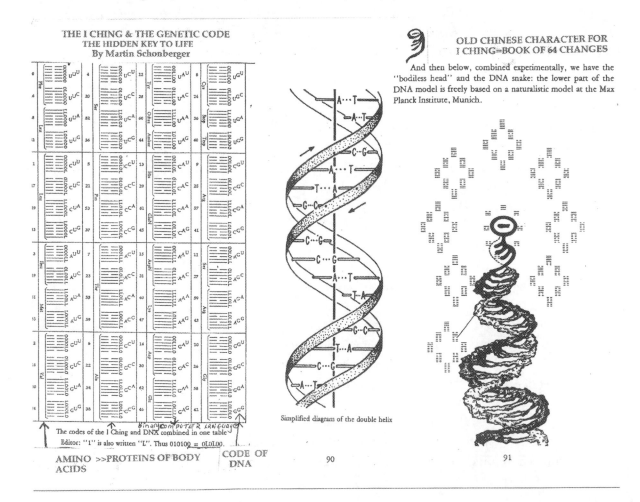

THE I CHING & THE GENETIC CODE
THE HIDDEN KEY TO LIFE
By Martin Schonberger

The codes of the I Ching and DNA combined in one table
Editor: "1" is also written "L". Thus 010100 = OLOLOO.

AMINO >>PROTEINS OF BODY   CODE OF
ACIDS   DNA

Simplified diagram of the double helix

OLD CHINESE CHARACTER FOR
I CHING=BOOK OF 64 CHANGES

And then below, combined experimentally, we have the "bodiless head" and the DNA snake: the lower part of the DNA model is freely based on a naturalistic model at the Max Planck Institute, Munich.

90   91

Today's DNA Findings

The latest DNA research written about in German in *Vernetzte Intelligenz*, a book from Russia, summarized by Baerbel, says that *"my DNA is not only responsible for the construction of my body, but also serves as data storage and communication."* This is what the "useless" 90% of the junk DNA is translating into. Fosar, G., Bludorf, F. (2001), Baerbel (2006)

"The Russian biophysicist and molecular biologist Pjotr Garjajav and his colleagues have explored the vibrational behavior of DNA. In brief, the bottom line was, *"Living chromosomes function just like a holographic computer using endogenous DNA laser radiation."* This means that they managed, for example, to modulate certain frequency patterns (sound) onto a laser-like ray, which influenced DNA frequency, and thus the genetic information itself. Bacrbel (2006)

"Since the basic structure of DNA nucleotide pairs and language are so similar, no DNA decoding is necessary. One can simply use words and sentences of the human language also. This too is experimentally proven." Fosar, G., Bludorf, F. (2001), Baerbel (2006)

In a causing and effecting sort of way, *"living DNA substance (only in living tissues, not in test tubes) will always react to language modulated laser rays and even to radio waves, if the proper frequencies to sound are being used. This finally and scientifically explains why statements, music, microwaves, and the like can have such strong effects on humans and their bodies. It is entirely normal and natural through my DNA to react to my language."* Fosar, G., Bludorf, F. (2001), Baerbel (2006)

This is a good background explanation of how Heartwaving and such similar techniques may be transforming my being and my health, possibly through my DNA also.

"They even captured information patterns of a particular DNA and transmitted it onto another, thus reprogramming sounds to another genome. They successfully transformed, for example, frog embryos to salamander embryos simply by transmitting the DNA information patterns. This way the entire information was transmitted without any of the side effects or disharmonies encountered when cutting out and reintroducing single genes from the DNA." Fosar, G., Bludorf, F. (2001), Baerbel (2006)

Though this is an example of an experiment with cause and effect, doesn't it follow that *as I change my own information pattern, since I am being in entanglement with others, as in this example, I may then have the ability and the gift of global transformation or transfiguration? The implications of an entanglement through my DNA as an incode decode key might be that I can then make my universe as I desire in every moment of my life.*

"This experiment points to the immense power of wave genetics, which obviously has a greater influence on the formation of organisms than the biochemical processes of alkaline (nucleotide bases) sequences."

"The DNA has been shown to be able to create magnetized wormholes. Wormholes are tunnel connections between entirely different areas in the universe through which information can be transmitted outside of time and space. The DNA attracts and projects my bits of information and passes them on to the universal consciousness. In Russia, they call this hyper-communication." Fosar, G., Bludorf, F. (2001), Baerbel (2006)

I would choose to call it quantum entanglement or quantum communication.

Focusing on memories gets in the way of entanglement. Memories can be a source of my stress as they are often a hidden source of my judgments. Without giving attention to memories, I am not limiting myself to my past.

Quantum physicists have realized that as I shift my 'present' moment, not only do I shift the future, I surprisingly shift my past along with my feelings about it. In Bathwaving, I am replacing the belief of past limitations, with something active like 'My living exists in this (emergent) moment beginning anew'.

An illustration of aware dream entanglement

In the Russian research, they mention that humans have encountered sudden access gains to information that is outside one's knowledge base and give some examples, such as the 42-year-old nurse mentioned in Chapter 19. Fosar, G., Bludorf, F. (2001), Baerbel (2006)

The nurse's dreams would merely be his openings with entanglement to the virtual information of the universe.

I tend to want to personify such happenings and call them 'channeling from other 'mostly dead' people', which I don't need to invoke with entanglement.

Entanglement is always the state I am in with something or someone that has virtual physical existence. Remember that a wave is physical even though I cannot see it.

DNA is a twoness as virtual (wave) and adorned (particle)

The wave pattern, which DNA can hold, remains for a short while once the DNA is taken away much the way the leaf pattern remains after a leaf was cut as demonstrated with kirlian photography.

I use the concept of wormholes in science to talk about this ability to assist or live outside of cause and effect. However, I can see with the concept of the quantum world's entanglement that it is one of my natures of quantum reality to retrieve informotion from anywhere in the universe. This is akin to the wave nature of my atomic building blocks.

Let's return to the concept of morphogenetic fields, which are written about by a British evolutionary biologist Rupert Sheldrake. Sheldrake defines morphic resonance fields as invisible fields of informotion that are fundamental to all living matter.

A New Zealand clinician, Robin Kelley, in his book, *The Human Antenna: Reading the Language of the Universe in the Songs of Our Cells*, wrote:

"As in our entanglement scenario, these fields exist in a dimension apart from our known concepts of space and time. According to the theory of morphic resonance, the fields are the reasons why flocks of birds fly and turn in perfect unison, why hundreds of fish within a massive shoal turn together spontaneously... Kelly, R. (2006)

Kelley hypothesizes that these fields formed the very template, or matrix, upon which our physical bodies are formed. This describes the patterns I have written about, which I have the ability to create through our BATHWAVEs.

I am excited and encouraged by the entanglement 'synchronistic' flowerings that occur while I'm writing this book. People appear who wish to read it and edit it who have been editors. I live on the most remote island in Hawaii in a rural cowboy town. People who I thought I would like to do illustrations for this book, show up at a concert and agree on the spot that they will illustrate after having said no on the phone. These are only a couple of examples of some current entanglements.

The universe is never in my way and uses my components/constituents (ingredients) from an unlimited pool that I have selected from, by how I live my life with my BATHWAVEs to 'entango'. My desire to have help writing this book was manifested in an EEEZY way.

When I live the resplendent way, doors open that I didn't even know were there.

The BATHWAVEs that I am living moment to moment are made from some of the constituents of which I speak. These constituents then are entangoing with my universe to create things that I have never dreamed of, to access information I have never known. My DNA molecule carries qualities of superconductivity. Sheldrake's theory of morphic resonance carries this concept, as Kelly writes, "into the wider domain of shared, non-local fields that carry with them the ancestral presence of the past. And the new studies on DNA and microtubules give us some understanding on how I convert these fields of quantum information into the miraculous living, breathing, growing reality of my bodies." Kelly, R. (2006)

Kelly continues, "My DNA is responsible for processing and coordinating this quantum information, projecting a four dimensional holographic matrix upon which my physical body grows and regenerates. It is at the same time connected to my ancestral past, through my genetic code and my current environment, receiving vibrational messages of light and sound. Meanwhile, many trillions of microtubule antennas are involved in downloading timeless quantum fields (the consciousness of the cosmos) into data I recognize as my physical reality. The microtubules are in constant non-local communication with my DNA and all the other intracellular antennas.

Robin Kelley also has experienced the ability to be in entanglement with his clients with only thoughts, and to use his thoughts in service of the common perceptions through his interactions with clients. Kelly, R. (2006)

The purpose of the book is to provide you with practical tools to awaken you to live this quantum resplendent 'eeezy' way. This quantum communication with realms outside of my time space model is allowing me to retrieve and create information, which is used moment to moment in emergent new ways.

When I use my BATHWAVE mirror-calls to directly understand my living patterns I am producing moment to moment, I am then using my 'Living I Ching'.

Relationshifting gives you the tools to begin reading my own personal I Ching in my symptoms, relationships, dreams, energy patterns (as shown on my magical tongue map) and daily events.

I 'entango' to translating more mirror-calls (miracles) in my love letters I give myself moment to moment. In 'resplendence' without trying I write love letters with awareness as I desire moment to moment.

CHAPTER 23

HOW LOW CAN YOU LIMBIC OR A
YOYO AS A MULTIPLE ORGASM

The Limbic System

Deep in the brain lies the limbic system, which functions closely with the brainstem (or reptilian brain) and the body to co-create my basic drives and emotions. It has much to do with my attachments and relationships.

Within the limbic system are the amygdala, associated with the fear/anger response, and the hippocampus which weaves together information from many parts of the brain into coherent memories and my own stories. My memories are more pliable than I realize. Also in the limbic system lies the hypothalamus, master regulator of the endocrine system, especially the sexual, thyroid and adrenal glands. The latter, under stress release cortisol which is an emergency response, activating the metabolism, for a flight or fight response. For long term, cortisol can be neuro-toxic. Chronic neural firing is dangerous to my health.

Soothing the flight-fight-freeze responses of the brainstem or the emotional responses of the limbic system is possible utilizing the more highly evolved parts of the brain.

The neo-cortex I share with higher mammals (elephants, apes, cetaceans).

The prefrontal cortex is a unique evolutionary shift, giving us the ability to think in abstract concepts such as awareness, expansion, evolution, empathy and more. "The middle prefrontal region creates links among...the cortex, limbic areas and brainstem....and internally distributed nervous system of the body proper. It also links signals from all those areas to the signals I send and receive in my social world. As the prefrontal cortex helps co-ordinate and balance the firing patterns from these many regions, it is profoundly integrative." Mindsight (2011) Daniel J. Siegel.

Scientific research has recently reported that my limbic brain has been shrinking an average of 1 millimeter a year, probably from lack of use. I am amazed that this important part of my brain is so unused in my culture since it sits right under the neo-cortex. Having said that, I realize that I was probably one of the people who had not been using their limbic system, and as a teenager, began to be attracted to the limbic system stimulators, like movement, touch, dance, qigong, walking and jogging. Most importantly, the limbic brain responds to relationship.

Relationshifting is really the technique to help you to develop the limbic brain and strengthen this bridge from my intellectual thinking life, to my feeling and living. I believe that Relationshifting is initiated in the pre-frontal cortex and soothes and 'rewires' the limbic system.

Developing the limbic system requires us to be responsive to my life, which means, developing and transforming myself; since this a relationship with myself, in regards to the limbic system, and I am like two people, a personalbeing (PB) and an eternalbeing (EB) as an eternal theme (ET). The indirect allusion to extraterrestrial being (ET) is on purpose, as I am mostly alienated from this awareness of my unique theme, that I am manifesting or resisting, whichever the case may be.

Whichever it is, getting to know my ET using information presented in Chapter 11 Eternalbeing Reading and Naming reminds me of the song "Getting to Know You". Discovering my eternal theme helps "ET to go home." Or in this case, it helps PB to go home to ET. If you haven't seen the movie "ET", I apologize.

My limbic system responds to mirror-calls

My limbic brain is very responsive to the mirror-calls in my life. My limbic system and its development is entangled with how I feel and respond or react to these prompts. When I am reacting or believing that my experiences 'shape us', I am in the old mode of being. If I face and embrace what's going on in my life, which is really a mirror reflection of "me" happening in whatever I'm doing or living, then I become able to change my footprint as I choose.

I want to bring my brains along with me as I Relationshift, and as I work with my information matrices. In the past I've mainly been using my domination schemes which are parts of my 'reptilian', old-lower brainstem. With pre-frontal awareness, these domination patterns become obvious and embraceable, or "engraceable". The quantum shift for domination would be "I maintain my own authority in all relationships". This shift has assisted me in all my working relationships and, recently, in writing this book.

My lives have become repressed, oppressed, suppressed, and depressed by my own self-unawareness. This can be embraced and all the emotion that it may elicit.

Shifting in the moment

I feel a little sadness now, writing this, and so I am embracing as I dictate. Embracing that I have felt the sadness in this state of self-pity and self-unawareness and I am ready to transform this now. I am also muscle testing whether I still feel sad around these words, or do I feel angry around them? Do I still feel afraid around them? Do I still feel hateful? Do I feel apathetic or numb in relation to these words? In relation to these words, am I ready to shift?

I am open to total responsiveness and expressiveness in living. My muscle test revealed that expressiveness is still weak in my life, so I am going to quantum–shift right now.

As my hand strokes my midline, I say:

"I can be open to expressiveness in living. I will be open to expressiveness in living. I am open to expressiveness in my living. I AM open to expressiveness in my living".

I muscle test whether this is strong now: "I am open to expressiveness in all aspects of my living and writing." I get a very strong rush now, of expressiveness.

Bathwaving and shifting in the moment helps me with writing this book. I thank my universe for giving me this bathwave while I'm writing. It's very easy to show you how I apply bathwaving as a way of life now; only a one-minute technique and it is extremely beneficial as it has inspired my writing.

In the quantum world I don't really need to "work things out with others". I need to work my things out with myself possibly by Bathwaving. Being expressive in a more understanding way is my new option. I have studied Non-violent Communication (NVC) but have felt unable to apply it, and now I understand why. I had been stuck in reacting and emoting instead of expressing the authority of myself in my relationships. I now feel ready to integrate these aspects of my communication training with my day-to-day living.

Do I feel free to do whatever I desire…dance and frolic? Do I feel free and enlivened in my self-expressions? If not, I might want to stop right now and do a few Heartwaves. This book is a workbook, not a book to read quickly through. It's a book to live through, to embrace myself through, to grace myself through.

Perhaps I can add a new salutation. I can go to bless you or grace you, or en-grace you. Or more specifically: en-grace me! And then I can bless you and mean it.

A strong limbic system helps us free our jungle

In weakening my limbic system, I am diminishing my Garden of Eden, and begin to create a jungle. With Relationshifting, I am reclaiming the Garden of Eden. Believing that mirror-call of resplendency means being in the Garden. I am always resplendent.

I am becoming more interactive and integrated with living. I am evolving in the true sense of the word. If you do word morphing as a technique of entanglement: turn evolve around and separate into two words, evlove: eve – love; this is the place I want to be prior to the choice of judging and if I live the Garden, the Garden manifests around me.

I can begin to play, to notice where I may be stuck. Take a walk and notice if you are prowling or marching on my hike. Cross-crawling and bi-lateral movements help to integrate the brain and can be learned through educational kinesiology and added to my playtime.

Books to help build the limbic system

I would like to recommend to you some books here. Dr. Carla Hannaford, a prominent physiologist and educational kinesiologist writer, has *Awakening the Child Heart: A handbook for global parenting* from which I can learn to re-parent and re-child myself, embracing and becoming those parents in full maturity. Then, *I will not need a parent anymore.* Her second book, *Smartmoves,* is a practical must for teachers. Her third, called *Playing in the Unified Field,* is a bio-quantum mechanical delight for shifters. Hannaford, C. (2002-2010)

Moishe Feldenkrais' awareness through movement, known as the Feldenkrais Method, is also rich in its imagery for Relationshifting, for he writes about and uses thumb sucking to mature and integrate the system. I experience great delight and pleasure in using Feldenkrais' information, as my body rewrites itself through a greater expansion of awareness.

Although it is not necessary, finding a companion to do this work with may be very beneficial at some point. Especially a best friend who's unconditionally loving and present, and will not obstruct, judge, structure, critique or overly praise anything I am doing.

Sophia Foster is the author of movement work with babies. All of the research with babies has revealed that touch stimulates bonding hormone, and with teenagers, they've shown that any kind of touch, even wrestling in the mosh pits, stimulates hormones that encourage limbic and other brain development. Swimming, floating, and bathing are also useful in transformative work. That's why it's wonderful and no accident that the acronym for the eight components which express myself is BATHWAVES—Beliefs, Actions, Thoughts, Habits, Words, Attitudes, Values and Emotions.

Therapies to support the limbic system

The name of Bathwaving reminds me that stroking the body in the bathtub as I scrub children, is one of the movements that almost always will transform an unhappy child. Adults can transform their stuckness and even their unawareness of their stuckness, with a quick shower or a trip to the local pool, spa, river, lake or ocean. I grew up in Niagara Falls, New York, so I didn't do much swimming in rivers and was limited to bathtub shifting!

All the new body work modalities help this focus on releasing emotions held in the body. Massaging, rolfing and other practices like cranial sacral therapy can trigger or integrate my BATHWAVEs spontaneously along with the use of Bathwaving.

I highly recommend bodywork. My masseuse is so aware and participates in my process. She is an excellent intuitive reader in her own right, and allows me and encourages me to shift whatever is coming up as she works on my body. My son, Mark, a massage therapist, is a totally aware masseur and supports my transformation because one massage from him and I am an emergent resplendentbeing again! He encourages connecting with self and deep relaxation.

Friend, family member, lover, therapist—may you find such delightful body workers to play with and help your transformation with their awareness and support of expansion. This can increase the delights of your life.

Mirror-neurons do the unexpected

In my teaching of Bathwaves, it becomes very obvious that as I face and embrace my patterning, my body responds with delight in various ways that I don't recognize are quite pleasurable. For instance, yawning is quite common in Heartwaving, and I have made up a word for it: "yo" which is short for yawn orgasm. It means that our blood volume has increased and the new blood needs to be oxygenated. Blood is vital emotions.

As I yawn, someone else who is entangled with me, nearby will usually shift with me. This is a perfect example of entangling. As I am energizing my new awareness with the yawn, the person next to me being entangled with me, is also getting the shift and yawning in their co-shifting. Their mirror neurons inspire the yawn in response to me—and perhaps their shift goes along with it!

I call it a yo-yo, and as we all know, when I let go of my yoyo, it returns to me. Hence, the sharing of yawning is like multiple group orgasm and is what happens in Heartwaving. Some people notice that burping occurs in shifting and so I call those "bobo's"—burping orgasms. There are many other bodily functions that may occur, so have fun making up my orgasming acronyms. I have at least 15 now. Use my imagination.

Bathwaving in the moment

The ability to focus on what I am doing in Bathwaving, is encouraged by the fact that I use at least three or four of my senses in doing it; touching my bodies, speaking out loud, hearing myself, visualizing the situation and feeling the emotion during the embrace of the BATHWAVE.

It may be difficult but beneficial to do Bathwaving when I am multi-tasking. For parents of little children, this doesn't mean I have to ignore my child. Since my child is entangling with me, I may notice that as I heartwave, the child or baby will be engaged and possibly, shifting with me.

Let's say I have a fear for my children's safety. Bathwave that fear and I can begin to Bathwave with my children around you. Embrace my fears and my worries around my children and since my children are mirror-calls of my creativity, my Heartwave might sound like:

"I am embracing that I am worried that my creativity is not safe or in jeopardy," or "My creativity is worried about expressing itself, because of fear of failure, or of being rejected in its expression."

Move on to the quantum shift, midline stroke, in the three tenses, replacing it with:

> I can enjoy expressing my creativity safely.
> I will enjoy expressing my creativity safely.
> I enjoy expressing my creativity safely.

I muscle test present tense only to make sure it is strong which means it went into the 'heartdrive'. If necessary, I mature my quantum shift as previously explained.

Bathwaving in the moment calms the limbic system.

Breathing calms the limbic system

To complete this chapter, take a deep breath.

Breathing slowly to a count of 6 or 7, in and out, throughout my day, synchronizes my breath with my heart coherent waves. This means, that my heart rate variability (HRV) is a sine wave which, if I breath in phase or in conjunction with the up and down pattern of the HRV wave, otherwise known as my heart coherence wave, I experience a greater sense of health and wellbeing. Dr. Daniel Astinoti in New Zealand calls this Heartbreath, and is doing research on this breathing technique. Using Heartbreath has benefited me, as I breathe slowly and deeply. The challenge is remembering to do it!

I think I will do a Heartwave on myself right now. As I write this book, I can definitely sense some fears of rejection of these ideas, this way of life, as a bridge to living my full resplendency. After embracing this BATHWAVE of fear and rejection over my whole body, my quantum shift becomes: I am confidently living and communicating my resplendency as I desire.

Thank you, dear book, for being a mirror-call of my resplendency.

How low can you limbic? I hope with every breath you take.

CHAPTER 24

DESCRIPTIONARY OF MIRROR-CALLS
OF THE "WISDOM OF THE BODY"
OR
OUTPICTURING IS INPICTURING IS OUTPICTURING IS INPICTURING

How I perceive and feel about everything is what my body reveals:

See it first in the chemistry or rapport of relationships

The quantum world teaches me that what is materialized or 'particularized' is a reflection of the observer; this means that what I bring to life is what I have in life.

How I feel about what is in front of me is nothing more than what I bring to it. I may choose to shift what I bring as I understand my mirror-calls.

In a relationship, if I am looking for chemistry, I can bring MY chemistry to the situation. In other words, give the chemistry that I desire toward the other person, and when it matches (entangos) with their chemistry, if similar, the magic is double the fun. When not a match, I still experience my own chemistry which is still fun. That is all I need to do.

I cannot wait and see whether a person has chemistry for me. It's my chemistry that sets the level of relationship chemistry. There may be ups and downs in the person's response or reactions, but that has to do with that individual's life's issues. Each person is responsible for that. I am only responsible for what I bring to the relationship.

I happen to life; life never happens to me.

In the quantum world, the quantum waves do not ever impact or 'cause and effect' the particle. The wave is simultaneously the particle. I impact the wave and the particle which cannot be separated.

This is love: the open space that receives….

In relationships, what the other person is doing is not the mirror, **the mirror-call is my response or reaction to what they do that is about me.**

If a person pulls away and I still love them and care for them and desire them, then I merely need to maintain my own desires in reality. As the person goes through their baggage or stuff, this is called "holding a container" for the other person. The container could be called love in this case.

This container is what is spoken of in the TV series *Kung Fu*, as the master is showing Grasshopper the definition of love in an hourglass. The master turned the hourglass up-side-down and said, "Grasshopper," as he pointed to the bottom part of the hourglass, **"This is love; the open space that receives the sand from the other half."**

That is the meaning of the container; the open space that I can hold for the other to fill. No matter what is happening at the moment.

This does not only apply to love, this applies to all of living and life.

Do the eternalbeing dance

In living my life, when I **focus on eternalbeing, I am basically focusing on what I bring and desire to bring to life. Also in focusing on that, I create the reality shape of the wave. The wave is always there.**

I cannot undo that quantum nature of myself; that virtual wavebeing exists. Being aware of what I desire and bring is the creative benefit of resplendence, even if it starts only as being the open container for personalbeing expression–that is still an eternalbeing. In fact, being an open container is one of the most difficult to live as anyone, including long time meditators, tells me. How I am an open container is what I am looking for.

There is always a theme of the eternalbeing even if it is to bring the open container of the virtual wavebeing–my openness–to the other and to all those who approach me.

It is very important to me that I have an awareness of my eternalbeing (what I am **offering to life**). To think about it is not the quantum world; that is the personal world's business.

Prior to intention

The word intention worked in the old days for the closest explanation of virtual wavebeing that I had. But now it is not sufficient.

Because "intention," by nature of its definition has an agenda; whereas, eternalbeing has no agenda, is not trying to cause or effect anything in life. It can't.

Eternalbeing has awareness which personalbeing gives existence. I guess I could say it is what is prior to intention. To be aware of this and live the EEEZY TOOLs is resplendency.

The virtual wavebeing nature from the quantum world differs from "intention." Intention is a good beginning. Doing my reading of my eternalbeing is an important part to begin understanding. Being correct is not necessary since I can refine my eternalbeing's understanding as I live my chosen eternalbeing. Looking at the accomplishments that I am proud of is the strongest vision of the eternalbeing that I can have.

Know that my eternalbeing expands to something new as I desire. I am not held to a particular expression of eternalbeing.

As I perceive that which enhances my self-esteem, I have a point of reference, which is necessary, as Einstein described when he said, "One can only know the universe from a point of reference." That point of reference is me.

The point of reference of my eternalbeing is only a third of me. Denying the existence of my eternal can wreak havoc in the system as all sorts of conditions. I just haven't known any better. The personalbeing is the other third which I know somewhat. Awareness of only personalbeing isn't enough either. It is only a third of the story; and I have been living that third of the story a long-o time.

It is time to live the whole story, and that means more than body, mind, and spirit; spirit is not the eternalbeing. My spiritedness belongs to my personalbeing. The eternalbeing is the awareness that I can cultivate by looking at my list of accomplishments to begin with and later verifying it in every aspect of my living.

Aspects of personalbeing can nudge myself over the bridge to awareness.

What if…

What if the whole existence of illness was to provide mirror-calls of my resplendence?

What if I need to learn to understand illness, without judging myself?

What if when I get the message of what my illness is telling me, I no longer need to repeat it?

This has been my experience for four decades of observation: all of our BATHWAVES (beliefs, actions, thoughts, habits, words, attitudes, values and emotions) manifest the real world and especially my body.

From my BATHWAVES I create my life, my body, my health and my well-being or my illnesses, disorders and disabilities. It all depends on the BATHWAVES.

My physical body and well-being are patterned by me and they're a confirmation of all I am thinking or believing about myself and others. My body is an image, a mirror-call image, of me and my way of life. My body's well-being or seeming frailties have nothing whatsoever to do with luck or misfortune.

The universe always supports and accommodates what I desire, what I am living and offering. Free will is pre-eminent. My body is a living picture of what I am doing.

Shift what I am doing and I will see changes in my body immediately, not over time like in cause in effect.

A client story

Two days ago one of my clients, whom I'll call Ginger, came to my office itching. It has been two years since Ginger was diagnosed and treated for breast cancer. I had treated her for allergies a week before. The allergies had improved but she was itching everywhere over her body, and she told me in an email she was taking Benadryl for the discomfort.

I said, "Stop the Benadryl and come in please."

When Ginger arrived, I described how in Chinese Medicine what was going on is that 'wind' was being released from her body and there were many forms of wind; itching, tumors, allergies, arthritis, pain, convulsions and so on.

In the BATHWAVE world, itching relates to judging good and bad; actually all wind involves judgment. I began looking for which organ in which the wind rose in the body as her symptom, and I began translating these into Bathwaves.

With 15 minutes of Bathwaving, the itching was 50% diminished. At that point she had two spots, one on her head and one on her instep, that were still itching on the left side of her body. Putting that together with what I had been shifting, it was clear that she had been judging that she didn't deserve to take care of herself, and so she would take care of everyone else but forget and neglect herself.

This is a variation on a classic outpicturing of women; I have only met one male nurse who had a breast tumor. By the way, after treatment he became a great Traditional Chinese Medical doctor.

Ginger and I worked to shift her lack of self 'worth' to being able to care for herself first as well as she takes care of others. With that shift her itching was gone completely, 100%. Ginger is a brilliant biology teacher at one of the best high schools in Hawaii. She was astounded and amazed, as I always am, at how quickly we got results. But with every shift, it's a confirmation that I am made up of the informotion of my BATHWAVES.

Using Relationshifting is quite an exciting new form of medicine which I am calling Epigenetic Medicine because it's outside of the genes, even though the genes may be the vehicle for some of the entanglement. It is not the central dogma of biochemistry; I used to think of it as an equality of gene to body part and/or condition. No longer do I believe that...and some of my colleagues agree. Lipton, B. (2005)

With these new understandings it becomes important to begin simplifying and forming an image of the lifestyle you truly desire and live that desire. Living as you desire is what eternalbeing is about.

This understanding of eternalbeing is such a big difference in the way I function that some people have to take a week or so off from their routine to reorient themselves. For that new lifestyle, combined with any medical and/or alternative relief and treatment that is needed, will emergently change everything within and around me.

Descriptionary of the body wisdom

The descriptionary is concerned with the BATHWAVEs (beliefs, attitudes, thoughts, habits, words, actions, values and emotions) I'd choose as a way to activate and express myself in life.

My outpicturing of beliefs inpicture myself. The inpicturing of myself outpictures my beliefs. Einstein knew that the observer influenced all they were observing.

My outpicturing of my body is what I am BATHWAVEing which is beyond even the concept of influence. It is the entanglement and emergent nature of reality. My outpicturing, whether of illness or well-being, simultaneously outpictures the inpicturing of what I believe, think, feel, say and do.

This means my body reveals the information instantly of:

- what I believe I was believing, thinking, feeling, saying and doing,
- what I think I believe, think, feel, say and do,
- what I say I believe, think, feel say and do
- how I actually am doing myself in life.

It's the actions themselves that are important, not the what's or the why's– although some of the why's may give us clues as to the how's of the actions.

This may seem involved and complicated. Simply reading the love letters that I give myself in my body really are gifts of my resplendence.

One of my clients, Carla, in New Zealand came in with a rash and her story is written up in the chapter on reading and naming my eternal being. Her rash had been around for two weeks and was very disturbing, red, welty and itchy. By the end of our work session, she came up with the correlation the how's and why's of her actions and "rashionalizing" her life, and clearly shifted everything. She walked out 90% better and by the next day the rash was gone. Some of her BATHWAVES were quite straightforward and easy, since she could pinpoint when the rash had started. Using common sense will serve well in seeing what BATHWAVEs need to be shifted.

Mirror-calls offer the keys to prevention

If I catch conditions in the beginning, which is what TCM, Traditional Chinese Medicine, always attempts to do, I can prevent harsh diseases from occurring. For example, my liver cancer diagnosis was a lot of the repression of anger that I had done in the first 50 years of my life. Anger is the main emotion of the liver. Through years of Bathwaves, herbs and acupuncture, but Bathwaves mostly, Relationshifting of course, and living resplendently, the liver cancer was relieved.

There are many faces of anger–I have discovered twenty–among which are guilt, disappointment, frustration, resentment, boredom, and so on, needless to say a lot of stuff to shift. It is all shifting and now I live to tell about it 20 years later. How much easier it would have been if I had understood my love letters from the beginning!

Do I now more fully understand how–my outpicturing–consisting of my BATHWAVEs, like Carla, is my symptoms? And that I am rashing those same symptoms in every aspect of myself in life?

Take heed of this awareness and stop the BATHWAVE of rashing. If I doctor and treat a physical rash while I continue the activities of rashing, I may soon have a severe rash on my face, which indicates that I am irritated by having to face my irritation…lol. Or, the face rash may signal I am unwilling or unable to face my irritations, as well as that I am rashionalizing and agonizing over what is the right thing to do.

These following simple questions can lead me to profound understanding of myself in life. Insert my symptom and its location in the logical places:

Am I irritated?
Am I unwilling to <u>face</u> my irritation?
Am I <u>rashing</u> over the right thing to do?

With this understanding I can heartwave my BATHWAVEs to make a real change in the whole system.

To return to the rashing example, perhaps I shift problems with my boss/supervisor and the rash clears up…but I continue these rashing attitudes about my life work, my purpose, my relationship, my feelings of being unsupported and unfairly judged, or my own judgments of myself.

With these continued rash attitudes I may out-picture a chronic illness such as asthma. Is that what I want to continue?

The descriptionary offers you questions to understand yourself 'mo bettah', as we say in Hawaii. The attitudes and beliefs are not really causing, nor will they cure, the pain and illnesses. However, they ARE the condition…and the pain and illnesses are simultaneously revealing to me how I am living my life in an out-picture which certainly includes my BATHWAVEs among other things.

The out-picturing of pain and illness is not a judgment of how I am living my life. My life in-picturings and symptoms are the same thing. I am not being judged.

Pain and illness are entanglements.

With the right constituents, pain and sicknesses are always emergent and cannot be withheld, but those constituents do not cause the ailment, they are the ailment. They are the sicknessing, the paining, the asthma'ing, the rashing.

The MRI chart that you see in the figure shows you words that will be useful in translating the love letter of my aches, pains and diseases.

There is a web site for more information for this symptoming approach: **www.wisdomofthebody.net**

MRI = Mirror-call Reflecting Image

HEAD ~ Consciousness, embodied thoughts

NECK ~ Transforming and embodying awarenesses and mindful thoughts or that which connects my thoughts and dreams to the body of my life. Pains in the neck are disbeliefs that I can live our dream and my thoughts.

SHOULDERS ~ Carrying commitment choices, duties, responsibilities, burden

ARMS ~ Reaching out, putting choices into action, giving to life

HANDS ~ Holding, handling, offering, receiving, acting upon

ELBOWS ~ Flexibility, uniting powerful and exciting actions ~ Joints are flexibilities in my lives. Swelling would mean emotion blocking the flexibility.

FLUIDS ~ The emotions of my life

BIOLOGICAL FLUIDS ~ like blood, Spinal fluid, saliva, tears, etc. ~ Vital emotions

FLUIDS OF SICKNESS, LIKE MUCUS ~ Undesirable emotions that don't serve us anymore.

CELLS ~ Beliefs.

BONES ~ Convictions.

LUNGS ~ Attitude

INHALING ~ Taking in, vitalizing and inspiring attitude.

EXHALING ~ Releasing undesirable, inappropriate attitudes, judgments or other matters.

HEART ~ Empowerment of emotions and feelings.

ABDOMEN/DIGESTION ~ Examining and assimilating nourishing matters.

HIPS ~ Putting self-empowerment into action.

LEGS ~ Motives, desires, intention, purposes.

KNEES ~ Flexibility, uniting our intentions and purposes.

ANKLES ~ Flexibility, uniting, understandings, desires and intentions

FEET ~ Understandings.

TOES ~ Reaching forward with my understanding.

BODY ~ mindful, spirited, fully embodied.

BACK ~ the past.

SIDES ~ the present.

FRONT ~ the future.

RIGHT SIDE of the body ~ appropriate, worthy, good, desirable or concept of right.

LEFT SIDE of body ~ inappropriateness, wrongdoing, unworthy, undesirable, bad, and no.

The MRI

Translating the Wisdom of the Energy Patterns

The next part of this book will be about understanding the five element/organ relationships, and will give you informotion about the wisdom of my energy by using the five element system from Traditional Chinese Medicine.

Take a few minutes to fill out the Five Element Questionnaire on the next page. Follow the guidelines below to translate the wisdom of the energy patterns.

Guidelines

After you have filled out the five-element questionnaire, the elements with the largest number of items selected will give you more information about your energetic patterns that may be challenging your awareness of resplendence. The larger the number of items in an element, the more attention that area needs.

For attention needed in the following areas:

Earth:	See Chapter 26
Metal:	See Chapter 27
Water:	See Chapter 28
Wood:	See Chapter 29
Fire:	See Chapter 30

As you are able to express your resplendency, these challenging energetic patterns no longer maintain themselves. Many clients, such as Ginger who walked into my office itching all over, got to experience instant relief with shifting the 'rash' judgments (itching) of herself to the new stance that, for the first time in her life, Ginger is valuing and taking good care of herself.

When I have symptoms which persist after my quantum shifts, the next step could be to look at my tongue and find my tongue markings within the next five chapters. You may have to use a few of the chapters since it usually takes two to entango. You may have a few organs in the element system that are issues in my life. There is also a quick reference tongue chart in the appendices.

After you connect your tongue "love letters" to certain organs, you can look at the BATHWAVE chart for those organs in that chapter and then muscle test for which BATHWAVEs are relevant for you to shift. All quantum shifts are provided.

Be sure to write them all down on my BATHWAVE form and say out loud my new quantum shifts for 21 days. During that time, I will see a greater sense of my well-being and energy, which is of course useful in living my desires.

If all the numbers in the five-element questionnaire are similar, say only one number different at the most, then you may have a yin yang imbalance that is standing in my way. Yin and Yang are basically understood as your femininity and masculinity. You can ask some simple relationship questions about them in you and go from there. The information on yin and yang is also in the car metaphor that might help you with that shift.

Enjoy the exploration of my energetic bodies and the transformation of my energetic atoms—a transformation that will make living my desires so much easier and attractive to do.

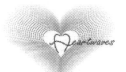

Five Element Questionnaire

Listed are the common TCM word associations with the five elements. Circle one or more words that mostly fit you. Create a five element chart. Fill it in using the totals below. The largest number of items in an elemental area indicate the element's organs which need to be focused on with Heartwaves, nutrition and herbs.

	Wood	Fire	Earth	Metal	Water
Senses affected	a. sight	b. speech	c. taste	d. smell	e. hearing
Body parts affected	a. nails	b. skin color	c. lips	d. abnormal body hair or skin condition	e. head hair
Liquids emitted (too much or too little)	a. tears	b. swat	c. saliva	d. mucus	e. urine
Body odor	a. rancid	b. burnt	c. fragrant	d. fleshy	e. putrid
Temperament	a. depression	b. up and down	c. obsession	d. anguish	e. fear
Emotion	a. anger	b. joy	c. sympathy	d. grief	e. paranoia
Flavor craving	a. sour	b. bitter	c. sweet	d. hot	e. salty
Sound of voice	a. loud	b. laughy	c. sing-song	d. weepy	e. groany
Weather that bothers you	a. windy	b. hot	c. humid	d. dry	e. cold
Seasons you like	a. spring	b. summer	c. mild summer	d. autumn	e. winter
Skin hue and color	a. green	b. red	c. yellow	d. white	e. black

TOTAL of Items circled in each element category:

# Wood	# Fire	# Earth	# Metal /Air	# Water

Five Element Questionnaire

PART THREE:

UNDERSTANDING THE ENERGY
OF YOUR TRIUNITY

The Five Elemental Relationships

I Auto know what's the metaphor My Body's ENERGY.

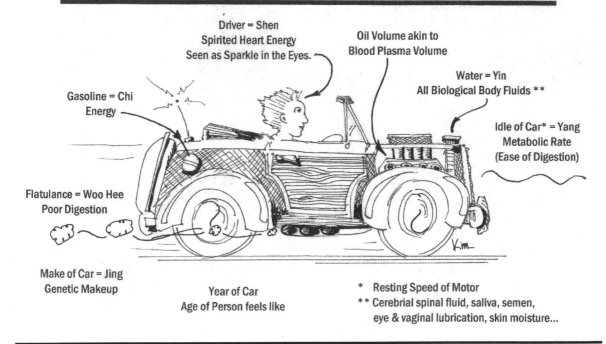

Driver = Shen
Spirited Heart Energy
Seen as Sparkle in the Eyes.

Oil Volume akin to
Blood Plasma Volume.

Water = Yin
All Biological Body Fluids **

Gasoline = Chi
Energy

Idle of Car* = Yang
Metabolic Rate
(Ease of Digestion)

Flatulance = Woo Hee
Poor Digestion

Make of Car = Jing
Genetic Makeup

Year of Car
Age of Person feels like

*   Resting Speed of Motor
** Cerebrial spinal fluid, saliva, semen,
     eye & vaginal lubrication, skin moisture...

CHAPTER 25

RELATIONSHIPS ARE ELEMENTAL, MY DEAR WATSON
OR
UNDERSTANDING THE FIVE ELEMENTAL RELATINGS

Getting into the glow of relatings

To better understand how to read the love letters we're giving ourselves with our bodies, it helps to know about the relatings between each of the main body organs. These five elements are all in multiple natural relatings with each other.

As part of my Traditional Chinese Medicine training, knowing about the five element glow of relatings has never ceased to amaze me in its efficacy. In support of Relationshifting, I have noticed that the physiological organ relatingss reflect social relationships like our Relationshifting mirror-calls. This is consistent with quantum theory presented earlier.

It seems to me that the ancient Chinese were probably aware of this quantum universe in using these relatings in medicine. Let's begin this explanation of the elemental relatings:

The Mother/Child Relatings

To begin with, the circle called the Shen or Chen cycle of the Mother/Child Law tells us about the supportive, nurturing and creative relating of a mother and a child.

If we start at the top of the circle with the **fire** element, we know that as fire burns, it generates ashes and therefore, **earth**. Therefore, fire would be the mother of earth.

As earth compresses, it forms **metal and air**, which is its child. The metal and gases inside the earth such as hydrogen and oxygen condense, becoming its child, **water**.

Moving around the circle, water as it falls on the earth's seeds, gives birth to its child, **wood** and the plants. When we strike the wood against itself, it gives birth to its child, **fire**.

We've created a full circle of these five elements and the Mother/Child relatings.

Resplendence of 5 Relationships
Particularizing 5 Elements:

① Mother - Child
② Father - Child
③ Beloved Partners

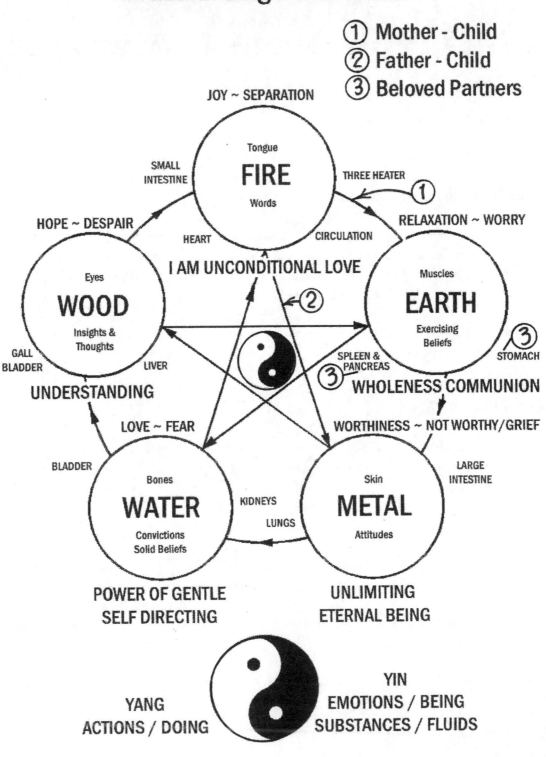

JOY ~ SEPARATION

Tongue
FIRE
Words

SMALL INTESTINE

THREE HEATER ①

RELAXATION ~ WORRY

HOPE ~ DESPAIR

HEART

CIRCULATION

I AM UNCONDITIONAL LOVE

Eyes
WOOD
Insights & Thoughts

Muscles
EARTH
Exercising Beliefs

GALL BLADDER

LIVER

②

③ STOMACH

SPLEEN & PANCREAS

③

UNDERSTANDING

WHOLENESS COMMUNION

LOVE ~ FEAR

WORTHINESS ~ NOT WORTHY/GRIEF

BLADDER

LARGE INTESTINE

Bones
WATER
Convictions Solid Beliefs

KIDNEYS

LUNGS

Skin
METAL
Attitudes

POWER OF GENTLE SELF DIRECTING

UNLIMITING ETERNAL BEING

YANG
ACTIONS / DOING

YIN
EMOTIONS / BEING
SUBSTANCES / FLUIDS

The Father/Child Relatings

Within the circle, you can see the form of a star, which is the guiding or disciplining cycle. As long as you can draw a 5-pointed star without picking up your pen, this will be easy. The direction your pen flows as you connect the elements, gives you the direction of the fathering.

For instance, the child, **fire**, is cooled by its father, **water.**

Water is then contained and channeled by its father, **earth.**

The **earth**-child is held together by its father, **wood**'s roots.

The **wood**-child is pruned by its father, **metal**, or the axe.

The **metal**-child is melted by its father, **fire** and we're back again to the fire-child, cooled by its father, water.

These cycles are very easy to remember and are useful to remember since all the organs relate to each other within this framework. I recommend drawing them on paper once or twice a day for a week and they will be yours forever.

The Beloved Cycle with the Elemental Organs

Within each element, there is a beloved partnership between a yin and a yang organ. Yin and yang are the basic phenomena of the dance of the two basic forces of energy in the universe.

Yin is described as feminine and receptive and is associated with the qualities of coolness, wetness, darkness, contraction, and nighttime and earth. In the body, Yin manifests as all biological fluids including blood, saliva, cerebral spinal fluids, semen, etc., low blood pressure, pale color, chronic conditions and the parasympathetic, relaxing nervous system, to mention a few.

Yang, on the other hand, is described as the masculine energy and is demonstrated by heat, dryness, light, projection/expansion, day and heaven. Yang energy manifests in our bodies as fevers, energy, the digestive and immune systems, acute conditions, high blood pressure, redness in any part of the body and the sympathetic central nervous system, which is the fight or flight aspect.

Understanding that these two forces are always dancing polarities and not opposites, is a really important distinction from Western ideas of these qualities. In Chinese medicine, these forces are beloveds. Yin and yang support one another. They are absolutely necessary for and flow into each other, as characterized by the popular yin yang symbol shown in the figure. **These are my training wheels and do not relate to the quantum world; I use them to describe the direction of glow, namely incoming and outgoing quantum waves in my workbook.**

Yin and Yang: back to the five elements

Within each element there is a cherishing beloved cycle of organs. Their gender can be remembered with a simple rule that the yin organs are generally more solid as compared to their yang partners that appear hollow.

Within **fire**, there is a partnership between the yin heart organ and the yang small intestine organ, each written inside or outside the large Creative cycle in the figure.

Earth's partnership on the inside of the big creative cycle is the yin spleen/pancreas system which is partnered to the yang stomach organ.

Within **metal/air's** partnership is the yin lung organ partnered to the yang large intestine organ.

Within **water's** partnership, we find the yin kidney married to or partnered to the yang bladder organ, written outside the creative circle.

In the **wood** partnership, the yin organ is liver on the inside of the mother-child cycle and in the outside, we see the yang organ, gall bladder. These partnerships are flowing within each element.

This whole five element picture, if it could be seen with its 'five color' energies in motion, would be quite dynamic, like a swirling rainbow star. These arrows in the diagram show a glow of energy that is constantly happening within our dancing bodily systems.

There is a chapter devoted to each element's organ relatings in detail and their respective BATHWAVEs.

Also, see the appendix and connect your tongue maps, BATHWAVEs, and five element relatings.

(The Five Elemental Relationships)
Resplendency is Elementally EEEZY!

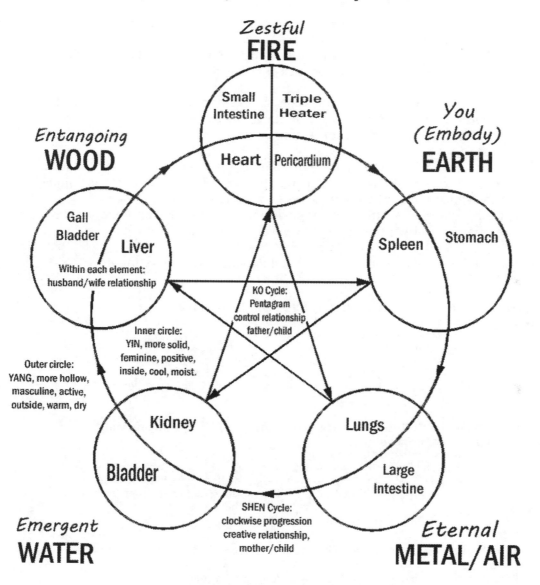

Eternal Metal/Air nurtures Water
Emergent Water nurtures Wood
Entangoing Wood nurtures Fire
Zestful Fire nurtures Earth
You embody Earth nurturing Metal/Air

Theory of Five Elements

Dr. Angela Longo

Theory of Five Elements

The flow chart of the five elements is a Relationshifting tool that can be used to understand and improve our energy and relationships.

The theory of the five elements describes all the relationships in our world: mother/child, father/child, beloveds, grandparents, and so on. It also describes our relationship with our natural environment of the elements. The names of the elements describe more than just physical substances.

- The energy of Wood is about wise understanding which moves our life forward in a transforming yet discerning way.
- The energy of Fire represents expanding, nurturing, harmonizing and pleasuring.
- Earth energy is about uniting or connecting, relaxing and being content.
- Metal is the heavy energy of condensation which describes our valuing or that which we wish to release when it doesn't serve us.
- Lastly, Water energy is an empowering, trusting, flowing and gently freeing movement which opens to our self-direction.

There are three main cycles or relationships which we will define now:

Creative Circle Cycle (the mother/child relationship)
Wood burns to create its child, fire...
Fire whose ashes create its child, earth...
Earth which compresses to form its child, metal/air...
Metal air which through condensation creates its child water...
Water which grows its child, wood...
These are the mothers and their children.

Guidance and Disciplining Star Cycle (the father/child relationship)
Wood child is pruned by father metal...
Metal child is melted by its father fire...
Fire child is cooled by its father water...
Water child is contained and channeled by its father earth...
Earth child is held together by its father's roots wood...
These are the fathers and their children.

The Cherishing Beloved Cycle within each element (the supportive equal partnership)
Wood's partnership is Yin liver organ married to Yang gall bladder organ...
Fire's partnership is Yin heart married to Yang small intestine organ...
Earth's partnership is Yin spleen/pancreas married to yang stomach organ...
Metal/Air's partnership is Yin lung married to Yang large intestine organ...
Water's partnership is Yin kidney married to Yang Bladder organ...
These are the beloved equal partners of Yin and Yang organs.

CHAPTER 26

GROUNDING MY EARTHEN
ELEMENT OF WHOLENESS
OR
SPEAKING IN MAGICAL TONGUES:

"Mirror, mirror on the wall,
What's the mirror-call for all?"
"Just open your eyes tall."

"Mirror, mirror on the wall,
What makes me feel so small?"
"Only you, and your judgment call."

"Mirror, mirror on the wall,
How can I get on the ball?"
"Resplendently do as you enthrall."

ESSENCE OF EARTH: The earth is the solid element that supports growth of food for our nurturance. Formed and warmed by the fire of its mother, earth is composed of years of mineral formation. It supports our embodiment. It serves us without taking credit. It is solid in its accountability and integrity.

The food it produces fulfills our needs. It reminds me how to express myself in satisfying nurturing ways. The earth by its nature is self- sustaining. We are composting, renewing, resting, and restoring as earth shows me how to energize myself.

The stomach receives the food of earth and dissolves it into the components that can be absorbed by our bodies. The pancreas prepares us to see the sweetness of living and integrate that into our bodies. The spleen is the largest lymph node showing us the safety of our selves well protected and filtered.

Can happiness find a home in me? Can I melt into the lava of living? Can I flow and solidify wherever I land…all of this is the essence of earth.

YIN/YANG EARTH ORGANS:

SPLEEN/PANCREAS, the feminine (yin) partner
STOMACH, the masculine (yang) partner

SPLEEN/PANCREAS MOTION:

Spleen is relaxing. Pancreas is sweetening.

STOMACH MOTION:

Stomach is nurturing and satisfying.

SACRED QUALITY OF EARTH:

Networking wholeness.

Weaving the web of our living.

MANIFESTATIONS OF EARTH ENERGY:

In body: Lips and muscles.
Sense commanded: Tasting.
Fluids: Saliva.
Bodily smell: Fragrant.
Flavor craving: Sweet.
Sound of voice: Singsong.
Weather that bothers you: Damp.
Season you like: Mid-summer.
Color of skin: Yellow.

OUR EMOTIONS OBSCURING FLOW:

Feeling obsessive, embittered, alienated, isolated, worried,
overwhelmed, exhausted, anxious.

OUR EMOTIONS ENHANCING FLOW:

Feeling centered, self-nurturing, fulfilling,
being grounded in reality, relaxed, rejuvenated, accountable, supportive.

RELATIONSHIPS TO ORGANS:

Spleen is the child of the mother heart.
Spleen is the child of the father liver.
Spleen/pancreas is mother to the child lungs.
Spleen/pancreas is the father to the child kidney.
Stomach is the child of the mother small intestine.
Stomach is the child of the father Gall bladder
Stomach is the mother of the large intestine.
Stomach is the father of the bladder.

TONGUES:

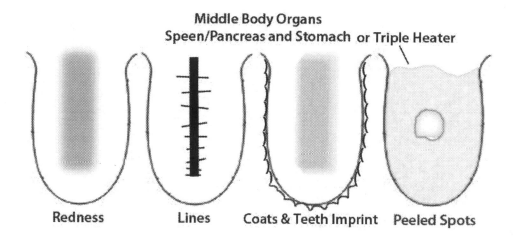

Middle Body Organs
Speen/Pancreas and Stomach or Triple Heater

Redness   Lines   Coats & Teeth Imprint   Peeled Spots

Shifting Beliefs

PART I: BATHWAVE

▫ Embrace all of your body, saying the sentence and the intention of loving and changing it.

PART II: Quantum Shift.

▫ Say the new belief 9 times while stroking your midline.

▫ 3x "I can..."

▫ 3x "I will..."

▫ 3x "I am..."

Element **EARTH**		Organ SPLEEN/PANCREAS/STOMACH
	PART I. BATHWAVES **Face and Embrace**	**PART II. HEARTWAVES** **Replace with Grace**
BELIEFS:	I worry.	I am trusting and optimistic about my living
ACTIONS:	I am weary for the turmoil.	I am enlivened and content in doing my best.
	I can't stomach life/people.	I am content.
THOUGHTS:	I am anxious.	I am safe secure and satisfied.
	Living is not sweet.	Living is sweet.
HABITS:	Things don't work out for me.	I am grateful that the universe nurtures me with abundant gifts.
	Living is not very fulfilling.	I am living a fulfilling life.
WORDS:	What I say doesn't make a difference.	I acknowledge that I am worthy and appreciated.
	I don't value my words.	I express myself satisfyingly in fulfilling ways.
ATTITUDES:	I can't focus on myself.	I believe in and approve of myself and others.
	I am upset.	I am appreciative and safe.
VALUES:	I am disappointed that I don't have enough.	I am grateful that the universe provides exactly what I need right now.
	I don't value myself or others.	The other is me. (mirroring for relationshifting)
EMOTIONS:	I am depressed. I am obsessed with things that keep me from really living. I am dissatisfied. I feel sorry for myself. I am uncentered. I am ungrounded. I feel disconnected. I am not fulfilled in what I do. I feel foggy or scattered. This is too good to be true.	I am enthusiastic about living. I focus on what I desire. I am connected, energized and confident in myself. I am grateful and appreciate all I am creating. The universe is benevolent. The universe gives what I desire. I am content and fulfilling my trueself. I am open to knowing my eternalbeing. My eternalbeing is imaged in everything I do, think, feel and dream.

CHAPTER 27

PEDAL TO THE METAL ELEMENT
OR
SHIFTING MY AIRY FAIRY TO BEING WORTH IT

Shifting Beliefs

PART I: BATHWAVE
- Embrace all of your body, saying the sentence and the intention of loving and changing it.

PART II: Quantum Shift.
- Say the new belief 9 times while stroking your midline.
- 3x "I can..."
- 3x "I will..."
- 3x "I am..."

	Element **EARTH**	Organ **SPLEEN**
	PART I. BATHWAVES **Face and Embrace**	**PART II. HEARTWAVES** **Replace with Grace**
BELIEFS:	I believe I am separate from others	I believe the other is me.
	I believe bad things happen to people.	
	I am a stranger to myself.	
	I judge myself and I am hard on myself.	
ACTIONS:	I withdraw.	I willingly unite, reach out and connect.
	I react.	I reflect and respect.
	I isolate myself/divide.	I center myself.
THOUGHTS:	I am exhausting myself	I energize myself with everything I do
	I feel overwhelmed.	I focus on and dedicate myself to everything I desire.
HABITS:	I need to worry to live, Old habits repeating	I relax a little as I do what I desire to do.
WORDS:	My words separate, are divisive and nervous.	I express myself satisfyingly in fulfilling ways.
ATTITUDES:	I live in an environment which I create, obsessive and worrying.	I live in a self sustaining, supportive environment.
	I am a loner unwillingly.	I rejuvenate myself.
	I am disconnected.	I am one with my reflections and my creations.
	Shallow breathing.	I easily cooperate with others and myself.
VALUES:	I separate my body, mind and spirit. I value being separate.	I am one spirited mindful body. We are each a hologram of our one universe
	My masculine and feminine sides are separate.	My masculine and feminine communicate their values and embrace each other passionately.
EMOTIONS:	I sacrifice myself, I am a martyr, I hurt myself, I am alienated, stressed, worried, anxious, edgy, panicky, obsessed, fatigued.	I live refreshed, enlivened, renewed, rested, restored and revived. I am connected, energized and confident in myself.

The essence of the metal/air element

The essence of metal/air element is the eternal (recurring) compressing and concentrating within our earth that transfigures rocks into valuable metamorphic metals, gems and gases. Likewise, when we concentrate on and then share our value, it is like manifesting the valuable metals, gems and air of our being.

This is the essence of value as contained in the organ lung. It can be understood in our breathing. As in the compression of the earth into metals, gems, and gases that are released into the space of our atmosphere, one of these gases is our valuable oxygen. As we breathe, we take this oxygen from the air and turn it into energy or chi, which brings life to our bodies. This is the nature of lung's essence: to transfigure the compression of inhaling oxygen into a concentrated state binding it to hemoglobin. This concentration, in turn, expands into the energy of our whole body.

This energy and life will nourish and nurture everything that we do, bringing attitudes of enthusiasm and excitement, which would be our living 'environments'. Our attitudes are associated with the lung which provides us our real 'environment'.

Seeing the cycle

We exhale CO_2 (carbon dioxide) which turns the wheel of the 5 elements again as explained below. It is also one of the other gases released from earth's biological material: CO_2 (carbon dioxide). Metal is the father of wood. Metal gives the CO_2 to the plants of wood element guiding them toward expanding growth. This CO_2 is inhaled by plants (wood element) and made into food, which in turn exhale more oxygen for the energy cycle, initiated in the lungs (metal element). Wood is father of metal's mother earth. Oxygen is like the money (energy) which dad (wood) brings home to child earth to support mother earth's child (metal element's lungs). This is one-way earth contributes to her child metal, supporting lung with oxygen. Mother earth also brings its child (metal) nourishment directly through growing its nourishing foods.

Thus, in relation to the large intestine, as the compression and the concentration of food from its mother the stomach, gets denser and the valuable nutrients are prepared for assimilation expanding into our blood and body with gases, which are also being released from our core colon. And these wasted products fall out of our bodies into the envirnment and also become part of our air. All of these scenarios are the cycle of compression turning around into expansion.

Through the concentration and the contraction, it circles around into expansion, which appears in the old science to be an opposite, but actually is a dance of polarity where one becomes the other.

We again see this cycle continue in the expanded air namely as hydrogen and oxygen becoming concentrated into water. This is the mothering nature of metal/air element birthing its child the water element explained in the next chapter on water.

I call the metal element the 'eternal' (reoccurring) element, since this process of breathing is repetitive throughout nature and ends with the expansion into energy. Our eternal nature is expansive just as the electron's wave nature is expanding in relation to its contracting particle nature (explained below). It begins to un-limit the part of us that is eternal. Eternal meaning reoccurring since we were born until after we die. Without breathing oxygen for energy, we would quite literally be dust.

Our zest for life or our enthusiasm to live is reflected in the metal/air element. It is surprising how many people visit me, and don't even know that they unconsciously have a desire to die or to leave the planet or leave their body. This is revealed with muscle testing and can be shifted with Bathwaving.

This air when ignited with great power, generates water, the child of metal/air, as the hydrogen and oxygen molecules come together with this empowerment. We generate flow of the water, so the metal/air is the mother of the water which is about self-empowering, which becomes our gentle (kidney) self-guidance (bladder). Now this lung attitude of self-value and worth is the life or the yin, and is complemented by the replacing of the recycling large intestine. It is logical and commonsensical to understand that the large intestine replaces what doesn't serve us, otherwise known as our "shit or excrement."

Replacing and recycling what doesn't serve us

As we are expanding and energizing ourselves, we also have to sift through what's nourishing us taken in through the stomach, and replace what doesn't serve us. This is reevaluating our desires. When we hold onto things from the past, we will limit and diminish our metal/air energy. As we Bathwave to shift 'holding on', we transform it to the quantum shift: "We replace the past to make space for transformation." Once again, there is the condensation and compression of the food within the large intestine; which then allows for the recycling of it, expanding more space within us to take more nourishment in through the stomach again.

The process of replacing, beginning with the compression of the food that nourishes us, also leads to the expansion of space within our being. The space creates the facility for transfiguration to happen. It's very important to understand this. These two movements of contraction and expansion are not opposite. Condensation and evaporation are not opposites in the universe just as yin and yang are not opposites but dancing partners. This dance of contracting and creating value like 'diamonds within us' leads us to understanding the expanding eternalbeing within us, and this is the sacred quality of the metal element.

Personalbeing, eternalbeing and metal

To understand the 'eternalbeing' nature of the metal element, we first have to understand the nature of the atoms of which we are constituted. The constituents of atoms and light have two distinct physical and natures. One nature is the nature of the particle which is like a solid ball (though not equivalent to a solid ball). The other nature is the quantum wave nature which has no resemblance to a ball and is hard to imagine. Physicists have been grappling with this wave nature which seems to be different to the particle nature. When they look at the photon particle nature of light, they don't see the wave nature of light. When they look at the wave nature, they don't see the photon particle nature. And yet, physicists know that they both exist and they're both necessary for the existence of the atom and light. This wave nature is quite physical, just ask any surfer.

To understand why I use this as an illustration of how we live I next invoke the 'wholographic' theory of the Universe. The theory that any pattern of the whole is in each part. And likewise, any pattern in a part is in the whole. So this wave/particle dance on the subatomic level pattern is repeated wholographically throughout life and the youniverse.

This pattern of two natures, particle and wave, must have some mirror, reflection or resonance within our own lives. We must have two distinct physical natures. The particle nature of us might be our original particularized expression of our self which we call our personalbeing (PB). The wave nature of us would be that which repeats itself just as a wave on water does. Picture a wave on water as it rises up and gives unique shape to our body. We will call it our unique eternalbeing, that aspect of us which is recurring.

This idea was new to me. How were we these two distinct physical 'beings' called personalbeing, (our particular expressions) and eternalbeing (our explained in detail in the first two parts of this book). These two exist together as light and atoms which is the stuff of which we are all made. The relating of these two, PB and EB, is called communion, and this communion is the source of our resplendency which means that aspect of us which 'is radiantly reaching out or shining'. This is reminiscent of gems and metals which 'shine'. Hence, the reason the essence of metal is intimately related to the communion of these two and resplendency.

For now, working to shift the BATHWAVEs of the lung and the large intestine will begin to prepare our awareness of communioning and living our resplendency. In a sense, this begins to unlimit our living so that we can be the fullness of ourselves.

Simply summarized, the lung helps us to energize ourselves as the female self might do in valuing our self through nurturing our self-esteem. As Swami Beyondananda says, we should take e-steam baths every day.

The large intestine helps us to release that which no longer serves us as the masculine self might do, guiding us to create space for our transfiguration. As Swami says that if you suffer from irregularhilarity, take a good laughsitive every morning. Beyondananda, S. (1999)

YIN/YANG METAL/AIR ORGANS:

LUNG, the feminine (yin) partner
LARGE INTESTINE, the masculine (yang) partner

LUNG MOTION:

Lung is about energizing ourselves with our self- value and worth.
Lung is also valuing the gifts and talents (mirror-calls) of others.

LARGE INTESTINE MOTION:

Large intestine is about recycling of our "shit", our undesirable material, (possibly, our judgments of ourself or others). In other words, large intestine is about replacing what does not serve us with our true desires.

SACRED QUALITY OF METAL:

Energizing value and unlimiting beliefs of eternalbeing

MANIFESTATIONS OF METAL:

In body: skin and unusual body hair.
Sense commanded: smelling.
Fluids: mucus.
Bodily smell: Fleshy, like bread or soil.
Flavor craving: hot and spicy.
Sound of voice: Weepy and breathy.
Weather that bothers you: Dry.
Season you like: Autumn.
Color of skin: White.

OUR EMOTIONS OBSCURING FLOW:

Feeling unworthy, grief, sadness, insecurity, hopeless, unhappy, despair, gloomy, intolerant, burdened.

OUR EMOTIONS ENHANCING FLOW:

Feelings of worthiness, generous, valuable, purposeful, enlivening, restored, revived, tolerant.

TONGUES:

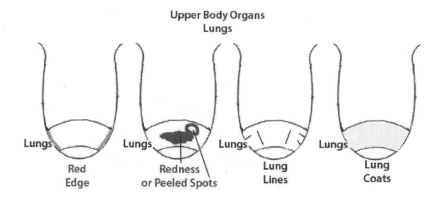

Upper Body Organs
Lungs

Lungs — Red Edge

Lungs — Redness or Peeled Spots

Lungs — Lung Lines

Lungs — Lung Coats

Lower Body Organ Signs

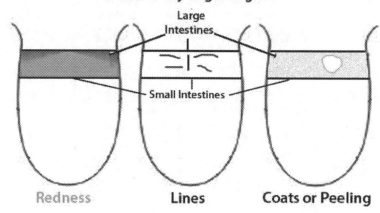

Large Intestines

Small Intestines

Redness   Lines   Coats or Peeling

Shifting Beliefs

PART I: BATHWAVE

 ▯ Embrace all of your body, saying the sentence and the intention of loving and changing it.

PART II: Quantum Shift.

 ▯ Say the new belief 9 times while stroking your midline.
 ▯ 3x "I can..."
 ▯ 3x "I will..."
 ▯ 3x "I am..."

	Element **METAL**	Organ **LARGE INTESTINE**
	PART I. BATHWAVES **Face and Embrace**	**PART II. HEARTWAVES** **Replace with Grace**
BELIEFS:	I have to hold on to what I no longer need.	I joyfully release the past to make space for change.
ACTIONS:	I deplete my resources	I use my resources appropriately.
THOUGHTS:	I block and sabotage my flow.	I yield to flow with living.
HABITS:	I have to be in control of my resources.	I create sustainable resources.
WORDS:	My words are powerless. I don't keep my promises.	My words are strong and meaningful. I keep my promises.
ATTITUDES:	My life feels stuck.	I flow freely through life.
VALUES:	I believe nothing changes.	I enjoy changing.
EMOTIONS:	I feel paralyzed and immobilized.	I freely dance with life.

237

Shifting Beliefs

PART I: BATHWAVE
    ⊠ Embrace all of your body, saying the sentence and the intention of loving and changing it.

PART II: Quantum Shift.
    ⊠ Say the new belief 9 times while stroking your midline.
    ⊠ 3x "I can..."
    ⊠ 3x "I will..."
    ⊠ 3x "I am..."

	Element **METAL**	Organ **LUNG**
	PART I. BATHWAVES **Face and Embrace**	**PART II. HEARTWAVES** **Replace with Grace**
BELIEFS:	I am a failure	I attract everything I need and desire.
	Failure exists.	Everything is useful.
ACTIONS:	I have to prove myself.	I am encouraging myself.
	I am resisting living fully.	I embrace living fully.
THOUGHTS:	I reject my values.	I value myself.
		I live by my values.
HABITS:	No body can teach me anything.	I am humble before the beauty and wonder of the Universe.
WORDS:	I am the only one who can speak the truth.	I value the words and needs of others.
ATTITUDES:	I feel sorry for myself.	I feel enthusiastic about living.
VALUES:	I am responsible for others feelings and needs.	I honor the feelings and needs of others.
EMOTIONS:	I feel sad.	I feel valuable and worthy.
	I am in grief and guilt	I feel refreshed and happy.
	I feel insecure and unworthy, discouraged, gloomy, hopeless, unhappy, despair and intolerant.	I feel significant. I feel purposeful and enlivening. I feel restored , revived, tolerant

CHAPTER 28

WATER UNDER THE BRIDGE ELEMENT
OR
CULTIVATING MY GENTLE POWER OF SELF GUIDING

Chapter 8 of Tao Te Ching:

Benevolent goodness is like water.
Water gives life to the ten thousand things and
does not struggle.
It glows in places men reject and
so is like the Tao. (emergent)
Water carries yin and embraces yang.

ESSENCE OF YOUR WATER ELEMENT:

Water (H_2O) is about the trust and confidence to be emergent (new and different) since water arises out of the two flammable gases, hydrogen (H_2) and oxygen (O_2), while not resembling either of them.

We are able to be emergent in every moment. This realization washes away worry. What's to worry about when we are able to begin again in the next moment?

As we begin again in every moment just as water rises up into waves over and over again, we are manifesting our true desires with greater creativity and consistency. It is easier to live without judgment of ourselves or others in this state of resplendent eternal reinvention. In living as a resplendent illuminatingbeing we are doing the eternal patterns we are willing to do forever and ever.

Water flows without question. Its power is in its confident persistence. In this sense it moves with full faith and honesty to itself. It moves with self-integrity. Yet, water also receives whatever enters it exhibiting openness and the ability to listen.

The essence of your water element is the gentle spirited power (kidney) of self-directing (urinary bladder) the information that I either desire to contain or wish to transform through the black holes of BATHWAVE recycling (urination). It is no wonder that the slang English word for urinating is 'pissing' which also means to be expressing one of the forms of 'anger'. When we are angry our urine turns a darker yellow helping us to recycle and, therefore, replace these emotions. When we are aware of our resplendence, we are less prone to be reactive, and are mostly self-expressive.

Another way of expressing the essence of our water element is self-empowerment. Water embodies the gentle strength for transforming the flammable, dispersing quality of the gases of hydrogen and oxygen into the condensing emergent flowing quality of a liquid. This is the power of our water element, the most yin of the elements in living, and yet, it can smooth a hard rock. One teacher said that our yin was the condensation of 'light'. Our vital emotions (understand from yin) are the 'light' of us. This is a mirror of the light's gentle self-directing energy of me. Water is unimpeded with resplendency or by expanding our awareness thru Heartwaving the BATHWAVEs of the water element (causing and effecting). See the chart of kidney/bladder BATHWAVEs.

One of the most important qualities of water is its ability to carry yin and yang within itself. It achieves this through its physical chemical structure (bonds). Water carries the charges of positive and negative within itself. The positive charge would be considered the more yang and the negative charge would be considered the more yin. This dipole is the quality that imparts the capacity to nurture life. One of the examples of this dipole property is that when it freezes, and the molecules slow down a little, they line up into crystalline pattern enabling its expansion into a lighter form that floats on top of its liquid form. This is why water is the substance that composes the ocean. When water freezes at the north and south poles it floats on itself which prevents it from killing all the marine life. No other liquid has this property of expansion on freezing.

This property of self-crystallization as pattern formation is one of the reasons we are composed mostly of water. Crystallization of water in our bodies into sphere-like clathrate structures are thought to contain and thereby enable oily molecules to interact. Liquid crystals in water can carry information of energy patterns which is an entanglement. This dipole attribute also accounts for some of water's cohesiveness.

The attributes of faith in oneself, confidence, trust, security, openness, and impeccable honesty create the strength of water's gentle self-guidance.

Kidney is about flowing the gifts and talents (mirror-calls) of myself and others in order to express myself. This would also indicate that we are able to listen deeply to the gifts and talents of others. This could also be expressed as entanglement (air/metal) to our emergent nature. (water)

In summary, our twenty water qualities are openness, emergent, expansive, confident, gentle, self-guiding, persistent, committed, believing in self, honest, secure, cohesive, receptive, competent, flowing, supportive, freeing, communicative, crystallizing, polarizing, networking, and with all these we are self-empowering.

YIN/YANG WATER ORGANS:

KIDNEY, the feminine (yin) partner
BLADDER, the masculine (yang) partner

KIDNEY MOTION:

KIDNEY IS BEING GENTLE WITH MYSELF IN FULL FAITH, CONFIDENCE, HONESTY, TRUST, WHILE DEEPLY LISTENING TO MYSELF WITH OPEN AWARENESS. DOING

AS I TRULY DESIRE. Kidney is about flowing with the gifts and talents (mirror-calls) of myself and others in order to express myself gently.

BLADDER MOTION:

BLADDER IS GUIDING MYSELF WITH FULL FAITH, CONFIDENCE, HONESTY, TRUST, WHILE DEEPLY LISTENING TO MYSELF WITH OPEN AWARENESS, DOING AS I TRULY DESIRE

SIMPLE SACRED QUALITY OF WATER:

Gentle self-guidance.

YOUR MANIFESTATIONS OF WATER:

In body: Bones, joints, hair on head.
Sense commanded: smelling.
Fluids: Urine.
Bodily smell: Putrid, rotten.
Flavor craving: Salty.
Sound of voice: Groany, monotone.
Weather that bothers you: Cold.
Color of skin: Dark bags.

OUR EMOTIONS OBSCURING FLOW:

Feeling fear, paranoia, doubt, distrust, insecurity, deceitful, closed, incompetent, giving up, jealousy, envy, the belief and feeling of victimization.

OUR EMOTIONS ENHANCING FLOW:

Feelings of gentleness, confidence, faith, trust, security, honesty, openness, competence, constant perseverance, free will, autonomy.

RELATIONSHIPS TO ORGANS:

Kidney is the child of the mother lungs.
Kidney is the child of the father spleen/pancreas.
Kidney is mother to the child liver.
Kidney is the father to the child heart and pericardium.
Bladder is the child of the mother large intestine.
Bladder is the child of the father stomach.
Bladder is the mother of the gall bladder.
Bladder is the father of the small intestine and triple heater.

Dr. Angela Longo

TONGUES:

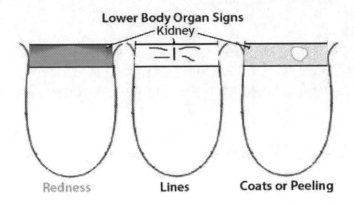

Redness   **Lines**   **Coats or Peeling**

242

CHAPTER 29

WOOD I OR WOODN'T I ELEMENT
OR
TRANCE FORMING ANGER TO UNDER STANDING

THE ESSENCE OF THE WOOD ENERGY:

Wood begins as a self-organizing seed of informotion and data of our recurring eternalbeing. The initiating self-supporting seed sprouts us to root in our personalbeing embodiment. We are fertilized by the entanglement of constituents and compost we amass. We water ourselves with the emergent yin fluidity of our vital e-motions. As we emergently expand our wisdom, our branches are pruned by our metallic shear valuing attitudes. All that remains is for us to pollinate our personalbeing with our eternalbeing so that ordinary resplendent fruit ripens daily as we share our self. The blossoming and ripening of our sweet resplendency is evident while transfiguring the moment into our fired up living.

YIN/YANG WOOD ORGANS:

LIVER, the feminine (yin) partner
GALL BLADDER, the masculine (yang) partner

LIVER MOTION:

Liver is understanding and planning.

GALL BLADDER MOTION:

Gall Bladder is deciding and timing.

SACRED QUALITY OF WOOD:

Understanding the wisdom of resplendence.

MANIFESTATIONS OF WOOD ENERGY:

In body: Eyes and nerves.
Sense commanded: Sight
Fluids: Tears.
Bodily smell: Rancid oil.
Flavor craving: Sour.
Sound of voice: Shout.

Weather that bothers you: Wind.
Season you like: Spring.
Color of skin: Green.

OUR EMOTIONS OBSCURING WOOD FLOW:

Feeling angry, disappointed, neglected, resentful, irritated, frustrated, guilty, bored, depressed, manic, hyperactive, upset, resistant, self-sabotaging, procrastinating, indecisive, nervous.

OUR EMOTIONS ENHANCING WOOD FLOW:

Feeling understanding, appreciative, calm, innocent, creative, excited, decisive, transformative, cooperative, engaging, self-supportive

RELATIONSHIPS TO ORGANS:

Liver is the child of the mother Kidney.
Liver is the child of the father Lung.
Liver is mother to the child Heart.
Liver is the father to the child Spleen/Pancreas.
Liver is the wife of her husband Gall Bladder.
Gall Bladder is the child of the mother Bladder.
Gall bladder is the child of the father Large Intestine.
Gall Bladder is the mother of the Small Intestine.
Gall Bladder is the father of the Stomach.

TONGUES:

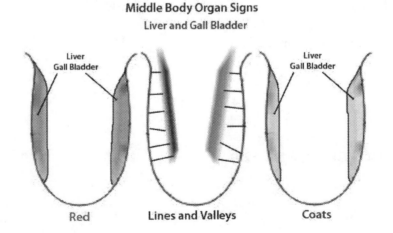

Middle Body Organ Signs
Liver and Gall Bladder

Liver Gall Bladder — Red

Lines and Valleys

Liver Gall Bladder — Coats

Shifting Beliefs

PART I: BATHWAVE
- Embrace all of your body, saying the sentence and the intention of loving and changing it.

PART II: Quantum Shift.
- Say the new belief 9 times while stroking your midline.
- 3x "I can..."
- 3x "I will..."
- 3x "I am..."

	Element **WOOD**	Organ **LIVER/GALL BLADDER**
	PART I. BATHWAVES **Face and Embrace**	**PART II. HEARTWAVES** **Replace with Grace**
BELIEFS:	I love that I am sabotaging my growing.	I am acting to benefit myself.
ACTIONS:	I love that I react.	I listen, reflect and understand.
	I put off deciding until it's too late.	I make approiate and timely choices.
THOUGHTS:	I embrace that I am resenting others or myself.	I recognize that every thing is beneficial.
	I love that I am disappointed in others or myself.	
	I have trouble making choices I desire.	I live my desires with ease.
HABITS:	I embrace that I am staying the way I am.	I always welcome changes as beneficial.
	I am addicted and stuck.	
WORDS:	I embrace that I use abrupt angry words.	I comprehend other's feelings and empathize with their needs.
		I hear what is alive for the other person.
ATTITUDES:	I am lacking in vital emotions.	I am filling myself with emotions of my heart's desire.
	I am irritated and irritating.	I breathe gratitude into every moment.
	I have difficulty making decisions.	I live my desires with ease.
VALUES:	I love that I use guilt to manipulate and control others and myself.	I am refreshing and free of coercion. I am innocent.
EMOTIONS:	I embrace that I am angry, enraging and burning myself up.	I am soothing and refreshingly buoyant.

CHAPTER 30

FIRED UP RESPLENDENT ELEMENT
OR
RADIANTLY REACHING OUT IN
CONDITIONS OF EXPANSION

THE ESSENCE OF THE FIRE ENERGY:

Now that we are resplendent with the communion of our personalbeing and eternalbeing the radiance begins. Our resplendentbeing enables us to be in entanglement with anything around us as conditions of expansion (COE) and then we "particularize" that as we desire. Radiance is this physical reaching forth thru entanglements in resplendency (without cause and effect) to conditions of expansion.

Intimacy becomes the entanglement of two resplendentbeings. Their emergent entanglement is the expansion of the universe.

The fire element is sparked with the wonderful realization that everything is a mirror-call of our resplendency. This is the dance of relationships, the dance of resplendency. Since everything in our living is relating as the dance of the expansion of our universe.

YIN/YANG FIRE ORGANS:

HEART, our feminine (yin) partner
SMALL INTESTINE, our masculine (yang) partner

HEART MOTION:

The ability to know and live our self in each moment.

SMALL INTESTINE MOTION:

The ability to absorb the nourishment in every moment as a mirror-call of our resplendent nature whether it is resisting or enhancing our resplendency. This encourages our maturing so that we can transform by any method that suits us to our resplendency.

SACRED QUALITY:

Unconditional resplendency.

MANIFESTATIONS OF FIRE ENERGY:

In body: Tongue and Transparent skin.
Sense commanded: Speech.
Fluids: Sweat.
Flavor craving: Bitter.
Sound of voice: Laughing.
Bodily smell: Scorched.
Weather that bothers you: Heat
Season you like: Summer.
Color of skin: Red.

OUR EMOTIONS OBSCURING FLOW:

Holding on to 'cause and effect' of the eight bottom lines of accuse, blame, complain lie, hide, deny, defend and justify withholds your awareness of your resplendent illuminatedbeing, RIB. Just as holding on to the particle nature of light prevents our perception of its exciting wave nature.

I use language as a symbolic structure or syntax of concepts. We need to use language to describe our reality because words can only describe what experience gives. We use language as a substitute for reality. That is why I need to describe more of what I am saying.

Other emotions: Feeling apathy, going numb, avoiding authenticity.

OUR EMOTIONS ENHANCING FLOW:

Feeling free of 'cause and effect', living emergent miracles, and 'at home in your skin' (yourself).

RELATIONSHIPS TO ORGANS:

Heart is the child of the mother Liver.
Heart is the child of the father Kidney.
Heart is the mother to the child Spleen/Pancreas
Heart is the father to the child Lung
Heart is the wife of her husband Small Intestine.
Small Intestine is the child of the mother Gall Bladder.
Small Intestine is the child of the father Bladder.
Small Intestine is the mother of the Stomach.
Small Intestine is the father of the Large Intestine.

Shifting Beliefs

PART I: BATHWAVE
 ☒ Embrace all of your body, saying the sentence and the intention of loving and changing it.
PART II: Quantum Shift.
 ☒ Say the new belief 9 times while stroking your midline.
 ☒ 3x "I can..."
 ☒ 3x "I will..."
 ☒ 3x "I am..."

	Element **WATER**	Organ **KIDNEY/BLADDER**
	PART I. BATHWAVES **Face and Embrace**	**PART II. HEARTWAVES** **Replace with Grace**
BELIEFS:	I am afraid of my own power.	I am not afraid to reach my potential.
	I am afraid of failure and making mistakes.	I am willing to explore new possibilities.
ACTIONS:	I am not in control of my living.	I am in control of myself.
	I am being hard on myself out of fear.	I am gentle and kind to myself first.
	I don't listen to other's opinions or needs.	I am open to listening to the opinions and needs of others.
	I over discipline myself.	
	I hold back my spirit for fear of...	
THOUGHTS:	I am not free.	I am free to choose
	I deceive myself.	I am aware of my own potential.
	I have no faith in myself or others.	I reflect on my inner wisdom and the wisdom of others.
	I doubt and question everything.	I believe in myself and others.
	I am controlled by forces or people stronger than myself.	
	I am indecisive.	I think clearly.
HABITS:	I am a victim.	I am committed to living a fulfilling life.
	I am scared to be anything.	I believe I am capable of fulfilling my dreams
	I am paranoid.	I am self assured and confident.
	I belittle myself and I give my power away.	I am willing to do new things to move forward.
	I am afraid to take risks.	
WORDS:	I am afraid to speak.	My opinion is worth hearing.
	I am shy and timid.	I am confident.
	I am tongue tired.	
ATTITUDES:	I have to please others.	I listen and follow my self-directing voice.
	I am afraid to live fully	I give my whole spirit to living.
	I am suspicious of others.	I follow my intuition.
	I distrust people.	I am discerning and trusting.
	I am closed.	I am open.
	Living is a chore	Living is easy.
VALUES:	I value other's opinions more than my own.	I listen and follow my self-directing voice.
	I take better care of others than I take care of myself.	I take care of myself first as well as well as taking care of others.
EMOTIONS:	I am jealous or envious.	I am good just the way I am.
	I am scared and afraid often.	I am confident and secure.
	I am fearful.	I and confident with the unknown.
	I am cold hearted.	I am generous and warm hearted.
	I doubt myself and others.	I believe in myself and others as I desire.

TONGUES:

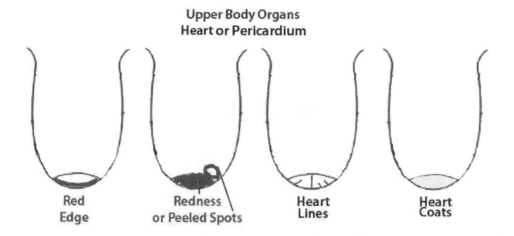

**Upper Body Organs
Heart or Pericardium**

Red
Edge

Redness
or Peeled Spots

Heart
Lines

Heart
Coats

Shifting Beliefs

PART I : BATHWAVE
 ▨ Embrace all of your body, saying the sentence and the intention of loving and changing it.

PART II : Quantum Shift
 ▨ Say the new belief 9 times while stroking your midline.
 ▨ 3x "I can ..."
 ▨ 3x "I will ..."
 ▨ 3x "I am ..."

Element **FIRE**	Organ **HEART**	
	PART I. BATHWAVES **Face and Embrace**	**PART II. HEARTWAVES** **Replace with Grace**
BELIEFS:	I want to be perfect.	I want to be authentic and real.
	I believe bad things happen to people.	Everything is a sacred mirror doorway of my enlightening self.
	I am a stranger to myself.	I know who I am now.
	I judge myself and I am hard on myself.	It is easy to love myself unconditionally.
ACTIONS:	I hide from myself.	I am awakening to who I am.
	I am shy or frightened.	I am safe and secure.
	I deny myself.	I appreciate myself.
	I withhold my love.	I express my love freely.
THOUGHTS:	I belittle myself.	I have uplifting thoughts about myself.
	I avoid thinking about myself.	I am open and aware of myself.
HABITS:	I run away from relationships and myself.	I am opening to relationships and myself.
	I am a loner.	I appreciate relationships.
	I ignore my intuition.	I follow my intuition.
WORDS:	I stifle and judge everything I say.	I express myself spontaneously.
	I find it hard to talk to others.	I converse easily with others.
	I cant find the words I want to say what I desire and I become tongue tied.	I speak my needs and desires appropriately to others.
	I stutter.	
ATTITUDES:	I avoid who I am.	I love myself.
VALUES:	I deny myself or others any value.	I acknowledge the value of our feelings and needs
EMOTIONS:	I hate what I do.	I am filled with joy and gratitude no matter what I do.

THE YANG SIDE OF FIRE:

Chapter 38 From the Tao Te Ching:
A truly good person is not aware of their goodness,
And is always beginning anew.
A foolish man "tries" to be good
And is therefore not good.
When one "tries" to do anything
One life becomes "trying". (exhausting)

A truly authentic person emerges without dissecting
The "thinking" of doing.
That leaves nothing incomplete (undone).
A foolish person is always <u>"trying" to do</u>
Yet much remains to be done.

When a disciplinarian does something and no one responds,
They roll up their sleeves in an attempt to enforce order.

Therefore, when the Tao (unconditional love which is emergent) is lost, goodness is born.
When goodness is lost, trying to be kind is born.
When "trying to be kind" is lost, justice is born.
When justice is lost, ritual is born.
Now ritual is a cover up for faith and loyalty,
The beginning of confusion.
Knowledge of the future is only a flowery trapping of your emergent nature that is the beginning of foolishness.

Therefore, the truly great man dwells on what is authentic
And not what is on the surface,
On the fruit and not the flower.
Therefore, support being emergent and
Transform your "trying"

Rewritten by Angela Longo

The yang aspect of fire element is about being bonded to the harmony of reality. (thanks to entanglement) Now, reality is always in harmony with ourselves, but we question that. When we realize the truth, we rest in the support of this reflection.

The other aspect of yang fire is the bonding we live within our <u>triUnity</u>. Our triUnity is made up of our personalbeing, our eternalbeing, and our resplendent illuminatedbeing. These three beings when bonded with each other create a strong safety net in which our heart can thrive. It gives our heart buoyancy just as the water balloon of pericardium gives heart an effortless way to keep beating. It is the waterbed of the manifestation of love in our lives. It is the fire of sexuality that provides the fertile groundwork of intimacy. This energy opens and receives another into our hearts and into our arms through a loving embrace.

YIN/YANG FIRE ORGANS:

PERICARDIUM, the feminine (yin) partner
TRIPLE HEATER, the masculine (yang) partner

PERICARDIUM MOTION:

The ability to bond with my selves and others.

Shifting Beliefs

PART I: BATHWAVE
  ▯ Embrace all of your body, saying the sentence and the intention of loving and changing it.
PART II: Quantum Shift.
  ▯ Say the new belief 9 times while stroking your midline.
  ▯ 3x "I can..."
  ▯ 3x "I will..."
  ▯ 3x "I am..."

	Element **FIRE**	Organ **PERICARDYUM**
	PART I. BATHWAVES **Face and Embrace**	**PART II. HEARTWAVES** **Replace with Grace**
BELIEFS:	I blame and accuse others	I release my misunderstanding of the nature of reality and I enjoy living responsible to myself.
	I believe others affect me.	
	I am not free to be me.	I am exited to be me, as I desire.
ACTIONS:	I love that I rejected my mother, father, nature and the world.	The Universe supports me abundantly.
	I love that I rejected my body, mind, feelings and my spirit.	I am a spirited mindful body.
	I love that I am needy for my mother, father, nature or the world's approval.	I nurture and guide myself without judgment.
	I am needy for either my body or mind or feelings or spirit.	I embrace that all of me is one.
THOUGHTS:	I believe I am not sexy enough.	I am a vital sexy being.
	I accuse others for my difficulties or problems.	I appreciate that everything is a sacred mirror doorway for my enlightenment.
	I blame others or myself for my difficulties or problems.	I appreciate that everything is a sacred mirror doorway for my enlightenment.
	I complain about others or myself and make things difficult.	I appreciate that everything is a sacred mirror doorway for my enlightenment.
	I believe that difficulties and problems exist.	Everything is a gift for my understanding.
	I believe that things are opposing me in the universe.	Everything supports me as I support myself.
	I use the thought of failure to motivate me.	I am successful, sharing, and inspiring. I desire to live my new, responsible self.
HABITS:	I am guilty	I am innocent
	I am resentful as I live.	I cherish everyone and everything I meet.
	I am overbearing in what I do.	I appreciate the input of others.
	I use force, control and power to manipulate to get things done.	I change myself and watch everyone and everything change with me.
WORDS:	My words are divisive.	My words express living the oneness.
	Other's words trigger me.	I unconditionally love and accept other's ideas, feelings and needs.
ATTITUDES:	Negative attitudes corrupt the clarity and strength of my self and life.	I conceive of myself as possessing true strength, which is personal change.
	I doubt my inner strength or wisdom.	Strength is always united with wisdom.
VALUES:	There is no free will.	I value my freewill and true strength to keep or recycle everything as I desire.
	The Universe is out to get me.	The Universe supports what I am creating now.
EMOTIONS:	Fear of failure paralyzes me.	I am clear and understand that there are no mistakes or failures. Everything I do is successful.
	I feel disoriented and out of my orbit.	I am fired up with enthusiasm.

TRIPLE HEATER MOTION:

The ability to see that the world is always in harmony with me. Every moment as a mirror-call of our resplendent nature. This encourages maturing so that I can see what is really going on.

SACRED QUALITY:

Unconditional resplendency.

Tongues: (similar to heart/small intestine) Different BATHWAVEs…muscle test or can look up symptomology for pericardium and triple heater.

MANIFESTATIONS OF YANG FIRE ENERGY: (same as yin fire above)

OUR EMOTIONS OBSCURING FLOW:

Inability to bond, arrogance, apathy, going numb, avoiding authenticity, alienation, disorientation.

OUR EMOTIONS ENHANCING FLOW:

Feeling free of 'cause and effect' and 'at home in your skin' (yourself).

RELATIONSHIPS TO ORGANS:

Pericardium is the child of the mother Liver.
Pericardium is the child of the father Kidney.
Pericardium is the mother to the child Spleen/Pancreas
Pericardium is the father to the child Lung
Pericardium is the wife of her husband Small Intestine.
Triple Heater is the child of the mother Gall Bladder.
Triple Heater is the child of the father Bladder.
Triple Heater is the mother of the Stomach.
Triple Heater is the father of the Large Intestine.

TONGUES:

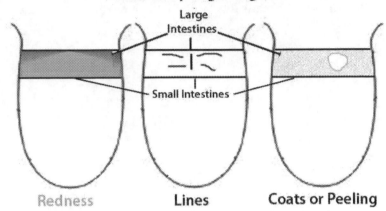

Lower Body Organ Signs

Large Intestines

Small Intestines

Redness · Lines · Coats or Peeling

Shifting Beliefs

PART I: BATHWAVE
- Embrace all of your body, saying the sentence and the intention of loving and changing it.

PART II: Quantum Shift.
- Say the new belief 9 times while stroking your midline.
- 3x "I can..."
- 3x "I will..."
- 3x "I am..."

	Element **FIRE**	Organ **SMALL INTESTINE**
	PART I. BATHWAVES **Face and Embrace**	**PART II. HEARTWAVES** **Replace with Grace**
BELIEFS:	Nothing is nourishing in my life.	I perceive everything nourishes me.
ACTIONS:	I block the participation in life.	I totally participate in my life.
THOUGHTS:	I am distracting myself from the fullness of the moment.	I am attracting everything I desire in the fullness of the moment.
HABITS:	I always negate my feelings.	I nourish myself with feelings I desire.
WORDS:	My words tend to justify, excuse and judge me or others.	My words emerge spontaneously and creatively.
ATTITUDES:	I have lost my desire to cook and live.	I cook and live with passion.
VALUES:	Life is meaningless or draining.	I ma amazes how everything nourishes me and gives the meaning that I choose.
EMOTIONS:	I am starving for warmth and nourishment in my life.	I am self-sustaining and the source of my own rejuvenation.

Shifting Beliefs

PART I: BATHWAVE

　▪ Embrace all of your body, saying the sentence and the intention of loving and changing it.

PART II: Quantum Shift.

　▪ Say the new belief 9 times while stroking your midline.

　▪ 3x "I can..."

　▪ 3x "I will..."

　▪ 3x "I am..."

	Element **FIRE**	Organ **TRIPLE HEATER**
	PART I. BATHWAVES **Face and Embrace**	**PART II. HEARTWAVES** **Replace with Grace**
BELIEFS:	I believe that my world is not in harmony.	The world reflects exactly where I am now and I am willing to change that.
	I still believe that I should judge.	I am willing to reflect and understand what is really going on.
ACTIONS:	I am always in the wrong place at the wrong time.	I am in the right place at the right time.
THOUGHTS:	My life and world is full of chaos.	I am in tune with flow of life. (Check the large intestine Beliefs if this won't shift)
HABITS:	I am always trying to change the world.	I am grateful and perceive everything as a gift in my life.
WORDS:	My words are cold and judgmental.	My words are warm and accepting.
ATTITUDES:	I am depressed and despairing at this disharmony.	I am full of elation as I dance with the flow of life.
VALUES:	My feminine side does not value my masculine side.	My feminine side (feeling, poetic, being side) values my masculine side (linear, logical thinking, organized doing side).
EMOTIONS:	I hate the disharmony of relationships.	I delight in stimulating relationships.
	I close my energy down in relationships.	I am open hearted to the beauty and security of real relationships.

CHAPTER 31

THE INTIMATE LOVE AFFAIR OF
RESPLENDENCY
OR
RESPLENDENCY IS EEEZY
OR
SIMPLY BECAUSE IT IS WHO YOU ALREADY ARE

You tell me who you want to be and I'll show you who you already are.

~Roger Cotting

You are already resplendent

Be who I want to become completely in one moment. In that moment I am totally the quantum me and resplendent. With awareness of the quantum world I can get out of my own way.

"Trying" always creates a "trying world to live in". That is one of the descriptions of stress which exhausts me. My favorite quote which you may remember if you watched "Star Wars" was by Yoda to Luke when he said: Do or do not do, but never try.

Tools in this book prepare me to be aware of living resplendently by helping me see my resplendency. 'Trying' to become someone gets in the way of 'being' who I already am... *because who I already am is resplendent.*

I have always been resplendent. Now I am aware of my resplendency and can live it. Knowing my eternalself pattern is a big gift.

"Becoming" usually limits me to the cause and effect world

Be who I want to be in every situation at this moment. I have to be who I want to be in order to get over 'trying to become' who I want to be. I am able to live as who I really already am, which is resplendent.

Wanting to be resplendent would be an obstacle...just like spending your life wanting to be someone else.

Living "wanting" gives you a "wanting life". Not much fun.

A list of the EEEZY tools

Emergent

Practicing Relationshifting until I AM minding and am aware.

Entanglement

The accessing of all which is to memory my nonce, or current, moment.

Eternal

Knowing the reoccurring 'virtual me that I discovered in my six doings (accomplishments) of which I am proud.

Zestful

The sharing of my unique resplendence using my own creative ways and gifts. Quantum communication is a mode of speaking to enhance the communion of my eternalbeing and personalbeing.

You

Understanding my unique resplendency and the intimate interaction of the triUnity of my resplendent illuminatedbeing emergent from the communion (love affair) of my personalbeing and my eternalbeing. It is the expression of de-light as my existence as 'spinning particle' and quantum wave, as distinct and as virtual, as the alpha and as the omega.

Relationshifting is a form of practicing 'minding' to emergent

As I trust enough to live as my illuminatedbeing, in hindsight I notice that relationshifting occurs automatically.

Wow!

'Minding' is motioning data and information around and together in relating. Relationshifting could be an example of manipulating the data and informotion I create in my day in order to see and be my self... eventually of deserving what coalesces or comes together dynamically.

As I motion data and information around, the motion creates the emergent moment. Keep putting relatings together, and I finally get something! The description of minding is that I am intentionally motioning my desirable data and information around, which invites emergent. (The data and information are accessed through entanglement). This 'minding' creates 'emergent-eyezing'. When I see and live what I desire, that gives me everything I minded and a whole lot more.

The 'whole lot more' is the emergent nature.

The example of putting together hydrogen and oxygen was an example of minding. What happens when I invite and move together hydrogen and oxygen is that in its relating, it is water. Water is emergent from hydrogen and oxygen. There is no cause or effect here. As water, I get whole lot more properties than I ever had with hydrogen and oxygen when they were separate. **The moving of things together is in a sense the real creative process.**

How you uniquely do 'minding' is an expression of my eternalbeing in resplendency.

Minding then would be the quantum world's way of manifesting, so I can mind with my speaking. I can mind in my doing. I can do minding in my thinking. It is not using the old-fashioned language way of 'subject causes object'. Using quantum communication or 'minding', I can describe and sometimes do declarative questioning about the moment.

In doing quantum communication, I am bringing together data and information in relatings. There is no causing and effecting. It feels effortless. It is full of creative surprises! That is a definition of emergent.

I have experienced this...I am in a sense particularizing and therefore manifesting. Where is this data and information coming from?

To memory is the verb of entanglement

The data and information comes from a function called 'to memory'. To memory is the verb or 'modus operandi' of entanglement. To memory, I am impacting my universe. By this I mean I am using my own encode, decode key, which is the declaration that I make as an eternalbeing, to gather information through the process which the quantum world calls entanglement. However, the entanglement happens spontaneously through my encode-decode key.

My particular encode-decode key is a function of my DNA. Your DNA is the vehicle to accessing the universe thru entanglement. All I have to do is ask questions that I desire to discuss.

To memory is to put an 'impact here and an impact there' as ME. **Here** an impact, **there** an impact, **everywhere an impact,** impact...

Entanglement occurs automatically, but the dynamics is determined by ME, so it is particularized around ME.

'To memory' or 'to memories', that is the question

On the other hand, if I do not bring myself to life and happen to my living, I will do entanglement by default. Letting life happen to me is living by default. Entanglement by default is what memories are. Memories are random entanglements.

Memories are reactions to the universe.

That is why **I bathwave all of my reactions until I finally stop reacting and discontenting my selves.**

In fact, I can bathwave facing and embracing what I react to and then quantum shift to 'I understand that **I am** the mirror-calls (miracles) that I am living' and that will put an end to the need for bathwaving eventually.

The pattern of reactive victimization was so old and deep in me that it took me years to see it clearly and shift it. I hope this benefits others from my efforts, to be able to shift it with less effort of time and energy.

That is, when I truly understand that all the mirror-calls (miracles) are me, I can stop reacting to them and get on with 'minding' my life as I truly desire.

When I begin to mind my life as I truly desire, I am beyond languaging.

The hazards of languaging or 'emergent' is nature's way of replacing languaging

Benjamin Whorf wrote that the way we speak these days, has become our way of living. It has limited us to not being what we truly want to be and that is why it is very important to recognize the presence of old languaging and begin to do quantum communication.

The first step in quantum communication is to just describe everything, especially that which I desire.

Secondly, in speaking with others it facilitates emergent to do declarative questioning as described in the chapter entitled 'quantum communication'.

The third step is to listen to my selves with the support of these tools as needed until I am automatically living what I am describing.

To describe again what I desire to do and what I desire to be so that finally I realize that it is Who I Am... as a RESPLENDENT, ILLUMINATEDBEING.

The intimate relationship of self

The triunity described within the text of this book is the basis of the intimate relationship that I am always living (though possibly unawares or by default) of the personalbeing, eternalbeing, and resplendent illuminatedbeing.

These three are separate just like the spinning manifestation, the vast quantum wave and the aware new wavicle, which provides for their intimate interaction or there would be no expanding universe.

Want to live potential linear evolution or definite universal quantum expansion?

Evolution is being enhanced by the quantum living of the intimate relationshift to the United States of Awareness (USA) beyond cause and effect. The old cause and effect way called it a tentative ' goal'.

It is important that we understand the huge difference between the old goal oriented thinking and the quantum world's way with miracles beyond cause and effect. The difference is authoritative simultaneity and emergent mirror-calls AS your BATHWAVEs, rather than 'caused or effected ' BY someone elses's BATHWAVEs.

It is the 'Land of AS' instead of the Land of OZ. Quantum expansion involves being aware in any way, beginning with feeling or doing or thinking. Recognizing expansion's importance in our lives is appropriate with the advent of the quantum awareness of our times.

CHAPTER 32

ENTANGLEMENT TALISMAN (ET)
YOUR WHOLOGRAPHIC SELF & QUANTUM COACHING

Objects as information

The science of psychometry has observed that objects contain virtual information as a wholographic film. The imprint that we leave in our environment transcends time and space. It occurs instantly as an entanglement. When we are aware of our resplendence, we can hold an object which another person has lived with and know things about that person that we haven't consciously been aware of. Psychics have demonstrated this all through history. This is the definition of what a talisman would be. It is an object that contains memories as entanglements of a selected moment.

What if an object contained the information of your resplendence and you keep that on you to remind yourself of resplendency throughout the day, especially when in need. By definition, the nature of your own declared virtual self would be part of the information that records your resplendency. Now if a person who already lives and knows their resplendency puts that information into an object, say a crystal or a piece of jewelry that can be kept on your body, then that information would resonate in your being as an entanglement of information.

This is why teachers give their apprentices a talisman to keep on their being to remind them of the awareness that the teacher has of the apprentice's resplendency. You could call this a resplendent mirror-call. When it is about who you truly are as a resplendent being, then it becomes a fixed point of reference for you in living your resplendency.

Einstein said that in order to know the universe, you must fix a point of reference. This fixed point of reference is you. In being a coach or a guide or a diamond in the life of another, as one instructs in these matters, one could give an object that the person can keep on them at times of awareness shifting. We may already have one or can give ourselves this object with the intention of it serving our awareness of resplendency. A friend of mine wears a necklace of a dove to remind her of her resplendency.

Quantum coaching

This book can be used as a quantum coach by asking it a question, opening to any page, reading and interacting with it. Choose a number 1-64 and read. Bathwaving can be used for transfiguring as desired.

Teleseminars

There are live discussions by the late Roger B. Cotting to freely share about resplendency. Constant replay is possible on emergentmiracles.net.

Quantum Wave Living Academy

There is a Quantum Wave Living Academy where programs for expansion of your awareness and becoming a coach are available. E-mail me for availability.

Awareness of resplendency is free of discontenting

Entanglement allows me to extract information from the environment. Dreams clearly show me how I am thinking and/or how I am judging. My dreams will also tell me when I am free of discontenting.

The only way to know whether I am aware and living resplendency is to see when I am free of discontenting.

However, we tend to lie, hide and deny our discontentings, which will manifest eventually as various illnesses or difficulties in relationships or situations or events of our life.

As we free ourselves to set the context of our life as our resplendentbeing to live our desires, we can be free of discontenting.

In my case, setting my life as networking resplendency as a statement of my eternalbeing, I can use this point of reference in everything I do. When what I do is not networking resplendence, then I will discontent myself automatically.

When I'm discontenting myself, I can simply ask: How could I be networking resplendency here and shift my doings, thoughts, feelings to one of networking resplendency?

With those two questions I shift my discontenting almost instantly.

Seeing wholey you

Time was personally constructed so that everything in our lives would not happen at once. In time it happens as bits and pieces. Time allows us to break up the whologram of us and then later we can re-sort it when we wish.

This is using life as memories. Sometimes we lose the ability to see the big picture, to see the whologrphic reality of us, which is our resplendent vision, or our emergent-eyes, which sees what is emergent.

When we look through our emergent-eyes, we see what is emergent, the wholographic picture.

Time still allows us to break it up into bits and pieces. I referred to this earlier when I described Mozart's way of perceiving a whole symphony of music in an instant. This was his resplendent ability. Then, as he said, it would take weeks or months to write it down on paper, which is using our personal self to reconstruct a resplendent vision. Mozart is known for not making corrections and getting it correct on first writing. This is the nature of the example of resplendency... also as in using arithmetic in a Chapter 15.

Personality grows by taking things in. Resplendency expands by radiating out.

If we choose five as our declared eternalbeing, then we can express it as 2+3 in this moment. That does not stop us from expressing it as 4+1 or 6-1 in the next moment. Those are the examples of using time to express our five-ish nature or our virtual nature as a five. This is an extremely simple but profound expression of resplendency. Though it is limited in its creativity on the five side, it is unlimited on the personal virtual two-part side.

Eternalbeing and personalbeing's interaction is what is giving us our five-ish way of being, which is our resplendent nature. The resplendent nature is radiant and has the ability to reach out and gather constituents and components or ingredients which we call our sacred state or our conditions of expansion.

Being who I truly want to be is my declaration. It is my five-ish choice. When I live that with all of my passion, I can begin to see around me who I really am. In living my resplendence, people will not discontent me. It is up to me as I begin to free myself to living this choice of my declared eternalbeing completely without discontenting myself. When free of discontenting, I find my resplendence expands and my life reaches all those who are desiring their own resplendence.

In sharing my resplendence with others, I expand my own resplendence. I inspire other resplendent beings with whom I am free to communicate and in that interaction, are creating more conditions of expansion which is resplendent expansion.

My eternal theme sings me home

Eternal theme (ET) is a gift of resplendence. It is interesting that I can use ET as a shortened version because ET, the movie, had a motto of going home. In a sense, resplendency is the home I were born into. In resplendency I rebirth my star again and again in this life into resplendency.

My memory of resplendency is a whole image which is not in time, not in bits and pieces. Some metals have a memory. Once the metal is shaped into a form, it retains that. When changed the metal will go back into its original form if allowed to. Some plastics also have this ability to maintain a memory. The quantum world is the level on which this kind of timeless, wholographic memory is contained. This memory of our resplendency is an illustration of entanglement.

People also contain this entanglement as my choices. My choices then access whatever we desire. DNA is the vehicle for expressing the memory we desire. This is a different way of using memory. It is not of the past and yet, because it is not in bits and pieces, it is a large picture.

The verb minding, on the other hand, is being emergent as I eternally express. To do this, I just need to focus on my constituents, my ingredients, and my components. I keep adding those ingredients which I desire to my life as memories in order to memory our life as we desire, as a wholographic picture.

I live using trial and error and my past memories until I get the clear picture of who I am. In clarifying my self-image as my resplendent illuminatedbeing, I am always ready to express that freely to all those who seek, knock, and ask.

Polishing the 'halo' or disentanglement and suscitation of resplendence

My master teacher of TCM, Dr. Lam Kong of Oakland, California gave me a tool among his abundant gifts, which is a method to use at the end of day or interaction that leaves you feeling discontented or less than your resplendent self.

The halo polishing exercise

Hands above the head, palms facing the ground, moving hands in twenty circles around the top of head, like tracing the 'halo' around the head for twenty circles. Bend over and shake your hands into the earth three times, avoiding the feet. Dr. Kong recommended five repetitions of the above after acupuncture or three times after massage. This exercise takes only a few minutes.

It may be a good practice for beginning anew and connecting to eternalbeing and resplendent illuminatedbeing especially in the evening.

Swinging arms exercise

A simple form of Chi gung, called swinging arms, energy resuscitation is also useful for energy renewing. It takes 10 minutes twice a day. See YouTube for instruction under 'swinging arms chi gung'. It can be done while saying your replacements out loud before bed and in the morning.

Mahalo to the kind generosity of Dr. Lam Kong.

Mahalo to you dear reader! May your sacred resplendent triunities shine and continue to expand the universe!

APPENDICES

Muscle Testing

Heartwaving Technique Checklist

Eight Basic Bottom Line Mirror Calls

Work/Play Page for Relationship Love Letters

Heartwaving Maturing Technique Checklist

Work Page For Reading and Naming Your Eternalbeing

Suggestions for Connecting With Your Eternalbeing

Your MRI: Your Mirror-call Reflecting Image

Five Element Questionnaire

Quick Reference Tongue Maps

Tongue Diagnosis Map

Your Eternal Gift to Others

Tool Box Chapters:

How to Heartwave: Chapter 4

Maturing Your Quantum Shift: Chapter 7

Eight Bottom Lines: Chapter 4

Relationship Love Letters: Chapter 5

Eternalbeing Naming: Chapter 11

Your MRI: Chapter 24

Five Element Questionnaire: Chapter 24

HEARTWAVES

Bathwave Loving Transformation (BLT)

Face / Embrace whole Body, especially when upset

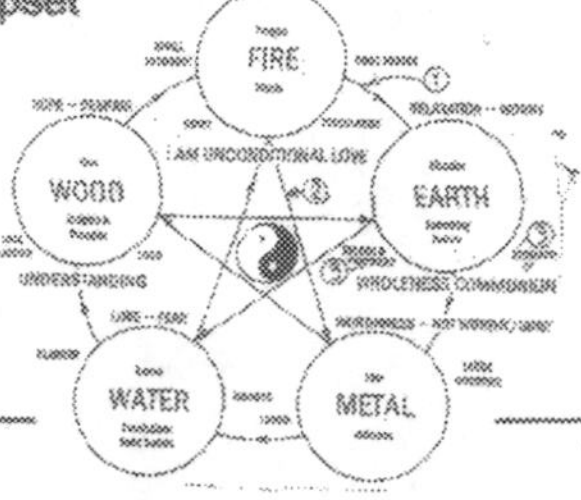

● _____

● _____

●Element: _____

_Organ: _____

●B. ALTH WAVE _____

● _____

● _____

● _____

● _____

● _____

Quantum Shift
3 x's Can-Will-Present tense each

Replace with Grace touch the central channel front and back.

Dates: Repeat Daily : _____

Weekly : _____

2 x's per month : _____

● _____

● _____

● _____

● _____

● _____

● _____

● _____

● _____

Muscle Testing

Put thumb and baby finger of your weakest hand together to form a ring.

Put index finger of your other hand in the center of the ring.

Say your name while moving your index finger against the connection of your two fingers forming your "o" ring. This movement will test the strength of your "o" ring bond.

The bond will be strong and hold if you have drunk enough water.

If the bond is weak, and your finger goes through the "o" ring, drink two or three ounces of water and try again.

Say " I am a cabbage" and test the strength of your "o" ring again.

It should test weak with your index finger breaking the bond, unless you are a cabbage!

Use the "o" ring test before and after Heartwaving and doing a quantum shift.

Muscle testing answers true/false and yes/no types of questions.

Be sure to stay hydrated as your muscles need water to perform this technique.

Hint: Practice using the "o" ring test with various statements to start to feel the difference between a weak and strong response.

Ace of Heartwaving

Bathwave Loving Transformation (BLT)

A QUANTUM MOLECULAR MOVIE SHIFTING TECHNIQUE

It's all shiftable material. Are you open and willing to shift?

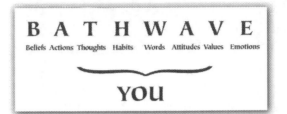

Part One:
Face It and Embrace It

- *Stroke body from head to toe*
- *Say, feel, and think of what you want to shift at the same time.*
- *Keep eyes open*

BACK = PAST
FRONT = FUTURE
SIDES = PRESENT

Don't miss a spot!

Part Two:
Replace It With Grace

- *Say what you desire three times:*
  - *with verb "can" (potential tense)*
  - *with verb "will" (future tense)*
  - *with present tense*

Quantum Shift

At the same time do a simple stroke across seven nerve hormone chakras:
With one hand on forehead and other hand on back of neck, move to top of the head, down to ears, to throat, past heart to lower abdomen while one hand moves to the bottom of the spine.

• Drink as much water as possible •

OPTIONAL MUSCLE TEST: *Put thumb and baby finger on your weakest hand together to form a ring. Put index finger from other hand in center of ring. Say your name and test the strength of your ring. It will be strong if you have drunk enough water. Say "I am a cabbage" and test. It will be weak (unless you are a cabbage). Use this test to test the efficacy before and after bathwaving and quantum shifting.*

Eight Basic Bottom Line

Mirror-Calls
(Miracles)

AWAKENING RESPLENDENCY
"Ace" / Heartwaving

PART ONE: *Bathwaves:* Face It and Embrace It;
Speaking and feeling while lovingly stroking body

PART TWO: Replace it with Grace/*Quantum Shift*
Circle mid-line with hands while saying quanta. Must test for shift.

Bathwaves →	*Quantum Shift*

1. ACCUSING
   I accuse people of things.
   I judge myself and/or others.
   I feel something is against me or blocking me.
   I feel accused or judged by others.
	1. I appreciate people or things.
	   I love myself and others unconditionally.
	   The Universe is good and benevolent and
	   works to help me.
	   I feel valuable. I feel gentle with myself.

2. BLAMING
   I am blaming others.
   I am blaming myself.
   I feel blamed.
	2. I bless others for the way they are a mirror-
	   call of my resplendency.
	   I bless myself.
	   I stop blaming myself.

3. COMPLAINING/CRITICIZING
   I am complaining about/criticizing myself
   and/or others or situations.
	3. I am complimentary with myself and others.
	   I complement and commune with myself
	   and others.

4. LYING
   I deceive myself and/or others.
	4. I am honest and open with myself at all times. I
	   am open and honest with others with discernment.

5. HIDING I am hiding from myself and/or others.	5. I am visible and speak my desires.

6. DENYING
   I have been burying things under and
   "unconscious" rug unknowingly.
	6. I am ready, willing and able to know
	   everything about me.

7. DEFENDING I am defending or explaining myself or others.	7. I am fine being just the way I am.
8. JUSTIFYING I am justifying and proving myself to others.	8. I do as I desire. I am good just as I am.

Work/Play Page for Relationship Love Letters

Here is a simple form for you to use in translating the love letters you are giving yourself. When Relationshifting your mirror-calls attempt to be specific with the issue:

_____ has an issue (_____) with _____.

Example:
Angela has resentment toward her mother.

- *Mothers* are about our (feminine side's) self-nurturance.
- *Fathers* are about our (masculine side's) self-guidance.
- *Partners and friends* are about our own beloved self of the gender that they are.
- *Children* are about our creativity...masculine or feminine, depending on their gender.
- *Authoritarian characters* might be about our self-guidance/discipline in the gender that they are.
- *Animals* pertain to what that animal means to us specifically. If you have no idea, look at some dream book imagery, such as:
    - Cats might be about your feminine side.
    - Dogs, about unconditional love in your life.
    - Horses might be high ideals.
    - Birds, transcending or bird's eye view.

Translation inserts:
My masculinity or femininity (whatever you physically are) has an issue with *translation of person* from basic mirror call list.

_____has an issue(_____) with _____.

_____has _____with _____.

Example:
My femininity has resentment toward my self-nurturance.

Muscle test should be strong. This is the complete BATHWAVE to take with you to the Heartwaving technique. After doing Part 1 of Heartwaving it will be easier for you to come up with a useful quantum shift for Part 2.

Heartwaving Maturing Technique Check List

Part One: Face It and Embrace It

Jot down BATHWAVE you wish to shift below.

_____

____ Muscle test.

____ Eyes open
____ Lovingly and compassionately stroke body from head to toe, back, front and sides
____ At the same time saying, feeling and thinking of what you want to shift.
____ Remember, eyes open.
____ Don't miss a spot!

Part Two: Replace It With Grace

____ Jot down your desired quantum shift below, stating as much in the positive as you can.

_____

While doing the quantum shift movements with eyes open,
____ State your desire in the potential tense: I can + verb...
____ State your desire in the future tense: I will + verb...
____ State your desire in the present tense: I + verb...

Quantum shift movement:
- Place one hand on your back behind your heart and other hand on your back from below your heart.
- Move top hand over the head midline, over the face to throat, past heart and lower abdomen past the groin while the other hand moves to the back bottom of the spine to eventually meet the other hand below the pelvis.
- If seated just move both hands to the chair and move the pelvis on chair to complete the cycle.

____ Muscle test your shift. See Appendix.

If the muscle stays strong you have shifted.

Muscle testing to mature the shift

____Ask by muscle testing whether you need to mature this shift through your life into your future. If the muscle is strong and the link holds that means yes.

____Start testing the shift at the age of five-years-old. If strong continue counting by 5's till it goes weak. Say the link broke at 20 years old. Then go back to 15 years old and count by ones, 16, 17, 18, at 19 it goes weak. Ask yourself what event or activity is significant to you at 18 years old? When something comes up proceed.

____Muscle test and ask if this is the action you are holding on to at 18. If strong, continue to the Part One: Face It and Embrace It step and Part Two step with an appropriate new twist on the quantum shift as above. With the new quantum shift ask if you are 20. Strong. 30? Strong. 40? Weak. 35? strong 36, 37, 38, 39 weak. Ask yourself what you are holding on to at age 38? When you think of something proceed below.

____ Muscle test the BATHWAVE at that age. If strong, repeat the Face It and Embrace it steps talking about the new situation. After you shift it come up with new quantum shift for Part Two steps as above.

____ Muscle test the new quantum shift for the age 38 starting at age 40 and continuing to age 100 or more. If the muscle is weak at any age, ask yourself again what might have happened at that age to you or what significance that age has to you. Continue repeating this process until the shift is clear at all ages.

Work Page for Reading and Naming Eternalbeing

List eight accomplishments of which you are proud in the order that come to mind.

1._____

_____

2._____

_____

3._____

_____

4._____

_____

5._____

_____

6._____

_____

7._____

8._____

_____

When possible, select a magazine cover for each accomplishment that captures the feeling or essence of that accomplishment.

Guidelines for the Person Doing the Eternalbeing Reading:

1. Find the action of the first accomplishment that describes eternalbeing's action.

2. Ask if the person would be satisfied doing this action for the rest of their lives, for themselves and for others.

3. Check each of the remaining seven accomplishments to see if they are compatible with the action of eternalbeing.

4. Give your eternalbeing a name that honors his or her accomplishments and eternal theme.

Suggestions For Connecting With Your Eternalbeing

- Practice believing you have an eternalbeing.

- Practice seeing and experiencing your relationships differently. This prepares for knowing or experiencing yourself as multiple relationships.

- Practice paying close attention to your dreams. We play multiple roles in our dreams.

- Practice being content. Being content is the absence of discontent

- Use your breath to bring matters into focus: Inhale what you desire. Inhale while thinking, "I bring myself to my eternalbeing. Conditions of expansion surround me."

- The greatest meaning of life is not that of serving others; it is offering to life, for in that action you draw to yourself. Offering yourself to life is the true meaning of self-ness.

- Begin observing and feeling yourself.

- Practice adding to yourself, i.e. add the dimension of eternalbeing. Fill your cup with new stuff to flush out the old stuff.

- Practice past story regression process that includes many avenues, from self-hypnosis to shamanic journeying.

- Practice standing outside yourself observing yourself.

- Step out of the old ways of doing things. Change your context to the ways of an eternalbeing. Get outside of your comfort zone, i.e. meaning get out of the context of a composed life.

- Practice putting everything you hear into images. We must be able to speak the language of eternalbeing.

- Practice being everything you do.

- Practice writing letters to your eternalbeing, and writing answers back to yourself as your eternalbeing.

- Practice considering and describing the partner and intimate relationship you would like to have for a lifetime.

- Practice not asking others for permission.

- Practice making connections.

- Practice thinking in eternal terms.

- Decide and declare (if only to yourself) that we are only meeting and experiencing our eternalbeing.

- Declare and commit in life. Do not struggle to achieve commitment. Instead stand content and carry commitments with you at all times.

- The highest state of enlightenment and wisdom is "not" a quiet mind; it is to keep yourself in a state of contentment.

- Tell your senses what you want them to sense, i.e. train your senses to sense your eternalbeing.

- What you want is not what you want until you make that what you already have!

- Practice expansive focusing!

- Practice maintaining your focus on another person, on an object, or on a task at hand, without relaxing or changing your focus to yourself!

- Create images in your mind and observe yourself creating those images.

- You already are an eternalbeing! So practice feeling yourself as an eternalbeing!

- Think of how living in the "now" deceives you.

- Develop your memory and self-awareness.

- Pay close attention to your attitudes and emotions.

- Practice watching people.

- Give yourself a direction to follow each day.

- Ask: What is mind?

- Practice not planning your life.

- Set aside time each day for involving yourself in preparing to experience your eternalbeing.

- Practice seeing others as eternalbeings.

- Practice directing energy around you to flow through you.

Suggestions For Connecting With Your Eternalbeing

- Practice believing you have an eternalbeing.

- Practice seeing and experiencing your relationships differently. This prepares for knowing or experiencing yourself as multiple relationships.

- Practice paying close attention to your dreams. We play multiple roles in our dreams.

- Practice being content. Being content is the absence of discontent

- Use your breath to bring matters into focus: Inhale what you desire. Inhale while thinking, "I bring myself to my eternalbeing. Conditions of expansion surround me."

- The greatest meaning of life is not that of serving others; it is offering to life, for in that action you draw to yourself. Offering yourself to life is the true meaning of self-ness.

- Begin observing and feeling yourself.

- Practice adding to yourself, i.e. add the dimension of eternalbeing. Fill your cup with new stuff to flush out the old stuff.

- Practice past story regression process that includes many avenues, from self-hypnosis to shamanic journeying.

- Practice standing outside yourself observing yourself.

- Step out of the old ways of doing things. Change your context to the ways of an eternalbeing. Get outside of your comfort zone, i.e. meaning get out of the context of a composed life.

- Practice putting everything you hear into images. We must be able to speak the language of eternalbeing.

- Practice being everything you do.

- Practice writing letters to your eternalbeing, and writing answers back to yourself as your eternalbeing.

- Practice considering and describing the partner and intimate relationship you would like to have for a lifetime.

- Practice not asking others for permission.

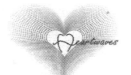

Five Element Questionnaire

Listed are the common TCM word associations with the five elements. Circle one or more words that mostly fit you. Create a five element chart. Fill it in using the totals below. The largest number of items in an elemental area indicate the element's organs which need to be focused on with Heartwaves, nutrition and herbs.

	Wood	Fire	Earth	Metal	Water
Senses affected	a. sight	b. speech	c. taste	d. smell	e. hearing
Body parts affected	a. nails	b. skin color	c. lips	d. abnormal body hair or skin condition	e. head hair
Liquids emitted (too much or too little)	a. tears	b. swat	c. saliva	d. mucus	e. urine
Body odor	a. rancid	b. burnt	c. fragrant	d. fleshy	e. putrid
Temperament	a. depression	b. up and down	c. obsession	d. anguish	e. fear
Emotion	a. anger	b. joy	c. sympathy	d. grief	e. paranoia
Flavor craving	a. sour	b. bitter	c. sweet	d. hot	e. salty
Sound of voice	a. loud	b. laughy	c. sing-song	d. weepy	e. groany
Weather that bothers you	a. windy	b. hot	c. humid	d. dry	e. cold
Seasons you like	a. spring	b. summer	c. mild summer	d. autumn	e. winter
Skin hue and color	a. green	b. red	c. yellow	d. white	e. black

TOTAL of Items circled in each element category:

# Wood	# Fire	# Earth	# Metal /Air	# Water

QUICK REFERENCE TONGUE MAPS

If you see the patterns below, go to Chapter 27.

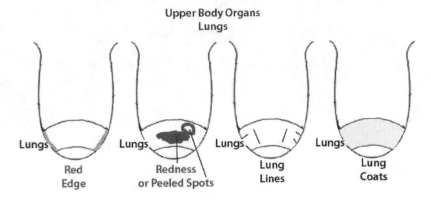

Upper Body Organs
Lungs

Lungs — Red Edge

Lungs — Redness or Peeled Spots

Lungs — Lung Lines

Lungs — Lung Coats

Lower Body Organ Signs

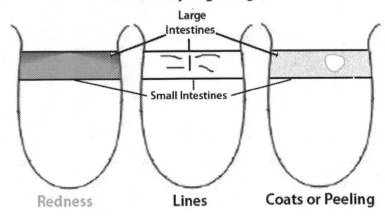

Large Intestines

Small Intestines

Redness

Lines

Coats or Peeling

If you see the patterns below, go to Chapter 26.

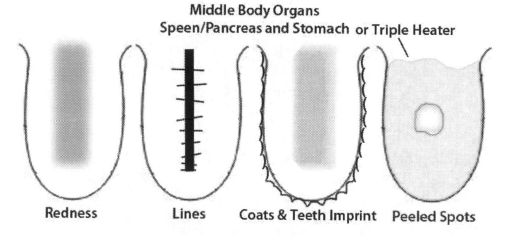

Middle Body Organs
Speen/Pancreas and Stomach or Triple Heater

Redness   Lines   Coats & Teeth Imprint   Peeled Spots

Note: For Triple Heater refer to Chapter 30.

If you see these patterns, see Chapter 28.

Lower Body Organ Signs
Kidney

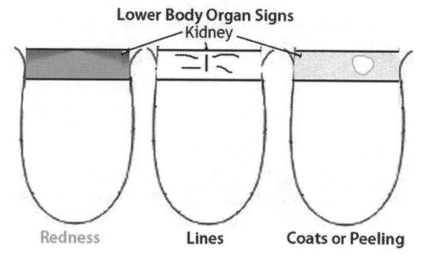

Redness   Lines   Coats or Peeling

For these patterns go to Chapter 29.

Middle Body Organ Signs
Liver and Gall Bladder

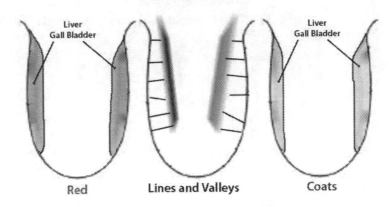

Liver
Gall Bladder

Liver
Gall Bladder

Red · **Lines and Valleys** · Coats

If you see these patterns go to Chapter 30.
Upper Body Organs
Heart or Pericardium

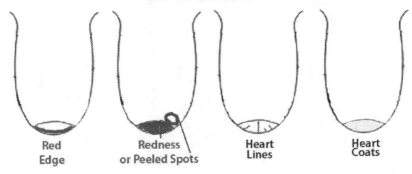

Red
Edge

Redness
or Peeled Spots

Heart
Lines

Heart
Coats

If you see these patterns go to Chapter 30.

Lower Body Organ Signs

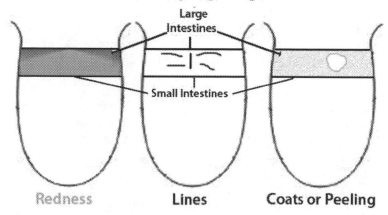

Redness   Lines   Coats or Peeling

Speaking In Magical Tongues:

The Love Letters We Are Giving Ourselves

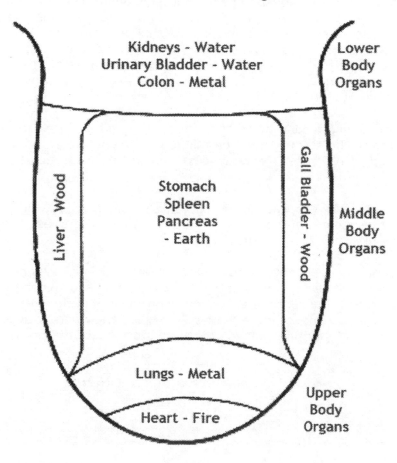

[Figure A.11]

Your Eternal Gift to Others

1. Life has not forsaken you! ...you have forgotten your eternalself and life! ...are you willing to fully live the eternalbeing that completely encloses and acknolwledges you? ...and feel this eternal awareness and presence and empowerment surging through you? ...overwhelming your fears and doubts ...and pushing them out of you?

2. The ego self and life and drama you are willing to defend and justify at all costs must be vital to you!? ...and it is! ...for it is your eternalself and life! ...actually, it is the very life and essence of your eternalself! ...which , before entering your life today, you promised to live and express openly!...to inspire and empower others to awaken their eternalself as well!

3. While many teachers declare that you mistakenly consider your ego to be who you actually are! ...it is those teachers who are mistaken! ... for your ego is exactly who you are! ...but you don't believe this because you've experienced too many problems and difficulties in living and expressing your ego ...isn't that right? ...and other people constantly remind you of that ...don't they?

4. Believe it or not, you experience problems and difficulties because you are giving birth to a self that doesn't speak your language of words! ...and needs you as an interpreter! ...how well are you doing? ...are you beginning to sense your tremendous role in life? ...this is not, alone, the reason for your being alive, this is merely your role in life that motivates you today ...and will offer even greater more fulfilling and enriching meaning and purpose as you form and birth your eternalself as you truly desire that to be! Are you willing to transfigure yourself to an eternal mortalbeing?

5. Since you understand that *what is composed will decompose* your Eternal Gift to Others, to be eternal, must be minded as a separate and different whole, not composed of old beliefs, experiences , and memories! ...nor as language is composed!

6. Do not demean your ego! ...put an understanding of your Eternal Gift to Others into everything you do ...as an offering! ...as an awareness and realization that inspires others to their eternalself!

7. The essence and ultimate nature of yourself today are synonymous! ...and that is clearly revealed in your continuously repeated and experienced beliefs-thoughts-attitudes-emotions-words-actions you identify with most strongly and securely! ...these do not compose your eternalself ...**they are your eternalself!** ...and the drama of your life today is the birth story of your eternalself ...as your gift to others!

What is your Eternal Gift to Others?

ACKNOWLEDGEMENTS

Did you ever think, that you were doing everything 'right', and then, all of a sudden, the universe strongly says, "Look again."And being Sicilian, I needed 'strong' wake up calls . . . is liver cancer strong enough for you? It was for me, since my Aunt Grace died of cancer, while gazing at a photo I had taken in college of light coming from behind trees in the shape of a cross . . . Well, this wake up call, woke up the mirror-calls (miracles) of Relationshifting and Quantum Resplendent Living.

With a Ph.D in Biochemistry from UC Berkeley, a 30 year successful clientele of Traditional Chinese Medicine(TCM) and a twenty year college of TCM I founded, I still faced this diagnosis of liver cancer. So after 20 years now, It just goes to show, that it's not what you know that 'saves' you, but what you don't know, AND you are willing to open to knowing, that keeps you in the glow. Oprah and my son have demonstrated that.

At 70 years old, I am bringing together, 48 years of TCM clinical work and teaching, scientific research in neurochemistry about glia & nerve protein communication, that was reviewed in Nature, a Ph.D. of Biochemistry, the study of quantum mechanics and living with Hopi Indians and their prophecy. I love reweaving a web, networking these fields of east and west, . . . north and south.

That's all the herstory you get. The rest of this book is a practical, and I wish, humorous, guide to reading the love letters, you are giving yourself, that will support you, being in your own unique eternal glow. It is edutaining', which is one of the words that the infamous comedian Swami Beyondananda, coined, in a conversation we had about developing sit down comedy for 'healers'. He is a star in a movie script I am writing turning my herstory into a triunistory.

This book is the sharing of my practical Relationshifting based on the quantum world, with 20 years of testimonial results. I am grateful to the great teachers who have been guiding me. My father, Angelo, who was an organic chemist and mother, Stella, an award winning teacher, who let me extract DNA from chicken livers in her kitchen in high school, and then mutate it with nitrous acid. My communioning personal, social self, has much gratitude for the relationshifting mirror-calls(miracles) that continue encouraging expansion and maturing. I am forever indebted to my first husband, Shanti Satterlee, for the embodiment of a son, Mark Angelo Longo, my forever inspirer, through thick and thin. Mark is the one who understands this work in his guts and finds his own ways as a strong thinker/feeler, to apply it. I love his work and his valuable mirror-calls to resplendency. He is especially there for me, when I forget my communion.

Dennis Spain, quantum physicist and tutor, earthen oxen and second husband, who slows me down as best he can and shares, as I apply what I am aware of as fast as an earthen rat can, in the chinese astrological sense. Elena Bonn/Dultz, clinical psychotherapist quoted in the book and younger sister, who kept us sane as children, singing & dancing and still does. My brother Dr. James F. Longo, MD has never ceased to amaze me from the time he played the Beatles songs and a sitar to how he raises his beautiful daughters that are like songs from his heart.

My high school science teachers, Sisters Monica and Dorothy (like in Oz). My favorite college organic chemistry professor, the late Dr. Jack Kampmeir, who brought out the 'poetic dance' of the electrons in the molecules and thereby saved my college career. My biochemistry graduate advisor, Dr. Ed Penhoet, who was courageous and believed in me enough, to give me a space in his virology lab to do my own brain chemistry thing. He surprised everyone when my discoveries were successful, reviewed in the prestigious journal named "Nature".

Next, my brilliant TCM professor, Dr. Lam Kong of Oakland who introduced me to the world of chi in healing, though I swore I would never be a doctor, converted me, and still does to this day, generously taking me into his family in the traditional chinese way.

And my inimitable, mystery school mentor, the late Roger B. Cotting and his composer wife, dentist, and co-creator, Misty Mistler. Roger, a retired successful architect, after thirty self-published books of philosophy based on science, still manages to keep me moving into "what I don't know", expanding into the context of 'what I desire to communion with eternally'. My quantum writing is inspired by Roger B. Cotting, and ET, my unique eternal theme. I am dedicating this second edition to Roger B. Cotting posthumously.

I am also grateful to the Kiwi Composer and close friend I admire, Jeffree Clarkson, whose music continues to bless and relax the treatments I give. My friend Scott Way, who proved how incredible TCM transforms one, in and of itself. and my favorite male cousin Chuckie Longo and his lovely family of Niagara falls N.Y., who play along with my wild schemes, from acupuncture to cooking. My Kiwi brothers, Tejas Engel, John Hamilton, Peter Azim Johnston, Ralph Cox and Brian Stoddard, who continue to amaze me and themselves with Relationshifting.

I thank my girlfriend mirror-calls from the bottom of my heart, to mention only a few, chronologically, or it would fill this book: Jaya Lalita, from upstairs apartment, who would keep me honest as she spun her beautiful wools into stories of hats and shawls that warmed our lives. Next, would be my first dancing teacher/sister, Lesandre Bailey/Ayrey, from the Royal Ballet Troupe of London, who taught me the elegant, international vocabulary of movement, beauty, and grace.

Catherine Nagelstadt, gorgeous opera singer of our hearts desires, who makes grown men cry from the touch of her heart's voice, incapacitating the one I hired to video her singing an Italian Song for TCMCH's 'funraiser', which I never got to hear. Jaiia Earthschild, a mentor and musical writing tantric sister, who was always walking along side my ventures in her own inimitably creative, healing, and inspiring way. Padma Laycock, my belly dancing poetic muse who encourages us to speak and dance what is alive for us.

Janine Seymour, Kiwi/ Aussie who has found and inspires us with her own voice, while using heartwaving relationshifting methods. Joy Farry, from Auckland, NZ, who combined these methods of transformation into her moving belly dance repertoire and life. I want to study more dance with you! And all my study sisters from TCMCH like Karen MacIsaac's heart of gold, Zizi Zolten, willing to transform herself to have children. Sharon Rincon's seven children, drinking herbs, eating and bearing the fruits of her study. Christine Bowden and her two daughters, Teal and Alexia, who at a young age studied along with their mother and shared everything they gathered with their friends. My favorite female cousins from Nancy Powell who studied at TCMCH with me, but didn't have to, since her presence did it all, and likewise for Claudia Claire's presence.

I will put the rest in another place, in my heart, as this page is too small for all the sisters and brothers who are moving me. My newest girlfriend and her husband, Maren and Mark Schmidt, Montessori Books author and online workshop leader, who inspired me constantly by editing this book as she lived what I was writing about and taught me everything I know about book composing.

Without her this book wouldn't have been half as much fun!

BIBLIOGRAPHY AND READING LIST

Armstrong. A. (2008). *Celebrating Partnership with Alison Armstrong: CD and Workbook*. Sherman Oaks, CA: PAX Programs Incorporated.

Armstrong, A. (2007*). Making sense of men*. Sherman Oaks, CA: PAX Programs Incorporated.

Armstrong, A. (2007*). Making sense of men*. CD: Sherman Oaks, CA: PAX Programs Incorporated.

Asimov. I. (1972). *The gods themselves*. New York, NY: Bantam Books.

Bach, R. (1962). *A gift of wings*. New York, NY: Ziff-Davis.

Baerbel. (2006). *DNA can be influenced and reprogrammed by words and frequencies: Russian DNA discoveries*. Retrieved July 21, 2012, from http://www.soulsofdistortion.nl/dna1.html.

Baron, R. (1994). *The enneagram made easy: discover the nine types of people*. New York, NY: HarperCollins.

Becker, R. (1990). *Cross currents: the promise of electromedicine, the perils of electropollution*. New York, NY: J P Tarcher.

Beerlandt, C. (1993). *The key to self-liberation*. Beerlandt Publications.

Beinfield, H. (1991). *Between heaven and earth: a guide to chinese medicine*. New York, NY: Ballantine Books.

Bethell, T. (2009). *Questioning Einstein: is relativity necessary?* Pueblo West, CO: Vales Lake Publishing.

Blackerby, R. (1993). *Application of chaos theory to psychological models*. Austin, TX: Performance Strategies Publications.

Bly, R. (2004). *Kabir ecstatic poems*. Boston, MA: Beacon Press.

Bonn, E. (2009). Turbulent contextualism: bearing complexity towards change. *International Journal of Psychoanalytic Self-Psychology*. Volume 5, Issue 1, pp 1-18.

Boissere, R. (1990). *The return of pahana: a Hopi myth.* Salem, MA: Sigo Press.

Braden, G. (2008). *The spontaneous healing of belief: shattering the paradigm of false limits.* USA: Hay House.

Brailsford, B. (2004). *Song of the old tides.* Christchurch, NZ: Stoneprint Press.

Brailsford, B. (1995). *Song of the stone.* Christchurch, NZ: Stoneprint Press.

Briggs, J. & Peat, F. (1989). *Turbulent mirror.* New York, NY: Harper and Row Publishers.

Bryuere, R. (1989). *Wheels of light: chakras, auras, and the healing energy of the body.* New York, NY: Fireside.

Campbell, J. (1989). *The way of the seeded earth: mythologies of the primitive planters: the middle and southern Americas.* New York, NY: Harper & Row.

Capra, F. (1996). *The web of life: a new scientific understanding of living systems.* New York, NY: Random House.

Cerney, J. (1974/1999). *Acupuncture without needles.* Paramus, NJ: Prentiss Hall.

Chia, M. (2006). *Chi self-massage: the Taoist way of rejuventation.* Rochester, VT: Destiny Books.

Childre, D. (2004). *From chaos to coherence: the power to change performance.* Boulder Creek, CA: HeartMath LLC.

Chopra, D. (1989). *Quantum healing: exploring the frontiers of mind/body medicine.* New York, NY: Bantam Books.

Coelho, P. (1993). *The alchemist.* New York, NY: HarperCollins Publishers.

Colton, A. (1973). *Watch your dreams: a master key and reference book for all initiates of the soul, the mind and the heart.* Glendale, CA: The Ann Ree Colton Foundation.

Connelly, D. (1979*). Traditional acupuncture: the law of the five elements.* Columbia, MD: Traditional Acupuncture Inc.

Croca, J.R. (2003). *Towards a nonlinear quantum physics:* River Edge, NJ: World Scientific Publishing, Co.

Csikszentmihalyi, M. (1997). *Finding flow in everyday life.* New York, NY: Basic Books.

Doidge, N. (2007). *The brain that changes itself: stories of personal triumph from the frontiers of brain science.* New York, NY: Penguin Books.

Davies, P. (1993). *The mind of God: the scientific basis for a rational world.* New York, NY: Simon and Schuster.

Dyer, W. (2005). *The power of intention.* USA: Hay House.

Emoto, M. (2005). *The hidden messages in water.* New York, NY: Atria Books.

Emoto, M. (2005). *The true power of water.* New York, NY: Atria Books.

Feinstein, D. (2003). *Energy psychology interactive self-help guide.* Ashland, OR: Innersource.

Feldenkrais, M. (1949,2005). *Body and mature behavior: a study of anxiety, sex, gravitation, and learning.* Berkeley, CA: Frog, Ltd.

Feldenkrais, M. (1972). *Awareness through movement: health exercises for personal growth.* New York, NY: HarperCollins.

Flaws, B. (1995). *The secret of chinese pulse diagnosis.* Boulder, CO: Blue Poppy Press.

Fosar, G., Bludorf, F. (2001). *Vernetzte Intelligenz.* Aachen, Germany: Omega Verlag.

Frankl, V. (1946/1997*). Man's search for meaning.* New York, NY: Pocket Books.

Fulghum, R. (1991). *Uh-oh: some observations from both sides of the refrigerator door.* New York, NY. Villard Books.

Garfield, P. (2001). *The universal dream key: the twelve most common dream themes around the world.* New York, NY: HarperCollins.

Gangaji & Tolle, E. (2007). *The diamond in your pocket: discovering your true radiance.* Louisville, CO: Sounds True, Incorporated.

Geldard, R. (2007). Parmenides and the way of truth; translation and commentary. Rhinebeck, NY: Monkfish Book Publishing Company.

Gennaro, L. (1980). *Kirlian photography: research and prospects.* UK: East-West Publications Ltd.

Gillis, L., Suler, J. (2001). *Dream secrets: unlocking the mystery of your dreams.* Lincolnwood, IL: Publications Internationals, Ltd.

Gleick, J. (1987). *Chaos: making a new science.* New York, NY: Penguin Books.

Goertzel, B. (2006). *The hidden pattern: a patternist philosophy of mind.* Boca Raton, FL: BrownWalker Press.

291

Golomb, E. (1992). *Trapped in the mirror*. New York, NY: William Morrow and Company.

Goswami, A. (1993). *The self-aware universe: how consciousness creates the material world*. New York, NY: J P Tarcher.

Greene, B. (2004). *The fabric of the cosmos: space, time and the texture of reality*. New York, NY: Vintage Books.

Gutheil, E. (1970). *The handbook of dream analysis*. New York, NY: W.W. Norton and Company.

Hannaford, C. (2002). *Awakening the child heart: handbook for global parenting*. Captain cook, HI: Jamilla Nur Publishing.

Hannaford, C. (2010). *Playing in the unified field: raising and becoming conscious, creative human beings*. Salt Lake City, UT: Great River Books.

Hawkins, D. (1995). *Power versus force: the hidden determinants of human behavior*. Sedona, AZ: Veritas Publishing.

Hay, L. (1991). *The power is within you*. USA: Hay House.

Hay, L. (1999). *You can heal your life*. USA: Hay House.

Hoff, B. (1982). *The tao of Pooh*. New York, NY: Penguin Books.

Hoff, B. (1992). *The te of piglet*. New York, NY: Penguin.

Huang, A. (2004). *The complete I Ching: the definitive translation by the Taoist master Alfred Huang*. Rochester, VT: Inner Traditions. Iovine, J. (2000). *Kirlian photography: a hands-on guide*. USA: Images Publishing.

Jantsch, E. (1980). *Design for evolution: self-organization and planning in the life of human systems*. Elmsford, NY: Pergamon Press.

Johnson, S. (2004). *Emergence: the connected lives of ants, brains, cities and software*. New York, NY: Scribner.

Kelly, R. (2006). *The human antenna: reading the language of the universe in the songs of our cells*. Santa Rosa, CA: Energy Psychology Press.

Lane, E. (1975). *Electrophotography*. San Francisco, CA: And/Or Press.

Laskow, L. (1992). *Healing with love: a physician's breakthrough mind/body guide for healing yourself and others; the art of holoenergetic healing*. Mill Valley, CA: Wholeness Press.

Leu, L. (2003). *Nonviolent communication companion workbook*: *a practical guide for individual, group, or classroom study.* Encinitas, CA: PuddleDancer Press.

Liangyue, D. (1987). *Chinese acupuncture and moxibustion.* Beijing, China: Foreign Languages Press.

Lipton, B. (2008). *Biology of belief: unleashing the power of unconsciousness, matter and miracles.* USA: Hay House

Lipton, B. (2009). *Spontaneous evolution: our positive future (and a way to get there from here).* USA: Hay House.

Long, M.F. (1948). *The secret science behind miracles.* Camarillo, CA: DeVorss & Company.

Longo, A. & Penhoet, E. (1974). *Nerve Growth Factors in Rat Glioma Cells.* Proceedings of the National Academy of Sciences Vol. 71, No. 6, pp. 2347-2349, June 1974.

Longo, A. & Penhoet, E. (1974). *Nerve Growth Factor Synthesis in Rat Glioma Cells.* Federal Proceedings, 33, (5) 1409.

Longo, A. (1978). *Synthesis of Nerve Growth Factor in Rat Glioma Cells.* Developmental Biology 65, 260-270, 1978.

Lonsdale, E. (2010). *Cosmic weather reports: notes from the edge of the universe.* Berkeley, CA: North Atlantic Books.

Mahoney, M. (1966). *The meaning of dreams and dreaming: the Jungian viewpoint.* Secaucus. NJ: Citadel Press.

Mann, F. (1962/1971). *Acupuncture: the ancient chinese art of healing and how it works scientifically.* New York, NY: Random House.

Marcher, L. Fich, S. (2010). *Body encyclopedia: a guide to the psychological functions of the muscular system.* Berkeley, CA: North Atlantic Books

McTaggart, L. (2002). *The field.* New York, NY. HarperCollins.

Martini, F. (1993). *The meaning of your dreams.* Baltimore: MD: Ottenheimer Publishers.

Mitchell, S. (1992). *Tao te ching.* New York, NY: Harper Perennial.

Moalem, S. (2007). *Survival of the sickest: a medical maverick discovers why we need disease.* New York, NY: HarperCollins Publishers.

Montagu, A. (1971). *Touching: the human significance of the skin.* New York and London: Columbia University Press.

Moritz, A. (2001). *Lifting the veil of duality: your guide to living without judgment*. USA: Ener-Chi Wellness Press.

Moss, T. (1980). *The body electric: a personal journey into the mysteries of parapsychology and kirilian photography*. Los Angeles, CA: J P Tarcher.

Nuernberger, P. (1981). *Freedom from stress: a holistic approach*. Honesdale, PA: Himalayan International Institute of yoga Science and Philosophy Publishers.

O'Hanlon, W. (1995). *Stop blaming, start loving: a solution-oriented approach to improving your relationship*. New York, NY: W. W. Norton & Company.

Osho. (1978). *The tantra experience: evolution through love*. Rockport, MA: Element Inc.

Pearce, J. (1977). *Magical Child*. New York, NY: Bantam Books.

Pearce, J. (2002). *The biology of transcendence: a blueprint of the human spirit*. Rochester, VT: Park Street Press.

Pearsal, P. (1998). *The heart's code*. New York, NY. Broadway Books.

Peck, M. (1987). *The different drum*. New York, NY: Touchstone.

Pelletier, K. (1977). *Mind as healer, mind as slayer*. New York, NY: Dell Publishing Co.

Pert, C. (1997). *Molecules of emotion: why you feel the way you feel*. New York, NY: Scribner.

Quintin, J. (2011). *The unity of geometry*. DVD: NZ: self-published.

Radin, D. (2006). *Entangled minds: extrasensory experiences in a quantum reality*. New York, NY: Pocket Books.

Reps, P. (1968). *Gold and fish signatures*. Rutland, VT: Charles Tuttle Company.

Roth, G. (1998). *Maps to ecstacy: the healing power of movement*. Novato, CA: New World Library.

Satir, V. (1976). *Making contact*. Millbrae, CA: Celestial Arts.

Satprem. (1982). *The mind of the cells*. New York, NY: Institute for Evolutionary Research.

Scheele, P. (1996). *Natural brilliance: overcoming any challenge – at will*. Wayzata, MN: Learning Strategies Corp.

Schonberger, M. (1992). *I Ching and the genetic code: the hidden key to life*. Santa Fe, NM: Aurora Press.

Shayac, T. (2010). DVD: *I Am*: USA: The Foundation for I Am.

Siegel, A. (1996). *Dreams that can change your life: navigating life*. New York, NY: Berkley Books.

Siegel, B. (1986). *Love, medicine and miracles*. New York, NY: Harper & Row.

Siegel, D. (2011). Los Angeles, CA: Mindsight Institute.

Simon, S. (2002). *The force is with you*. Charlottesville, VA: Hampton Roads.

Smith, C. (unknown). *Descriptionary: inpicturing, outpicturing*. USA: Forever Living Manuscripts.

Starwynn, D. (2002). *Microcurrent electro-acupuncture: bio-electric principles, evaluation and treatment*. Phoenix, AZ: Dessert Heart Press.

Steiner, R. (1959). *Cosmic Memory: Atlantis and Lemuria*. Blauvelt, NY: Rudolf Steiner Publications.

Stone, R. (1989). *The secret life of your cells*. West Chester, PA: Whitford Press.

Tanner, W. (1988*). The mystical, magical marvelous world of dreams*. Tahlequah, OK: Sparrow Hawk Press.

Tebo, B. (1993). *Free to be me*. New York, NY: Bantam Books.

Thakar, V. (1974). *Five talks by Vimala Thakar on the general subject of the nature of human consciousness, its challenges and problems, and its transformation through meditation*. Claremont, CA: The Blaisdell Institute.

Tiller, W. (1997). *Science and human transformation: subtle energies, intentionality and consciousness*. Walnut Creek, CA: Pavior Publishing.

Tiller, W. (2001). *Conscious acts of creation: the emergence of a new physics*. Walnut Creek, CA: Pavior Publishing.

Tiller, W. (2005). *Some science adventures with real magic*. Walnut Creek, CA: Pavior Publishing.

Vitale, J. & Behrend, G. (2004). *How to attain your desires by letting your subconscious mind work for you*. Newport News, VA: Morgan-James Publishing.

Warren, R. (2002). *The purpose driven life: what on earth am I here for?* Grand Rapids, MI: Zondervan.

Waters, F. (1963). *Book of the Hopi: the first revelation of the Hopi's historical and religious world-view of life*. New York, NY: Ballantine Books.

Weiss, K. (1984). *Women's health care: a guide to alternatives*. USA: Reston Publishing Company.

Wheeler, J.A. (2004*). Science and ultimate reality; quantum theory, cosmology and complexity.* Cambridge, UK: Cambridge University Press.

Wilhelm, R. (1967). *I ching.* Princeton, NJ: Princeton University Press.

Woolf, V. (1990). *Holodynamics: how to develop and manage your personal power.* Tucson, AZ: Harbinger House.

Xuemei, L. and Jingyi, Z. (1993). *Acupuncture patterns and practice.* Seattle, WA: Eastland Press.

Yap, S. & Hiew, C. (2002). *Energy medicine in CFQ healing.* USA: iUniverse.

Zukav, G. (1989). *The seat of the soul.* New York, NY: Fireside.

ABOUT THE AUTHOR

Dr. Angela Longo received her doctorate in biochemistry from UC Berkeley in 1976 doing original research discovering glial cell Nerve Growth Factor synthesis in the nervous system. This opened up many new fields in glia-neural and small peptide research. Her traditional training in Chinese Medicine is from Dr. Lam Kong, in Oakland California, a teacher with a legacy of ten generations in Chinese Medicine. As professor of interdisciplinary holistic science at San Francisco State University and founding a Traditional Chinese Medicine College in Hawaii with 48 years as a teacher and practitioner, she brings a wealth of knowledge to her new field "Quantum Wave Guided Living".

Dr. Longo and her team teaches Quantum Wave Guided Living as Relationshifiting and Resplendencyinternationally and offers one-on-one coaching and trainings of 9 modules. Kamuela, Hawaii and Chiang Mai, Thailand are her main bases.

Contact her at angelalongo1@gmail.com.

Visit angelalongo.com

Printed in the United States
By Bookmasters